Religious Pluralism
in the Academy

STUDIES IN

EDUCATION & SPIRITUALITY

Peter Laurence and Victor Kazanjian
General Editors

Vol. 2

PETER LANG
New York • Washington, D.C./Baltimore • Bern
Frankfurt am Main • Berlin • Brussels • Vienna • Oxford

Robert J. Nash

Religious Pluralism in the Academy

Opening the Dialogue

PETER LANG
New York • Washington, D.C./Baltimore • Bern
Frankfurt am Main • Berlin • Brussels • Vienna • Oxford

Library of Congress Cataloging-in-Publication Data

Nash, Robert J.
Religious Pluralism in the Academy: opening the dialogue / Robert J. Nash.
p. cm. — (Studies in education and spirituality; vol. 2)
Includes bibliographical references and index.
1. Religious pluralism. 2. Religion in the public
schools—United States. I. Title. II. Series.
BL85 .N27   291.1'72'071173—dc21   2001022294
ISBN 0-8204-5592-X
ISSN 1527-8247

Die Deutsche Bibliothek-CIP-Einheitsaufnahme

Nash, Robert J:
Religious Pluralism in the Academy: opening the dialogue / Robert J. Nash.
–New York; Washington, D.C./Baltimore; Bern;
Frankfurt am Main; Berlin; Brussels; Vienna; Oxford: Lang.
(Studies in education and spirituality; Vol. 2)
ISBN 0-8204-5592-X

Cover design by Dutton & Sherman

The paper in this book meets the guidelines for permanence and durability
of the Committee on Production Guidelines for Book Longevity
of the Council of Library Resources.

© 2001 Peter Lang Publishing, Inc., New York

Printed in the United States of America

Table of Contents

Acknowledgments

I will come right to the point. Without the help of four special groups of students in my "Religion, Spirituality, and Education" seminars during the years 1998–2000, I probably could still have written this book, but it would have been missing something truly essential: a heart and a soul.

In more generic terms, if what I have written here has any worth at all, it is because of the inspiration I have gained from many wonderful students, colleagues, and friends at the University of Vermont during a 33-year teaching career. I find particularly valuable the associations I have had with supportive colleagues and students in Foundations of Education, and Higher Education and Student Affairs Administration.

Most precious, however, have been my relationships with *all* the excellent students who have found their way to my courses for over three decades. Not only have they given me much grist for my writing mill, but many have served as exemplars in my own continuing quest for something worthwhile to believe in.

I am an aural learner. What I hear, I rarely forget. Thus, I am deeply grateful for the privilege of being able to listen to so many extraordinary people willing to share their religious stories with me, particularly over the last few years. I want each of them to know that I truly tried to hear them, that I deeply respect the integrity of their spiritual journeys, and that I hope I accurately captured some kernel of truth from their accounts that even remotely resembles what it is they were attempting to communicate to me. I also hope that they will forgive me if they are offended by some of my unintended distortions of their thinking. I take full responsibility for filtering their wisdom through my less than wise ears and intellect. I want to thank them for everything.

The list that follows includes the names of students and colleagues who have been *directly* involved in some way in this particular project. I am sure that all of the people on my list will recognize the extent of my indebtedness to them. I only hope that I have done justice to their striking insights. I list their names alphabetically:

Judith Aiken, Janine M. Allo, Amy Barrett Apgar, Julie Berg, Judy Branch, Jennifer F. Cernosia, Roddy O'Neil Cleary, Paula Cogan, Susan Conrad, Jake Diaz, Tom Dodd, Kyle Dodson, Merin Eglington, Rebecca Flewelling, Joe Gervais, Corynn Gilbert, Susan Girardin, Hillary Hazen, Jennifer Helvik, Julie W. Innes, Jon Jankowski, Kathleen Kesson, Connie Krosney, Christine Leslie, Gary Margolis, Paul McLoughlin, Mollie Monahan, Laurie Mossler, Warren Nord, Toni Oceguera, Kate Paxton, Ray Quirolgico, Judy Raper, Tom Robinson, Jeff Schulman, Carney Strange, Jena Strong, Tammimarie Wallace, Kelli L. Woodfork, and Jason Zelesky.

I also want to express my gratitude to two people whose special contributions to my well-being were crucial in my being able to continue work on this manuscript: Paul Foxman, Ph.D., and Lindsey A. Kerr, M.D.

I wish to thank the members of the Executive Board of *The Vermont Connection* (2000), made up of graduate students in the Higher Education and Student Affairs Administration (HESA) program at the University of Vermont, for inviting me to write The Final Word article, "It Is Time for HESA Professionals to Talk Openly About Religion in the Academy," the template for the present book.

I am especially grateful to Peter L. Laurence, General Editor of the Education and Spirituality Series for Peter Lang Publishing, Inc., for inviting me to publish this book, and to Heidi Burns, Ph.D., for her excellent editing.

Finally, I wish to thank my wife, Madelyn, for her presence in my life. She actually attempts to live the kind of spirituality I only write and teach about. She is truly the *sine qua non*, the absolute prerequisite, for all that I say in these pages, especially because she does not always agree with me. Our moral conversations on many of the issues I raise in the book have, at times, been heated, but always instructive and loving.

Chapter 1

The Cry for Meaning

One of the great problems of humankind is that we suffer from a poverty of the spirit which stands in glaring contrast to our scientific and technological abundance. The richer we have become materially, the poorer we have become morally and spiritually.
—Martin Luther King, Jr., *The Words of Martin Luther King, Jr.,* 1983

For too long we have been dreaming a dream from which we are now waking up: the dream that if we just improve the socioeconomic situation of people, everything will be okay, people will become happy. The truth is that as the struggle for survival has subsided, the question has emerged: survival for what? Ever more people today have the means to live, but no meaning to live for.
—Viktor E. Frankl, *The Unheard Cry for Meaning,* 1978

There is a place where we are always alone with our own mortality, where we must simply have something greater than ourselves to hold onto—God or history or politics or literature or a belief in the healing power of love, or even righteous anger. Sometimes I think they are all the same. A reason to believe, a way to take the world by the throat and insist that there is more to this life than we have ever imagined.
—Dorothy Allison, *Skin: Talking About Sex, Class, and Literature,* 1994

Taking the World by the Throat

I have wanted to write this book for many years. I am a senior professor of educational philosophy at a major state university—a so-called "public ivy"—who has taught thousands of undergraduate and graduate students during a 33-year career as an educator. The courses I teach deal unavoidably with highly controversial, even soul-wrenching content. Among my areas of intellectual and pedagogical competence are moral and character education, religious and spirituality studies, applied ethics, and philosophy of education. Not a single day goes by in my teaching without students wanting to talk in some way about their struggles to create, or to find, personal meaning. I am not referring here to what too frequently happened in my classes during the decades of the 1970s and 1980s at the hands of the navel-gazing, values-clarifying, catharsis-seeking "Me-Generation." That generation's quest for meaning was unabashedly therapeutic and mostly apolitical. Rather I am talking about hearing a different cry for meaning during the mid- to late 1990s and, now, into the third millennium; one that at times includes the psychological to be sure, but, even more, one that takes on a definite *moral, religious, and spiritual* tone. In fact, this cry for religious and moral meaning has become so loud in my classes that, at times, it is deafening.

I am a philosopher of education who teaches both undergraduates and graduates in a college that trains educators as well as a variety of other human service professionals. The majority of the courses I teach are electives. Certainly, the very content of these courses—philosophy, morality, ethics, religion—tends to spark this kind of soul-searching conversation. However, I believe that there is still some deeper human need that evokes the cry for meaning among my students of all ages. They seem more desperate than students in past decades, in Dorothy Allison's (1994) words, to find "a way to take the world by the throat" (p. 181) in their pursuit of a life that has enduring integrity, meaning, and purpose. I could not agree more with Viktor Frankl's observation that though most students today have the means to live, very few believe deep-down that they have any genuine meaning worth living for. In fact, even those who do profess to believe in something lasting and worthwhile often lack the "confident assurance" mentioned in Hebrews (11:1) that what they hope for with all their hearts will ever be realized. Their "conviction about the things [they] cannot see" is excruciatingly fragile.

Dorothy Allison says it well: We all need "something greater than ourselves to hold onto," a "reason to believe." Students in my classes today, in spite of what too often seems to be a tunnel-visioned drive to become well-paid, well-placed professionals, still crave a safe dialogue zone on campus to explore the possibility that there might be "more to [their lives] than [they] have ever imagined." At some level, most of my students, whether creators, seekers, finders, or losers of meaning, suffer from Martin Luther King's "poverty of the spirit." They know this all too well, and they do not like it.

Despite their philosophical and temperamental differences, most students I meet these days possess a genuine sense of religious wonder. They want to inch toward the discovery of some fundamental moral truths.

Some are hungry to belong to stable, church-based communities, especially if they are, or intend to become, parents of young children. Others prefer the more private path of cultivating a richer interior life, a life of the spirit. Still others strive to give generously of themselves in furthering the cause of social justice, a cause they believe to be profoundly religious at its core. Even the religious doubters, who see all too clearly that excessive religiosity has produced much demonstrable human misery throughout history, are eager to engage in conversations about meaning that might enlarge and enrich their secular worldviews.

Taking the Plunge

Because I wanted to spend an entire semester dealing solely with questions of *religious* meaning with my students, in 1998, I took the plunge and created what I thought would be a onetime, intensive course called "Religion, Spirituality, and Education," the first of its kind ever in the history of my university. In spite of many well-intended warnings from some of my colleagues that such a course would be unlikely to draw enough students to justify its existence, or that it would simply prove to be "too hot to handle," or that it would only attract the "lunatic religious fringe," the course has played to full houses in the five consecutive semesters I have offered it. Moreover, it has drawn as philosophically and religiously diverse a group of students as I have ever had in over three decades of teaching. Because each semester I always end up with a lengthy waiting list of curious students, I feel compelled to offer the course yet one more time to answer what appears to be a virtually insatiable need for religious exploration in the academy.

In early 1999, I published a book—*Faith, Hype, and Clarity: Teaching About Religion in American Schools and Colleges*—and, surprisingly, in a period of just a few months, the invitations to speak on this topic at universities throughout the country began to flood my phone-mail and e-mail. Equally as surprising, the book won a 1999 American Educational Studies Association Critics Choice Award, was named a Choice Magazine scholarly book of the year, and was also nominated for the prestigious Grawemeyer Award in Education, an international honor of great merit. I intentionally use the word "surprising" to describe these events, because, while writing the book, I honestly did not think an extended, pedagogical essay that advocated teaching about religion in secular classrooms would even be marketable, let alone worthy of intellectual acclaim. I am deeply grateful for all the attention.

More important than the honors, however, the book touched a highly responsive chord among many university administrators—particularly student affairs leaders—throughout the country. They wanted to know how they might begin to open a campus-wide dialogue on religion, *in venues both inside and outside the classroom*. I wrote *Faith, Hype, and Clarity* primarily for high school teachers and college professors, but the majority of invitations to deliver workshops and public lectures around the country came from college personnel administrators, campus ministers, and directors of Higher Education and Student Affairs graduate programs. These "out-of-classroom" campus leaders felt that, in some way, I was speaking directly to them.

I soon came to realize that I could have written the book for a much larger audience: administrators as well as faculty, student leaders and campus ministers, as well as professional scholars; professors of higher education, policy and leadership, and educational foundations, as well as religious studies and philosophy professors. These are all the groups I want to reach now. Thus, the kind of book that the reader will find here speaks both to nonprofessorial educators and to professors, primarily at the college level, but with several implications for secondary public school teachers and administrators as well. The book also addresses the faith needs of students. My general goal is to combine in equal measures methodological, theological, philosophical, and personal elements in laying out a rationale, and a model, for opening the dialogue about religious pluralism across campus in secular colleges and universities. I intend for this book to be both analytical and applied.

My overall argument is that American universities ought to enlarge their understanding of pluralism to include open, challenging, spiritually and educationally revitalizing conversations about *genuine religious difference*. Furthermore, I am advocating that higher education adminstrators ought to take the lead in furthering this objective. Working in tandem with qualified scholars and professors from a number of academic disciplines, campus ministers, members of college religious groups, and off-campus religious leaders, higher education administrators have an opportunity at this particular moment in time to transform the academy into a designated space for robust and respectful religious dialogue. This is a space that encourages what I call "unbounded religious dialogue." Religion is such a fundamental part of human existence that to exclude it from the ongoing dialogue about meaning in the American university, either intentionally or unintentionally, is to ignore, deny, or trivialize what has meant so much to so many for at least three millennia of human history (Boorstin, 1998).

The unhappy state of affairs on most secular campuses (and even on many sectarian ones as well, according to the respected, Notre Dame historian of religion, George M. Marsden, 1996, 1997) is that, although religious difference is an important piece of pluralism, it too often gets ignored, conveniently marginalized, or sugar-coated in higher education. Somehow, we feel we are on safer, more righteous, more politically acceptable ground when we are are advocating the merits of racial, ethnic, class, sexual, and gender differences.

The fears are understandable. Some educational leaders mistakingly believe that the First Amendment requires a strict separation between church and state, religion and the academy. It does not (Noonan, 1998; Nord, 1995). While secular schools and colleges, like the state, must avoid favoring, as well as discriminating against, religion, they are free to *study* religion. It is my position that, particularly in the academy, religion must find an educationally appropriate voice. This is not a voice that panders, promotes, proselytizes, or practices. Rather, it is a voice that students must explore openly for its narrative strength and weaknesses, just as they have with any other kind of "voice" in the curriculum. In the *Abington School District v. Shempp* Supreme Court decision in 1963, Supreme Court Justice Thomas Clark declared that "Nothing we have said here indicates that such study . . . , when presented objectively as part of a secular program of education, may not be effected consistently with the First Amendment" (quoted in Nord, 1995, p. 117).

I sought in my earlier book to achieve a salient balance between representing the pros and cons of religion. I worked hard to construct a to-and-fro, critical conversation between and among the four contrasting religious narratives—fundamentalist, prophetic, alternative spiritualities, and post-theist—which I examined. In retrospect, though, I think I could have been a little more positive and generous, and a little less polemical toward each. In fact, after two years of using my book in courses, I am convinced that its general tone was subliminally angry, even though most students (and reviewers) tend to disagree with my self-assessment.

Moreover, in *Faith, Hype, and Clarity*, I talked about my own approach to teaching controversial material in a bit more detached manner than I would have liked. What was essentially missing was the personal touch. This current book attempts to be more self-revealing. My own personal voice will be apparent throughout, but not, I hope, in a way that is overpowering or unnecessarily distracting. At times, I will be candid regarding what I believe is injurious about religion. However, I will also be reconciling, and often laudatory about what I believe is worthwhile. I will be speaking from the heart as well as from the head. I will strive always for the kind of even-handedness that Supreme Court Justice Thomas Clark urged regarding the study of religion in secular institutions. However, because I am human, I know that I am bound to fail as often as I succeed.

Inescapably, this book, like the others I have written, is as much about me as it is about my students and colleagues. I believe that, in the end, all of us are asking similar questions because we are all plagued by the same kinds of existential doubts and buoyed up by the same kinds of existential hopes. At some point, our own diverse cries for meaning converge. I am fully aware that in these pages I will be walking a writer's tenuous tightrope of trying to be both a seeker and a finder, a reporter and a philosophical analyst, a narrator and a scholar, an advocate and a critic, a teacher and a student. I can only pledge to the reader that I will try very hard not to abuse the honor I have had of spending many years talking about religion and spirituality with thousands of students, colleagues, and workshop attendees both at home and throughout the country.

One further word about an author's personal voice is necessary here. I value what Raymond Hedin (1995), a former Catholic seminarian, says about formal academic writing in his semi-autobiographical *Married to the Church*:

> I became convinced that I could not write another impersonal, magisterial sentence. I had come to feel that the omniscient voice of academic writing . . . was a dishonest construct; after all, it is always the author whose ideas lie behind the mask of impersonal authority, so why not admit it and take the heat as well as the credit? . . . . I found myself drawn to Emerson's ideal of "man thinking," someone who brings everything in his experience to the questions he addresses and who acknowledges his engagement by speaking openly in his own voice; authority, Emerson realized, is inseparable from vulnerability. (p. 249)

The pages that follow are far more vulnerable than authoritative because I refuse to write them from the perspective of the detached academic. I, like most of my students, have strong personal opinions about religion. Therefore, I construct each chapter from the vantage point of my own lived story as a teacher, seeker, and student. As the pages sometimes embarrassingly reveal, I am hardly omniscient. Like all my students and colleagues, I am struggling mightily to make sense of my existence. Furthermore, like most of them, I hope, I do this knowing that *exitum in dubio semper est* (the end is always in doubt).

Student Affairs Professionals: The "Hidden Educators"

There are currently tens of thousands of student affairs personnel working in colleges and universities throughout the country. They represent a powerful, albeit hidden, educational force in the academy. Although many faculty often marginalize and demean these professionals as being superfluous to the academic mission of a university, nevertheless, they constitute a powerful educational infrastructure. Their work with students is often at the grass roots level, meeting and engaging them around questions of meaning and purpose in sites far removed from the classroom. Few professors I know ever take the trouble to know these people and to visit these places.

These locations include student activities offices; deans of students offices; judicial affairs offices; outreach and service learning centers; student unions; residential life departments and residence halls; campus ministry, spirituality, and alternative worship sites; centers for cultural pluralism, international students, and multicultural affairs; offices for student life; health and wellness centers; career planning centers; academic counseling centers; teaching and learning centers; counseling and testing centers; management enrollment, financial aid, development, and admissions offices; among a host of others.

Throughout three decades of experience in working with thousands of these professionals, both as students in a very prestigious Higher Education and Student Affairs Administration graduate preparation program at my university, and as respected colleagues whom I meet in my other roles as a speaker, workshop presenter, and as a director of a graduate degree program in Interdisciplinary Studies, I remain convinced that, as a result of their efforts, "true" education can happen anywhere on a college campus, and often does. These non-professorial educators are frequently there—whether or not they want to be—whenever students experience the gnawing pain, confusion, and tongue-tied inarticulateness that comes from seeking meaning; whenever students yearn for something morally solid in which to root their lives, something that does not disappear into the thin air of hedonism, relativism, or subjectivism; or, once again, in the words of Viktor Frankl, whenever students realize that they might indeed "have the means to live, but no meaning to live for."

Unlike many faculty, these hidden educators frequently hear what touches students at the core of their lives, because students tend to drop their guards whenever they leave the faculty advisor's office, the formal lecture hall, or the seminar room. Safely beyond the immediate concern about grades and the need to impress, students are more likely to raise those personally vexing, existential questions. These are the insistent questions that cry out for attention at all age and grade levels, even though they defy any final resolution. These are questions of ultimacy, purpose, finitude, vocation, love, value, good and evil, and social justice. Where better to discuss these issues openly and honestly, humbly and without academic posturing, than in a residence hall setting, a campus minister's office, a human wellness center, a counseling center, a service learning site, or in a center for cultural pluralism?

To mention but a few examples: After reading *Faith, Hype, and Clarity*, one student activities leader at a large mid-western university asked me to help his division develop, and implement, a "core-values" component on "spiritual growth." There were simply not enough campus ministers available at this university to meet the overwhelming need to nourish students' spiritual appetites.

Another was "desperate" for me to help her residential life staff deal with all the religious differences—along with the controversies that often accompany them—that were starting to surface among students in her university's dozens of residence halls. Offensive, anti-religious graffiti was beginning to show up on dormitory bulletin boards and walls, as well as on anonymous e-mails. Evangelical students at this university often felt they were being singled out for criticism by sarcastic, nonbelieving faculty and students. Conversely, agnostic students and faculty recoiled from them because of what they perceived to be a rampant and overly aggressive anti-intellectualism practiced in the name of religious evangelization.

In still another case, a respected higher-education faculty member in one of the most prestigious higher education programs in the nation asked me to speak on how student affairs educators might help students throughout the campus to foster what he called "compelling spiritual narratives" in their lives. According to him, huge numbers of students were inundating his campus's counseling center asking questions that revealed all too clearly the "metaphysical vapidity" at the center of their lives. They were "fed up" with the educational rat race of career credentialing, the whirligig of self-indulgent partying, and the hell-bent acquisition of meaningless, inflated grades that fill too many young people's lives today on campuses throughout the nation. Depression, binge drinking, marijuana abuse, date rape, internet addiction, and plagiarism had surged out of control on this campus. In his words:

> Students here walk around campus, from class to class, and from party to party, like zombies. The vacant looks in their eyes reveal the empty souls that form the basis of their existence. And, to make matters worse, we don't know how to respond to what you are calling the "cry for meaning." Where in the world do we ever get the training to do this? What do we need to know? Can you help us?

Examples such as the above trouble me. Why in the face of these intensifying "cries for meaning," I will ask in the chapters to follow, have most of us in the university, and particularly in higher education administration graduate programs, shied away from—in fact ignored—the growing reality of spiritual and religious need on our campuses? Why is it that we have failed to systematically address the *religious* pleas for meaning that are becoming more and more widespread among students everywhere? Why have we not incorporated core courses on religion and spirituality into our professional leadership curricula? Why is it, particularly in colleges of education where we train students to become higher education administrators, that we do not enlarge our conception of multiculturalism to include religious pluralism?

Why have higher education administrators, multiculturalists, student activities directors, campus ministers, and even foundations of education and humanities professors—usually the "official" advocates of diversity on racial, ethnic, gender, and sexual-orientation issues throughout the country—been so obviously reluctant to deal directly with the ever-increasing expressions of *religious* pluralism that find their way onto our nation's campuses? Why have we not paid as much reverent attention to "faith communities" on campus as we do to other communities of difference?

I fear that those of us in higher education preparation programs throughout the country have defined diversity and pluralism in such a way as to systematically exclude religious considerations. In speaking to several graduate classes in higher education leadership during my off-campus visits to other universities, the same students who willingly and enthusiastically register their every opinion regarding the better known types of diversity on college campuses become strangely mute whenever I attempt to involve them in a discussion about religious diversity. After one of my more notably abortive attempts at trying to stimulate a conversation about religion and spirituality, an African-American woman, a doctoral student in higher education administration, approached me somewhat furtively, long after her peers had left the room.

She said:

> You know, if you were to ask me what was the most significant aspect of my self-identity, I would say that my Pentecostal religious affiliation defines me to myself more than the fact that I am an African-American or even a woman. I would never admit this to my peers or to my professors, for fear of being dismissed as some type of religious fanatic who has forgotten her true racial and gender roots. I only wish I could be in a safe, like-minded environment where I could talk as much about my overriding love for Jesus Christ as I feel obliged to do about my political loyalties in other areas of my life.

The reason why we tend to duck religious issues on secular campuses is certainly not one of indifference or neglect by everyone in the university community. To mention one of the more proactive initiatives, Peter Laurence (1999) reports that in the fall of 1998, a national conference on educational transformation, spirituality, and religious meaning, hosted by Wellesley College, drew over eight hundred enthusiastic participants from all over the country. The organizers felt in the early planning stage that they would be lucky to get a turnout of three hundred. One other example: the Lilly Foundation (Wolfe, 1997) for the last three years has sponsored a wide-ranging seminar on religion and higher education that brings together religious leaders from church-affiliated colleges and universities to converse with secular academicians. The purpose of the seminar is to study ways that church-affiliated institutions, and religion in general, might play a more visible role in the American university. By all accounts, the seminar has been a huge success, and more are being planned for the future. Other projects are underway as I write (see Kazanjian & Laurence, 2000), but they are still very rare.

Overcoming Fear

The short answer to the questions I raise above is *fear*. This fear is rooted in not understanding, or taking seriously, the accelerating growth of religious interest that animates so many students on secular college campuses. Indeed, among a growing number of fundamentalist, Pentecostal, and evangelical Protestant and Catholic students, there is an outright spirit of religiosity and triumphalism; just as there is among many Muslims, Hindus, Buddhists, and Ultra-Orthodox Jews (Roof, 1999).

One of the worst-kept secrets in higher education is that too many faculty and administrators, in spite of their professions of appreciation for diversity, are latently religio-phobic (Marsden, 1997). This religio-phobia becomes apparent whenever conservative and absolutist expressions of religious fervor surface on college campuses (Wolfe, 1999). The fear is real, of course, because all too frequently proclamations of religious certitude in an academic environment can lead to suppression of honest doubt and critique. Academic freedom can wither in such an atmosphere, as is evident in many other countries where religious group is pitted against religious group in a frenzy of conflict and even bloody violence (Juergensmeyer, 2000). However, like it or not, college and university leaders must tune into the reality of a remarkable revival of religious interest all over America (Cimino & Lattin, 1998), but particularly in higher education (Wolfe, 1997). Moreover, this revival is here to stay. My contention throughout this book is that it will benefit all of us to formulate a coherent and compelling educational response to this revivial, because a very teachable moment is upon us.

Sadly, however, many of us, whether administrators or teachers, do not know *who* on campus is being victimized by subtle or explicit forms of anti-religious bigotry (Freedman, 1998). Neither do many of us know, or care to know, exactly *what* it is that students actually believe regarding the specific content of their ardently expressed faiths. The extent of comparative religious understanding among most faculty and administrators is alarmingly deficient (Marsden, 1997). Moreover, I suspect that few of us have ever taken the trouble, in intimate, face-to-face conversation, to understand just *why* some students cling so firmly to the religious convictions of their youth. How, some of us might wonder, is it possible for them, in the face of all the scientific and postmodern critique of religious belief that they frequently endure in their classrooms, to retain such seemingly impregnable faith?

Furthermore, I submit that most of us have no idea *how* to get people to talk respectfully, vigorously, and instructively about their deepest beliefs with each other, without worrying about offending. Here are the words of a vice-president for student affairs I met on one of my consultancies: "Why should we risk talking about this stuff when we might stir up a hornets' nest that will come back to sting all of us, in the form of costly lawsuits?" Finally, few of us know, or want to know, *when* the time might be right to engage students, faculty, and staff throughout the campus in an inclusive community dialogue on constructing meaning. This is a dialogue that must include dealing directly with spiritual and religious material because, whether we like it or not, this is the primary avenue that even Generation X students travel today in order to seek meaning (Beaudoin, 1998; Wolfe, 1997). Instead, we are content to hide our heads in the sands of blissful (often cowardly) avoidance.

I think that, when all is said and done, the main reason why we are reluctant to explicitly address students' cries for religious meaning and understanding on our campuses is that we honestly do not know how to do this without "stirring up the hornets' nest." I will argue in the pages to come that, ironically, significant learnings about religion and spirituality (like most content) are more likely to happen in university settings *when* the hornets are stirred up, *but only under certain, carefully prepared, pedagogical conditions.* These conditions include cultivating a cross-university climate conducive to generous sharing of beliefs, compassionate listening, courageous responding, candid inquiry, and, yes, constructive criticism and challenge, whenever this is called for.

I will also contend that students actually know very little about their own religious beliefs, and even less about others'. Most of my own experience in teaching undergraduate and graduate students from the dominant, mainline Christian denominations confirms the observation that not only are most college students disturbingly lacking in alternative religious or spiritual understandings. They are barely literate regarding their own faith traditions. I can remember vividly one of my doctoral students in higher education administration blurting out in class one day:

> How can you expect me to talk intelligently with others about *their* religious beliefs when I know so little about *my own*? My undergraduate college didn't even have a religious studies department. Moreover, I had no idea that religion was something that could, or should, be studied. I always thought that religion was a series of dogmas and rituals to be obeyed and practiced, rather than to be appreciated intellectually or examined critically.

I think another reason why many students, faculty, and administrators fear addressing religious issues directly in a secular university is the very real danger of somehow offending those who might believe differently. Some administrators who may otherwise be genuinely interested in responding to students' pleas for religious meaning on a college campus do not know how to do this in a way that they think must always be value-neutral or nonpartisan. They are rightly wary of imposing their beliefs (whether mainline, agnostic or atheistic, or lapsed) on those who represent a bewildering array of alternative American and non-Western religions. As graduate students in higher education administration programs, whenever the topic of religion got raised in their own seminars and in other settings, they were probably taught to adopt a stance of fastidious nonjudgmentalism.

I know in my own seminars, for example, that whenever the occasional Muslim, Buddhist, Hindu, or neo-Pagan talk about their beliefs publicly, my majoritarian Christian believers, along with the disenchanted ex-Christians—in the interests of civility and for fear of offending—will either remain silent, or else respond in an overly polite, but banal, manner. Although well-intended in their attempts to show empathy and respect for religious differences, often these students unwittingly send a clear message to the more articulate (and passionate) adherents of other faiths: They do not take them seriously enough to engage them in probing and extensive conversation about their religious and spiritual convictions.

I recall a former Catholic graduate student, who had recently converted to Quakerism, remarking to me once after class that he was "dying for dialogue" throughout the semester about the things he *used* to believe as compared to what he *now* believed. Sadly all he ever got from me and his peers was "polite, head-nodding, religious-correctness" whenever he talked. He practically dared us at times to involve him in rigorous engagement instead of responding to him from the stance of a studied religious impartiality. In this regard, I agree with a distinction that the comparative religion scholar, Diana L. Eck (1993), makes between *diversity* and *pluralism*. For most of us in higher education, multicultural diversity instinctively signals a respect for otherness, tolerance, noncriticism, and acceptance, indeed celebration, of difference. However, Eck believes that religious pluralism calls for something that goes far beyond what is often a mere gratuitous respect for difference. Eck asks: "What kind of faith refuses to be tested by real encounter with others? What kind of faith grows by speaking and proclaiming without having to listen, perhaps even be challenged, by the voices of others?" (p. 198).

Because my Quaker student never experienced Eck's kind of genuine encounter in my seminar, he was frustrated. He left at the end of the term intellectually and emotionally unsatisfied. He wondered out loud to me one day whether, when all the "posturing of inclusiveness" was over, if any of us really cared about what he believed, despite our warmhearted claims that we truly did.

What I am saying, at this early stage in the book, can be summed up once again by the four-letter word, *fear*. There are actually two ways of thinking about this word. The more common meaning of the term suggests a feeling of anxiety, uneasiness, or apprehension about trying something new—in this case, talking openly about religion in the secular academy when there is very little precedent to do so, and very good reason to avoid it entirely. In a deeper sense, however, the word recalls Rudolf Otto's (1923) Latin phrase *mysterium terrible et fascinans*. Otto depicted the phenomenon of transcendence as a "terrible and fascinating mystery" that simultaneously elicits the feeling of *fear* as terror and dread, but also as awe and reverence.

Otto's dual notion of fear, I submit, is a challenge for all of us in the university. Talking about religion in the academy looks on the surface to be terrifying because we are breaking new, controversial ground. However, upon closer examination, the project is also capable of inspiring great reverence and respect for genuine religious pluralism on a secular college campus. My hope is that, if convinced, readers of this book will make their own leaps of faith, and take some creative steps to open the dialogue about religious pluralism in the academy. This openness, of course, must candidly confront religion's potential for both good *and* evil, whenever our students inquire. It is irrefutable that many times throughout history organized religion has been a force for much that is noble in the human spirit. However, sadly, it has also been a force for much that is base (Easterbrook, 1998; Haught, 1990). This "leap" will take considerable courage, as I have said, because it entails that we move beyond a mere *respect* for religious diversity to encourage a *robust pluralism* in the American university.

Three Objectives in Writing This Book

I have three primary objectives in writing this book. First, I will attempt to construct a convincing rationale for administrators *and* faculty to address the needs of all students, both secular and religious, to make meaning. This is a meaning that incorporates, among other elements, a sense of transcendence, immanence, and mystery; an enlargement of the moral imagination; and a genuine respect for religious and spiritual pluralism. I will be concerned mainly with *religious and spiritual meaning*, because this is the crux of the new faith revival both in the larger society, and on college campuses everywhere, that cries out for attention from faculty and administrators (Cimino & Lattin, 1998; Wolfe, 1998; Kazanjian & Laurence, 2000).

Second, I will spend some time examining the actual nature and content of religious difference that exist on college campuses today. I will do this by examining a number of what I call religious "narratives" that I have found, as a result of my research and direct experience, to be present on college and university campuses throughout the United States.

Third, I will attempt to explore one particular way that we might effectively engage students, faculty, administrators, and religious leaders, both on and off campus, in genuine pluralistic dialogue around religious and spiritual matters. To this end, I will present a model for "moral conversation" (Nash, 1996a, 1997) throughout the academy, with the intent of establishing "unbounded religio-spiritual dialogue zones." It is here that I hope to encourage moments of "real encounter" in higher education, to use Eck's (1993) phrase.

As there are only a few college programs nationally that have attempted to open the dialogue on religion and spirituality beyond the classroom, of necessity I will spend little time citing such programs. This has already been done to some extent in an excellent volume by Kazanjian and Laurence (2000) that I discuss below. I am more interested in trying to develop a rationale, and a method, for promoting lively, cross-campus, diverse, educationally relevant conversations about religious matters, *both inside and outside the classroom,* and even beyond the campus. I will draw not only from the sparse, relevant literature but also from my own varied, professional experiences in trying to achieve this goal. Always, I will try to do this with humility and caution, because everywhere this project is no more than a rudimentary work in progress. The daunting challenge for all of us is to acknowledge honestly that there is so much to be done and so little precedent for how to do it.

At this time, I know of only four books that attempt, either directly or indirectly, to cover one or more of these goals. None covers all of them. The first, *Religion and American Education,* by Warren A. Nord (1995), presents an extremely detailed, philosophical and legal rationale for the teaching of religion in public schools and universities. What is missing in this very erudite and helpful book, however, is any attention to concrete suggestions for carrying out the author's excellent objectives. Also, the author speaks mainly to high school teachers and professors, and not at all to college administrators or student affairs personnel. Nord and Charles Haynes's follow-up volume, *Taking Religion Seriously Across the Curriculum* (1998), is more applied, but intended only for the use of elementary and secondary classroom teachers.

The second, *The Courage to Teach: Exploring the Inner Landscape of a Teacher's Life,* by Parker Palmer (1998), is less concerned with fostering out-of-classroom, cross-campus dialogue about religion and spirituality than it is in constructing what I would call a "spirituality of good teaching." Palmer has much to say about teaching that is elevating and wise. Because he is vitally aware of the central importance of a teacher's inner spiritual life, his primary goal in this book, as in his *To Know as We Are Known: A Spirituality of Education* (1983), is to "focus on the practice of teaching and an approach to the inner life that is open to the varied paths of the devoted teachers I have met" (p. xv).

Palmer does make many valuable suggestions about the type of dialogue that he thinks will encourage a "learning in community." Also, he emphasizes the very important point that unless university faculty and administrators are themselves spiritually conscious, open to the possibility of personal transformation, it is unlikely that students will be. However, Palmer is much less willing than I to talk explicitly about *religious* and *spiritual* difference, preferring like many in higher education to secularize meaning-making by talking mainly about interiority, "consciousness-raising," and "personal transformation." Nevertheless, I will build on some of his ideas in these regards in the pages ahead.

The third book (now out of print), *The Critical Years: Young Adults and the Search for Meaning, Faith, and Commitment* (1986), by Sharon Parks, is an examination of the "place of young adulthood and the role of higher education in the pilgrimage toward a critical and mature adult faith" (p. xvi). Parks is a developmental psychologist, and so her work draws upon the insights of such thinkers as Piaget, Erikson, Kohlberg, Gilligan and Keniston. What makes her book particularly relevant to *Religious Pluralism in the Academy,* however, is the author's interest in faith development, the construction of meaning among young people, and the explication and application of James Fowler's *Stages of Faith* (1981) and William Perry's *Forms of Intellectual and Ethical Development in the College Years: A Scheme* (1970). Parks's most recent book, *Big Questions, Worthy Dreams* (2000), extends her interests in these themes to include the function of mentoring young "twenty-something adults in their quests for meaning and faith in environments as diverse as universities, the workplace, families, and "religious faith communities."

In the current book, while I too am concerned with how and why college-age youths make meaning, I am less tied to the insights of developmental theory to explain this activity than Parks. In fact, I register my agreements and disagreements with the faith development theory of Fowler, and with the intellectual development theories of Kohlberg and Perry, in another chapter. More importantly, however, I am mainly concerned with faith as it is linked to *religious* belief and spirituality. Parks's take on faith, while valuable for her purposes, is more generic than mine—more psychological, and expressed exclusively in secular terms.

The fourth book, *Education as Transformation: Religious Pluralism, Spirituality, and a New Vision for Higher Education in America* (2000), edited by Victor H. Kazanjian, Jr., and Peter L. Laurence, is a volume whose purposes are highly compatible with my own. Kazanjian and Laurence are affiliated with the Education as Transformation Project, cofounded and directed by Laurence, at Wellesley College in Massachusetts. Their wide-ranging work in this project with college leaders from all over the country deals mainly with providing a model of religious and spiritual pluralism for other universities, based on the "multifaith programs" they have put together for their Wellesley campus. Kazanjian, an Episcopal priest, is also the dean of religious and spiritual life at Wellesley.

Education as Transformation is a rich collection of essays, constructed by individuals who are trying to implement on their own campuses a vision of higher education that "both scholarship and spirituality are essential to fostering global learning communities and responsible global citizens who can address the challenges of a diverse world." While some of the ideas I express in *Religious Pluralism in the Academy* intersect with Kazanjian's and Laurence's, our respective approaches to the material are somewhat different. I do not know whether both of the authors are religious believers, but I am an existential agnostic, also engaged in the process of respectful seeking, and reluctant to foreclose on any metaphysical possibility, including either belief or disbelief.

Even though the structure and organization of our two volumes is different, our treatment of the relevant issues is held together by a similar central thread: the need for all of us on secular campuses to overcome fear by encouraging students, faculty, and staff to talk openly about their religious explorations, their meaning narratives. I have chosen to write my book using a quasi-personal narrative style in which I am as much the storyteller as the teacher. Their book, with several wonderful exceptions, is a bit more concerned with policy, particularly in Part Three. I believe that *Religious Pluralism in the Academy* will make a very nice companion volume to *Education as Transformation*. I respect the authors' work very much, and I have been consistently inspired by it.

My Preliminary Credo

The following is a brief, explicit statement of some of my own beliefs about religion and pluralism. It is my initial attempt to provide some truth-in-packaging for the reader. It is my *caveat emptor*. These beliefs undergird everything I am about to say in the pages ahead about opening up the dialogue on religion on college campuses everywhere.

1. *This I believe*:

> Some fixed doctrinal apparatus is necessary for a religion. But faith in the possibilities of continued and rigorous inquiry does not limit access to truth to any channel or scheme of things. It does not first say that truth is universal and then add there is but one road to it. It does not depend for assurance upon subjection to any dogma or item of doctrine. It trusts that the natural interactions between man and his environment will breed more intelligence and generate more knowledge. . . . (Dewey, 1934, p. 26)

John Dewey, in *A Common Faith* (1934), was intent on emancipating what he called the "religious" inclination from the authoritarianism of "religion." Dewey's faith throughout his life was in human intelligence, not in blind assent to "some inaccessible supernatural" (p. 86). His faith, like my own, was in the ability of human beings to interact with each other in sustained dialogue in a mutual quest for "a religious faith that shall not be confined to sect, class, or race" (p. 87).

This never-ending, thoroughly democratic conversation about "conserving, transmitting, rectifying, and expanding the heritage of values we have received that those who come after us may receive it more solid and secure," was, for Dewey, profoundly religious. This "common faith of mankind" is the one faith that Dewey thought would lead to further growth in what he called the "moral imagination" (p. 87). *Students ought to have the opportunity to engage in an open-ended conversation about religion and spirituality, one that is positive, practical, dynamic, and critical. This is a conversation free of bias and wishful thinking, toward the end of reaching an agreed-upon consensus regarding a common heritage of values that will bind people together, instead of tearing them apart, both on and off campus.*

2. *This I believe*: Whether one is spiritual or religious, theistic or apatheistic, we are all engaged in a journey to discover and/or create a meaning that transcends the self and the tribe. This is a meaning that motivates us to give our hearts and minds to something larger than ourselves, to some mystery far beyond our secular range of vision. It is a meaning that fulfills the longing we have for the living presence that lies beyond or within all of creation. It is a meaning that combines seeking, practice, place, and community while, at the same time, it requires discipline, sacrifice, and attention. It is a meaning that nourishes our moral growth, and gives rise to the compassion and love which will allow us to live rightly with others. *Students ought to have an opportunity, if they wish, to discuss the personal meaning of this journey openly and publicly on college campuses, including both its benefits and its risks, its opportunities and its dangers, and its joys and its sorrows.*

3. *This I believe*: The words *religion* and *spirituality* are interchangeable parts of the same experience. One without the other is like possessing an intellect without a heart to soften and deepen it, or feelings without a cognitive intelligence to give them direction and purpose. The term *religio-spirituality*, though awkward, best encompasses this interaction, and avoids the artificial dualism so rampant on college campuses everywhere. Religion is too often seen as what we do with others; spirituality as what we do within ourselves. Students experience the former as public faith; the latter as private faith. In principle, I hold that neither one is inferior or superior to the other, and both are complementary. *Students ought to have an opportunity to use both their heads and their hearts*

in examining the best and the worst of what spirituality and religion have to offer them in the process of their meaning-making.

4. *This I believe:* "God is a hypothesis constructed by man [*sic*] to help him understand what existence is all about" (Aldous Huxley, cited in Mendelsohn, 1995). Thus, "God," "religion," and "spirituality" are words we arbitrarily give to everything in life that inspires depth, reverence, awe, and a sense of the numinous. They are generic terms that denote the profound solemnity of the cry for meaning that each of us emits during the ups and downs in our lives. Here is Paul Tillich (1948) on God:

> The name of this infinite and inexhaustible depth and ground of all being is *God*. That depth is what the word *God* means. And if that word has not much meaning for you, translate it, and speak of the depths of your life, of the source of your being, of your ultimate concern, of what you take seriously without any reservation. Perhaps, in order to do so, you must forget everything traditional that you have learned about God, perhaps even that word itself. (p. 24)

Students ought to have an opportunity to examine, construct, and to share with others alternative conceptions of God (or no-God), as one way to plumb the "infinite and inexhaustible" depth that gives shape and substance to their lives.

5. *This I believe:* "Ekam sat vipraha bahudha vadanti"—"Truth is one, but the wise call it by many names" (from the oldest and most sacred Hindu text, *Rig Veda* 1.64.46). Religion, spirituality, and God are the tentative and diverse answers we struggle to give to the following questions about meaning and the search for a liveable truth. What am I? Why am I? Where am I going? How should I act? What is worth knowing? What do I stand for? What should I believe? What should I hope for? Why should I believe? What is worth living and dying for? Whom should I love? Whom should I help? Who is my neighbor? To whom or what should I belong? What is my source of joy? What is my vocation? Why do I and others suffer? How can I further the cause of social justice and human compassion? *Students ought to have an opportunity to explore multiple conceptions of religious truth—including the postmodern conception that there might be no religious truth—in the company of believers and disbelievers.*

6. *This I believe:* A genuine faith must somehow find a way to wrestle with the demons of honest doubt. The goal is not to overcome the doubt, because this is neither possible nor desirable. The goal is to fully incorporate doubt into any final declaration of belief and call to action. A genuine faith, for some, finds expression in the humble understanding that when

everything is said and done, one's frail and wavering beliefs are all that are left to fill the interval between saying too much and saying too little about what is essentially incommunicable, but worth expressing nonetheless. No sentence about religion and spirituality should ever be regarded as an infallible pronouncement, but always as a humble question. *Students ought to have the opportunity to discuss openly the strengths and weaknesses of any meaning that might be grounded in revelation, dogma, skepticism, faith, doubt, reason, or certitude.*

7. *This I believe*: Religion is basically a story devised by people to give meaning to their lives in a particular place and time. Thus, one test of whether a particular religious narrative is true or false is whether the account still speaks to people's needs today. Does the story help us to understand who we are, whom we belong to, how we should behave, and how we might come to grips with the mystery of our existence? *Students ought to have an opportunity to critically examine a variety of religio-spiritual narratives on pragmatic grounds as well as theological, aesthetic as well as philosophical, political as well as creedal, and poetic as well as propositional.*

8. *This I believe*: Every faith tradition, despite major differences, has its universal elements. These exist mainly in the *spiritual* realm, and not in the *dogmatic*. It is in the *spiritual* realm, rather than in the *institutional*, that religious leaders throughout history have had little need for the stake, the gallows, the dungeon, and the rack in order to compel creedal conformity (Haught, 1990). Beyond all the ignorance, dogmatism, bigotry, injustice, tyranny, and hypocrisy that religions have spawned through the ages, however, their most noble aspirations are still in harmony. All the greater and lesser world religions, each in their own distinctive ways, sing the praises of love, compassion, mercy, charity, peace, wisdom, justice, moral discernment, and hope. *Students ought to have the opportunity to raise honest questions about religion's misdeeds throughout history as well as to celebrate religion's contributions to the welfare of people everywhere.*

9. *This I believe*:

Pluralism is the attempt to make America what the philosopher John Rawls calls "a social union of social unions," a community of communities, a nation with far more room for difference than most. Multiculturalism is turning into the attempt to keep these communities at odds with one another. (Rorty, 1999, p. 252)

To the extent that multiculturalism recognizes, legitimates, compensates, and empowers various minority groups whose human and civil rights have been trampled at the hands of dominant elites, it has been an invaluable movement toward equality and social justice in America and throughout the world. To the extent that multiculturalism stands for an obsessive emphasis on difference, separation, relativism, and Europhobia, then it becomes a threat to the pursuit of common religious and political ground, to any semblance of national unity, and even to the furtherance of the ends of democracy. Among these ends are freedom, responsibility, community, equality for everyone, and the right to debate the worth of all competing ideologies without *a priori* favoring any single one. *Students ought to have the opportunity to engage in the challenge confronting all multiculturalists: How to build a just and inclusive America (and a world) around a set of common public purposes without obliterating the uniqueness and diversity of individuals, groups, and religions that make the project a worthy one in the first place.*

Organization of the Book

Chapter 2 sets the stage for the chapters to follow. In this chapter, I am guided by a single question: What do educational leaders need to know about the paradox of pluralism before opening the dialogue on religion on college campuses? I also discuss the reality of religious pluralism on college campuses, the differences between pluralism and diversity, and universalism and particularism. Finally, I present a preliminary conversational framework for understanding, and working productively with, the reality of religious pluralism on college campuses.

Chapters 3 and 4 attempt to answer this question: What are currently the most common religious orientations on college campuses across America? In these two chapters, I present a rationale for adopting a "narrative" approach to dialoguing openly about religion, based on three decades of using this method to teach a variety of controversial subject matters. I also construct six broadly conceived, *mainstream* and *alternative* religio-spiritual narratives that my own experience suggests are growing in popularity in colleges and universities. In addition to explaining each narrative, I point out the opportunities and dangers that these narratives currently present to educators. I also suggest a number of questions that we in the academy might ask in order to capitalize educationally on the strengths, and the weaknesses, of each of these narratives. These two chapters are the heart and soul of the book, in that they summarize and analyze several kinds of religio-spiritual stories that students tend to tell on college campuses today.

Chapter 5 asks this question: What is the relationship, if any, between students' search for religious meaning and for fostering values on a college campus? I argue that the movement on most campuses today toward even a minimalist form of values education can only be enriched by a religio-spiritual dimension. In fact, I see the two as inseparable. In this chapter, I also talk about a capstone values-and-religion seminar that could help students, college educators, and administrators to open, and to sustain, the dialogue on religious pluralism throughout the campus. Finally, I present a brief annotated bibliography of relevant materials on values, ethics, and religio-spirituality that higher education leaders without any formal training in these areas will find helpful. My overall argument in this chapter is that while religion is certainly not sufficient for values education—for moral character and ethical formation—it is still a significant and vital force.

Chapter 6 poses several central questions: How can educators and students actually go about engaging in an open-ended, mutually respectful, yet intellectually challenging, cross-campus conversation about religious beliefs in a secular university setting? What ought to be the ground rules for such a dialogue? Can this type of conversation always be done in a manner that is instructive, constructive, and productive? Or is harmful fallout inevitable, given the intrinsically controversial nature of the subject matter? This chapter, forming the *methodological conclusion* of the book, presents a detailed account of one way to dialogue effectively about religion and spirituality in secular settings. I call this "moral conversation." I have taught this communication process successfully to a variety of constituencies in a number of locations for over thirty years. It is not without its problems, however, and I also address these in this final chapter.

A Note on Use of Resources

At times throughout this book, I present a series of written segments from students' journals and papers. I also recount a number of planned and impromptu conversations about religion and spirituality that I have had with students and colleagues, both at my own university and throughout the country. All of these written pieces and conversations are largely creative fictions, constructed and filtered through my own screen of understanding and interpretation, and dramatically shaped to make certain points. My references to these materials are imaginary composites of hundreds of students and colleagues whom I have met during the last three decades. The reader can rest assured, however, that the people and materials I create in this book represent near-perfect facsimiles of particular religious types whose stories I have heard for many years. Needless to say, my own personal disclosures, whatever their value, are authentic in every way.

Definitions of Several Key Terms

Finally, what follows, in no particular order, are several terms that students (and professionals) bring up time and time again in my courses and consulting. I will be using these words throughout the book. I offer them at this early juncture mainly to give the reader a sense as to how I employ religious nomenclature. The words are meant to be illustrative and not prescriptive. Think of each as a probe, a stimulus, a goad; or, better still, as a deliberate educational provocation. I append to each definition some of the questions that most frequently come up whenever these words emerge in classroom, and campus-wide, discussions. Making meaning together, especially religious and spiritual meaning, requires, at the very least, that educators begin their explorations with a common set of words. These terms will always precipitate animated discussion and dissent, however, because, invariably, interpretations of them differ among individuals and groups. The teachable moment is always just around the corner, because conflict and difference are the inevitable by-product of any candid, and mutually respectful, discussion about religion and spirituality. In my own work in the classroom, the words themselves are pedagogical tools that allow me and my students to probe more deeply into the subject matter at hand.

• *Meaning* (Middle English, *menen*, means to have a purpose, intention, or destiny in mind) is a difficult word to pin down. I like Irvin D. Yalom's (1980) distinction between "cosmic" and "terrestrial" meaning. Cosmic meaning "implies some design existing outside of and superior to the person" (p. 423), referring most often to a transcendent religious or spiritual reality. Whenever students ask a question such as "What is the meaning of *life in general?*" they are usually asking a cosmic question. The world's major religious and spiritual systems attempt to provide answers to cosmic questions of meaning, and many students turn to these traditions for meaning.

Terrestrial meaning may "have foundations that are entirely secular" (p. 423), devoid of a cosmic explanation. Whenever students ask a question such as "What is the meaning of *my particular life?*" they are usually asking a terrestrial question. While some might turn to the transcendental religions and spiritualities for answers to the more personal questions of meaning, many students today look inward to their own psyches, or outward to secular philosophies, nature, and community for the elusive answers they seek.

It is my contention that whether students look mostly toward the self, intimates, society, nature, community, ideology, philosophy, politics, or the supernatural for a sense of their own destinies, their own significance in the world—whether they are cosmologists or terrestrials—they have one thing in common. Like all the rest of us, they are meaning-making and meaning-discovering creatures. In terms of its origins, I remain agnostic as to whether this "cry" for meaning is biologically innate, culturally constructed, or supernaturally implanted. For what it is worth, I lean toward the middle explanation with a dash of sociobiology added for good measure.

My main point, though, is that when the academy ignores or makes light of this drive to construct and discover meaning, whatever its origins, it leaves many young people asking the questions that Tolstoy at age fifty asked as he contemplated the possibility of suicide: "Why should I live? Why should I wish for anything? Why should I do anything? Is there any meaning in my life which will not be destroyed by the inevitable death awaiting me?" (cited in Yalom, 1980, p. 420).

One intriguing concern about meaning that occasionally comes up in my classes is that students wonder if there might not be a *paradox of meaning*. Some are aware that any intentional search for meaning, like an intentional search for happiness or pleasure, is highly unlikely to produce it. Like pleasure, meaning might be something that one receives as a side effect from doing other things, such as getting into the "flow" of everyday life and just letting terrestrial or cosmic meaning happen without forcing it. A therapist I know calls this "going along for the ride and seeing where it will lead."

• *Transcendence* (the Latin, *transcendere*, means to cross a boundary, to pass beyond the limits, to be greater than) is a very controversial term in religious studies (Smart, 2000). From a traditional perspective, transcendence refers to any belief that describes a realm of being surpassing creaturely existence and understanding; a realm of being that presupposes a divine power allegedly exceeding the capacity of any natural reality.

The questions about transcendence that I hear most often are these (in my own words): Why must we "pass beyond earthly limits" in order to make contact with the divine? Why isn't it possible for the divine (or the ineffable) to be present *within* human existence rather than *above* and *beyond* it? Can't transcendence somehow incorporate both realms? Can't one be deeply religious or spiritual and not have any interest in transcendence? Don't secular humanists, or even atheists, have their own type of transcendence, perhaps a self-transcendence that goes outward (not upward) to others in the name of compassion, social justice, or just simple generosity?

• *Religion* (the Latin, *religio*, means to tie fast, to rely on) is another ambiguous, somewhat controversial term in religious studies. I sometimes use the term to refer to an institutional set of beliefs, values, and practices, based on the teachings of a spiritual leader or sect. These beliefs often include the cause, nature, and purpose of the universe. Religion, in the sense I define it, can include institutionalized beliefs in monotheism (belief in one personal God), polytheism (belief in many Gods), process theism (belief in a God who is imperfect, evolving, universe-dependent), and feminine deities, among others. The most frequent inquiry regarding this definition is: Why isn't it possible to be religious without being "tied fast" to, or "relying upon," a particular creed, leader, moral code, church, or any other type of corporate entity?

• *Spirituality* (the Latin, *spirare*, means to breathe the breath of life) is a more preferable term today for many people who might consider themselves "religious," but who reject what they see as the institutional excesses of organized religion. For these people, spirituality, more than religion, emphasizes the vital principle or animating force within all living beings, the "breath of life" that is incorporeal, the force that makes us truly who we are. For them, spirituality is private; religion is corporate and public. Spirituality is immediate and experiential; religion is doctrinal and traditional.

This definition raises several questions. Why does the term *religion* stir up such pejorative connotations on college campuses for so many young people? Does one need religion in order to be spiritual? Are there any parameters on spirituality, or is everything spiritual that is deeply felt? Does the dualism between religion and spirituality actually hold up in practice? Must spirituality always be contentless and nondirective? Must religion always be dogmatic and authoritarian? Is spirituality likely to draw people *away from* community and toward private, individual expressions of belief and practice? Isn't much of the emphasis today on a private spirituality among young people predictable, given the developmental need for most college-age students to individuate, to become their own persons, and to break from what they consider to be "irrelevant" traditions and restrictive communities?

• *Mystery* (the Greek, *myein*, means to shut the eyes or mouth, to contemplate, to intuit) appears to be at the core of all religions and spiritualities. In its more common religious usage, mystery is a term that refers to the infinite incomprehensibility of God (or gods) as well as to the explicit experience of the immediate presence of God (or gods). In technical terms, students often wonder whether mystery is *kataphatic* (Gr)—whether it can be spoken about and shared. Or whether it is *apophatic* (Gr)—whether it refers to something essentially detached and unspeakable. Or whether it is a complex combination of both phenomena.

Many students are fascinated by the *mystic*: the practitioner of mystery; somebody who has learned to "shut the eyes and mouth" enough to discern the mystery of existence; somebody who gains insight into the divine through direct communication, immediate intuition, or spiritual ecstasy. One question often raised by skeptics is this: Isn't mystery merely the name we give to something we do not understand, because, as yet, science has not given us the answer? Another question: Why can't Western religions have more of a sense of mystery about them?

• *God*, an Anglo-Saxon term of Teutonic origin, refers generally to any object(s) of religious worship. The meaning of this word, from an anthropological perspective, is as varied and as creative as the number of cultures that have used it throughout human history. The word refers to what social scientists call the *numinous* (from the Latin, *nutare*, which means to nod the head in assent to a divine power or presence). Numinous experience contains mystery and inspires awe. According to some theologians, in the presence of the mystery we call God, the most that we can ever do is "to nod the head in assent," or in Ninian Smart's (2000) words, to undertake a "faithful bow in silence before the solemn event" (p. 23). What constitutes an exact definition of a God will differ markedly, according to the definer. For starters, the highly respected *Dictionary of Philosophy and Religion* (1996), edited by William L. Reese, lists 75 different definitions of God, offered by 75 well-known philosophers and theologians.

Some questions that frequently come up in my work: Isn't *God* an arbitrary, even archaic, term that people use to explain the inexplicable? Why should particular churches, patriarchs, and sects lay an exclusive claim to the term? Isn't the only way (depending on one's perspective) that we can ever know God through a Divine Revelation? Or through unaided human reason? Or through intuition? If God is all-good, all-loving, and all-powerful, as most Christians, Jews, and Muslims believe, why does He allow the presence of evil in the world? (This is the problem of *theodicy* [Gr]—justifying God—that always comes up in discussions of religion.) Why can't one be religious, like Buddhists and Taoists, and not believe in a personal God?

- *Theism* (from the Greek, *theos*, meaning be|
atheism (from the Greek, *atheos*, meaning with
Godless), and *agnosticism* (from the Greek, a|
knowing). What is intriguing about these three w
obvious differences, they all share one sentim|
God-centered. Theism, a term dating back to seventeen...
gland as a way to counter atheism, signifies a belief in a personal God or
Gods as the creator(s) and ruler(s) of the universe.

Atheism, a word thousands of years old, is a denial of the reality of
God. Some atheists are *anti-theists*, militantly opposed to the idea of
God. Some are *agnostic*, authentic seekers with an open mind, because
they believe it is impossible to say one way or another whether there is a
God—until they possess sufficient evidence to demonstrate God's existence. To my mind, all three terms, each in its own way, are God-driven.
Hence, an atheist and an agnostic, at least in theory, can be as God-
obsessed as a theist. Whether or not they believe, their thoughts are God-
centered, either pro or con.

In contrast, I have coined a new term to describe certain students and
colleagues, *apatheism* (from the Greek, *apathes*, meaning unfeeling, and
theos meaning God) to suggest another perspective: one that denotes a
total lack of interest in, or concern with, questions of God's existence or
nonexistence. In my language, the apatheist is someone who expresses
no passion, emotion, or excitement regarding religious matters. In this
sense, apatheism is a disposition toward religion that sees it as nothing
more than an individual idiosyncrasy, a matter of personal temperament
or taste, only vaguely interesting in an intellectual sense, but nothing to
get too excited about. Each semester, I meet increasing numbers of
apatheists in my courses and throughout my campus. Ironically, I often
have the most charged religious exchanges with these people, in spite of
their professed unconcern about religious phenomena.

- *Faith* (from the Latin, *fidere*, meaning to trust) is an attitude of
trusting belief in something that goes beyond the available evidence.
Whether or not religious faith and reason are complementary or opposi-
tional is a perennial theological and philosophical question. Was Alfred
Lord Tennyson right when he said "There lives more faith in honest doubt,
believe me, than in half the creeds" (cited in Haught, 1996, p. 188)? Or
was Blaise Pascal? "Faith is God felt by the heart, not by reason" (cited in
Brussell, 1988, p. 190). Was Augustine? "I would not believe . . . if the
authority of the . . . Church did not compel me (cited in Mendelsohn,
1995, p. 53). Or was Susan Anthony? "Truth for authority, not authority
for truth" (cited in Mendelsohn, 1995, p. 43).

Revelation (from the Latin, *revelare*, meaning to unveil) suggests an "unveiling" of religious truths which cannot be reached by reason alone. In this sense, revelation stands in opposition to reason, much as does faith. An important theological question is whether there can be a *natural revelation* (religious truth derived from nature based on unaided reason) in addition to, or in contrast with, a *supernatural revelation* (a direct communication from God[s] by words or signs). The one question that both skeptical and believing students often raise is this: "Whose revelation? And according to what authority?"

In the next chapter, I explore what I call the paradox of religious pluralism on college campuses throughout America. One of the most difficult questions that concerns me about this topic is the extent to which, at times, we might actually need to initiate *a policy of intolerance* in order to sustain *a policy of tolerance* toward religious difference in higher education.

Chapter 2

The Paradox of Religious Pluralism

Are the citizens of a democracy obliged to tolerate those who, if they prevailed, would destroy the practice of tolerance—by saying paradoxically that the defense of tolerance may require some degree of intolerance?
—J. L. Sullivan, J. Pierson, G. F. Marcus,
Political Tolerance and American Democracy, 1982

The existence of fundamentalist Christian schools creates a paradox of pluralism in the United States. Paradoxes of pluralism testify to our ideological health. . . . [As a Jew] I feel anything but indifferent to the orthodoxy of fundamentalist Christians. I confess to fearing those who know they have the Truth and are convinced that everyone else would do best to hold this same Truth. I further confess to fearing those who apply their Truth with an implacable logic unmoderated by a need to be pragmatic, to compromise, to see things in terms of degrees. But I prefer the anomaly of the Christian school paradox to the alternative of harassing them or unjustifiably constraining their right to survive.
—Alan Peshkin, *God's Choice: The Total World
of a Fundamentalist Christian School,* 1988

How are we as a community, dedicated to pluralism, to find room for the different values and moral perspectives of different people and different groups? How, that is, are we to respect *particularism*? . . . How can we as a community, made up of diverse individuals and groups, find a way to transcend those differences in order to reach consensus on some matters of common human welfare? How, that is, are we to respect *universalism*?
—Daniel Callahan, "Universalism & Particularism: Fighting to a Draw,"
The Hastings Center Report, 2000

We have learned quite a lot, in the course of the past two centuries, about how races and religions can live in comity with one another. If we forget these lessons, we can reasonably be called irrational. . . . Insofar as "postmodern" philosophical thinking is identified with a mindless and stupid cultural relativism—with the idea that any fool thing that calls itself culture is worthy of respect—then I have no use for such thinking. But I do not see that what I have called "philosophical pluralism" entails any such stupidity. The reason to try persuasion rather than force, to do our best to come to terms with people whose convictions are archaic and ingenerate, is simply that using force, or mockery, or insult, is likely to decrease human happiness.

—Richard Rorty, *Philosophy and Social Hope*, 1999

The Reality of Religious Pluralism on College Campuses: Promise or Peril?

I want to propose in this chapter that before college and university administrators can do anything worthwhile about opening the cross-campus dialogue on religion and spirituality, they need to understand the complex nature of religious pluralism. My somewhat dramatic contention is that *religious pluralism, if left unattended, is a phenomenon that in the future will threaten to divide students, faculty, and administrators in a way that makes all the other campus divisions look tame by comparison.*

For example, I recently spoke to a remarkably diverse religious group on a secular college campus many miles from my own that included, by my count, fourteen different religious orientations, in addition to the Christian and the Jewish traditions. Among the invited students, guests, and staff members who attended my workshop were two Muslims, one Buddhist, one Sikh, one Hindu, one Unitarian-Universalist, one Unificationist, one Baha'i, one Sufi, one Theosophist, two Neo-Pagans and Witches, one practitioner of Native-American spirituality, and three outspoken members of the newly formed Campus Freethought Alliance. All of these participants were more than eager to tell stories of the insidiously silent forms of discrimination, alarming lack of understanding, and verbal abuse (mostly covert, but becoming more overt every day, according to their reports) that they experienced throughout their university from some members of the mainline religious groups.

To get us started, I opened the workshop with this question: "The local media are making a big deal about anti-religious prejudice on this campus. Is there any truth to these claims?" After a brief period of embarrassed and awkward silence, people began to respond. I was struck by the fact that there was actually very little overt whining about so-called "anti-religious oppression." Rather, the comments took on a matter-of-fact, what-else-can-one-expect? tone, as many of the participants recounted a number of what someone called "seemingly innocuous, but nevertheless hurtful, incidents."

For example, the Muslims were "fed up" with being perceived by some on campus as "Jew-hating terrorists," ready to participate in a holy jihad (a war against enemies of Islam) at the drop of a Western infidel's hat. Also, they had never met a Christian student who had read even one sentence from the *Qu'ran*, the sacred book of Islam containing Allah's revelations made to Mohammed. One of the Muslims, somewhat outspoken on campus regarding the merits of Islamic autonomy in the Middle East, particularly Palestine, had recently been the recipient of some very obscene e-mails on two separate occasions. Another Muslim wondered why a Jewish professor he had taken for three small seminar courses in his junior and senior years, someone he liked and admired greatly, had never bothered to learn his name, or ever looked him in the eye when responding to his questions. "Could it be just a coincidence or irrational paranoia on my part?" the student asked. "Or was it something more personal?" Nevertheless, this professor had the reputation of being one of the friendliest, most accessible instructors on campus.

While a few Western students at this university were openly experimenting with meditation and mindfulness practices, the Buddhists in the group were still unhappy over anti-Buddhist stereotypes circulating around campus. One of the Buddhist students was called a "spiritual elitist" by a sarcastic classmate, because she tried to explain to a comparative religion class how important the Four Noble Truths and the Eight-Fold Path were to her personal quest for enlightenment. The other Buddhist, a Tibetan, sat in a world-cultures course and heard a Christian student report on her research that all Buddhists were atheists, anti-materialist and anti-Western, and, what is more, impervious to pain and pleasure, because of their "other-worldliness."

Similarly, the Buddhists had met few students, or faculty, on campus who had even heard of the *Dhammapada,* a collection of verses attributed to the Buddha, or the originating *Prajnaparamita* texts of the Mahayana Buddhists, created by leading mystics from around 483 B. C. E. Also, while some Western students had heard of the Dalai Lama, the traditional ruler and highest priest of the Lamaist religion in Tibet and Mongolia, and Thich Nhat Hanh, the Vietnamese mystic, scholar, and peace activist, few had ever taken the trouble to read their works. The Buddhists felt that in order for Westerners to get the most from Buddhist meditative practices, they needed to learn something about Buddhist culture and Buddhist beliefs. Few Western students they knew were willing to extend themselves in this way.

The Hindu student felt negatively "judged" by Christian, Jewish, and Islamic monotheists whenever she talked about her "shrines" at home, or the more than 250 million Gods of Hinduism that she recognized, or the sacred marriage of Shiva and Shakti, the masculine and feminine creative powers that inspired so much of her worship. Also, she wondered why she was required to read sections of the Hebrew and Christian Bibles in an introductory world literature course, but the Christians and Jews in class were not asked to read sections of *The Upanishads*, the earliest living record (1300 B.C.E.) of Hindu spirituality, or *The Bhagavad Gita* (fifth-second centuries B.C.E.), the central text of the Hindu religion. Consequently, she made the intentional decision, after that course, to keep her religious beliefs free from Western influence and to herself.

The Neo-Pagans and the Witches in the group confessed to feeling "totally marginalized" on their predominantly Christian campus, and so, admittedly, they sought to become more visible by "deliberately playing to the more outrageous stereotypes assigned to them," as one put it. Furthermore, a member of the Campus Freethought Alliance was asked by his "brothers" to leave his fraternity, and the position of leadership he held in it, because, as an "acknowledged atheist," he was an embarrassment to them and to the national office. This merely confirmed for him his own stereotype that "Christians are bigoted, hypocritical, and anti-intellectual." Thus, his militancy in behalf of the cause of absolute freedom from all religious influences in public places like secular universities only intensified.

Even allowing for the inevitable hyperbole, paranoia, and copy-cat behavior that often accompany any airing of grievances in a group setting, I was still troubled by what I heard. Why hadn't these students been given the educational opportunity to talk with each other "*across* their differences *about* their differences?" Fortunately, the stereotyping that upset the students in my group had not yet spilled over into outright religious acrimony on this campus. However, the sad lesson of history is that anti-religious bigotry (like all bigotry) starts small before it grows tall. Stereotyping (no matter how trivial) frequently breeds counterstereotyping, born out of defensiveness and anger. Anger sometimes results in separation. Separation easily grows into separatism and isolation. Balkanization, in turn, can lead to a defiant exclusionism. Exclusionism can fuel an arrogant triumphalism. In addition, as religious history has demonstrated time and time again, triumphalism often gives way to a period of aggressive proseletyzing, forced attempts at conversion, and even violence (Juergensmeyer, 2000).

Even now, on many campuses, members of minority religious groups are asserting their rights to autonomy, and, in some cases, complete separation. Many Eastern religious groups demand their own faith centers instead of having to worship in formerly Christian chapels. Muslim students are angry because they do not have a prayer space of their own. They are tired of sharing space with Christians or Jews. They want prayer rugs not pews. So, too, Buddhists want a separate location for a meditation room. Jews want their own chapel sites complete with Torah scrolls. On some Catholic campuses, representatives of non-Christian religions are insisting on autonomous spaces for the full expression of their own devotions. In fact, several groups of evangelical Christians in secular universities are feeling ghettoized because their own worship areas are contracting in size, given the escalating demands for space by other religious groups (Kazanjian and Laurence, 2000; McMurtrie, 1999; Schreiber, 1999; Wolfe, 1999).

My worry is that unless these separate groups are able to come together to dialogue openly in designated, multifaith, dialogue spaces, then religious Balkanization, and the triumphalism and suspicion of others that are its inevitable by-products, will sooner or later threaten to fragment entire campuses. Since the immigration boom of the 1960s, for example, there are presently 5.7 million Muslims, two million Buddhists, and 1.2 million Hindus in the United States (McMurtrie, 1999). Their numbers are continuing to grow dramatically, and their children have reached college age. Also, the number of evangelical Christians has increased almost exponentially, not just in the United States but throughout the world, constituting in some parts of the globe one-fourth of the adult population (Smith, 1995). The real pluralism on college campuses today is religious, and this phenomenon presents us with an educational opportunity that is unique (Winston, 1998). Left untapped and misunderstood, the phenomenon can only bring us unmitigated grief.

Is Conflict Among Religious Groups Inevitable?

Sadly, grievances such as the ones I heard above remind me of Harold Bloom's grim but ominous prediction in 1993 that the twenty-first century will feature a full-scale return to deadly religious wars throughout the world. For Bloom, many fervent believers around the globe are so emotionally invested in their convictions that whenever their religious beliefs get combined with nationalistic, racial, ethnic, and political interests, then the result is bound to be continuing outbursts of violence and bloodshed.

This outcome appears inevitable because, historically, whenever organized religion aligns with the state, it always manages to produce epic bloodbaths (Haught, 1990).

Recent events throughout the world are proving Bloom to be prescient. Today, in northern Ireland, Catholics and Protestants continue to injure and kill each other. In New Delhi, militant Hindus of the Save Dara Singh Committee kill Christians. On the island of Cyprus, Muslims and Orthodox Christians continue to engage in 35 years of armed standoff. In Armenia, Christians kill Shi'ite Muslim Azerbaijanis and Shi'ite Muslim Azerbaijanis kill Christians. Sikhs in India bomb Hindu aircraft, and Hindus open fire on Sikh temples. Throughout the Middle East, Jews maim and kill Muslims, and Muslims maim and kill Jews. Sunnis and Shias slaughter each other in many Islamic states. Hindu Tamils in Sri Lanka massacre Sinhalese Buddhists, and Sinhalese Buddhists napalm Hindu Tamils. Furthermore, in Seoul, South Korea, rival factions of Chogye Buddhist monks fight each other with fists, rocks, firebombs, and clubs (Constable, 2000; Crossette, 1998; Easterbrook, 1998; Seok, 1998).

Whenever I recite this litany of atrocities to my students, they always ask if the violence perpetrated in the name of religion will ever stop, or if the decimation is inevitable, given what each of the aggrieved groups perceives to be at stake. Just what *is* at stake, I contend, is well worth discussing on college campuses. A simple question I often ask students always manages to precipitate heated dialogue: "Why do you suppose that so much violence has been, and is still being, committed in the name of religion throughout the world?" The diverse responses I get from students are both instructive and alarming. They give me an excellent opportunity to surface lingering religious stereotypes and promote deeper thinking about the violent proclivities of their own groups. I manage to keep the analysis in balance (not always) by reminding students that no group—political, religious, racial, ethnic, or otherwise—is completely immune to the seductions of self-righteousness and the horror that is often its consequence. Sometimes a personal question is all that is necessary to bring the point home: "How far would *you* go to defend something that you cherish with all your heart and soul?"

Here are the types of reactions I tend to get to my earlier question regarding the reasons for the apparent ubiquity of religious violence: "People have long memories of wrongs done to them by their religious enemies." "If you believe that your religion is the One, True Religion necessary for Salvation, then you'll go to any lengths to convert others, even using force, if you think it will save their eternal souls." "The stronger the religious conviction, the worse the cruelty. This is almost an axiom among zealots." "Religious difference breeds fear. Fear breeds resentment. And resentment breeds aggression." "The need for absolute certainty allows for no apostasy. Self-doubt and questioning among zealots are poisonous. Thus, heretics must be punished." "Religion gets all mixed up with ego needs, political agendas, and nationalistic feelings." "Some religious wars are necessary and righteous in order to stand up for the Truth, and especially to defend the integrity of a group's religion." "Satan hates people who love God, and so he stirs them up to hurt each other in God's name." "In the absence of give-and-take dialogue with those who think differently, believers tend to get more and more paranoid about who might be their enemies."

Many of these comments remind me of Friedrich Nietzsche's (1844-1900) wise, yet troubling, words: In spite of all the outward displays of love, generosity, and concern, *the underlying inclination of the monotheistic religions seems to be to "make the 'other' the 'same.'"* However, it need not be this way. While it is undoubtedly true that some believers find comfort and salvation in sameness, and turbulence and threat in otherness, not all do. It is my contention that the more we work to encourage open and probing multifaith, interfaith, and no-faith dialogue on college campuses, then the less believers and disbelievers will feel they need to "iron out" the "wrinkles" in religious differences. Often these "wrinkles," despite their untidiness, can effectively disturb, and eventually strengthen, belief systems. At the very least, they can force believers, and nonbelievers, to look a little more closely, and critically, at their own religious faiths, or lack of them.

I sometimes give my classes, and campus dialogue groups, a handout (created by a Unitarian Universalist student I once had) of an oversized, very colorful graph, vividly depicting the reality of religious difference throughout the modern world. In 1990, the World Development Forum (cited in Eck, 1993, p. 202) asked the following questions: "If our world were a village of 1000 people, who would we be religiously, and in which continent would we live?" The answer is that we would be a village of 329 Christians, 174 Muslims, 131 Hindus, 61 Buddhists, 52 Animists, 3 Jews, members of 34 other religions, and 216 would claim no religious affiliation at all.

Moreover, 564 of us would be Asians, 210 would be Europeans, 86 would be Africans, 80 would be South Americans, and 60 would be North Americans. Finally, as if to confirm Harold Bloom's prediction that religious wars are inevitable in the third millennium, in this same village of

1000 people, 60 would own one-half the income, 600 would live in a shanty town, 500 would be hungry at all times, and 700 would be totally illiterate. Revealingly, the vast majority of the "have nots" would be the most religiously zealous as well as the most angry; while the "haves" would be content simply to assume a stance of benign, bourgeois neutrality toward religion. I predict that in the next quarter of a century, even though an ever-burgeoning group of religious "haves" and "have nots" will achieve, at best, an uneasy truce at many of our nation's colleges and universities, many will also confront each other in open conflict. This is bound to happen *unless we begin to pay systematic attention to the promise and to the peril of religious pluralism everywhere in higher education.*

The following is but one recent example of religious conflict between a powerful dominant group and an aggrieved religious minority. In 1997, at Yale University, five Orthodox Jewish students filed a federal lawsuit (in 2001, the U.S. Court of Appeals for the Second Circuit ruled against the students, who planned to appeal to the full federal court) charging religious discrimination against the university for requiring all first- and second-year students to live on campus in integrated residence halls. To these five proponents of Orthodox Judaism, the Yale residential colleges "represent immorality itself, an arena of coed bathrooms, safe-sex manuals and free condoms, a threat to [their] very souls" (Freedman, 1998, p. 32). It was impossible for them to observe the Jewish requirement of *tzniut* or modesty. According to the five plaintiffs, they felt religiously misunderstood and, at times, mistreated by Yale administrators.

For starters, nobody at Yale seemed to know, or care, that Orthodox Judaism in this country had become increasingly factionalized in recent years between the so-called Modern believers and the *haredi* (the ultra-Orthodox). Haredi describes those ultra-Orthodox Jews who "tremble" before God, and while they are likely to accept the *technical* accouterments of modernity, e.g., higher education, and computer technology, they reject the *cultural* ones—e. g., permissive lifestyles, Godlessness, and sexual promiscuity. Regarding the Yale Five's bitter refusal to settle their suit against the university, Betty Trachtenberg, the Dean of Student Affairs and the primary defendant in the suit, could only mutter: "I don't understand; I just don't understand" (Freedman, 1998, p. 35).

In these litigious times, unfortunately, religious misunderstanding and ignorance in the academy can often result in expensive lawsuits, or worse. For a dean of student affairs (herself a Reformed Jew) at a major Ivy League university not to know that for many Jewish believers there are irreconcilable differences among the worldviews of Conservative, Reformed,

Reconstructionist, Orthodox, and Ultra-Orthodox Judaism is difficult to fathom. Even more difficult, however, is the lack of sensitivity on the part of a highly placed, student affairs official regarding such paramount religious questions as whether the *secular* should, in some extenuating circumstances, accommodate the *sacred*, or whether it should always be the other way around. As one of the plaintiffs, Batsheva Greer, a 19-year-old history major, remarked, "you never think people [Yale officials] will have such low regard for religion. Anyone can see we're serious about this" (Freedman, 1998, p. 32; also see Freedman, 2000).

The Paradox of Religious Pluralism

"Anyone can see we're serious about this!" says Batsheva Greer, the Ultra-Orthodox Jew. Now what? The perplexing dilemma for Yale administrators in this case is how to deal fairly with religious monists in an academic environment that prides itself on being religiously pluralistic. What does an administration do when a particular religious group believes unalterably that there is *One* Truth in *one* set of doctrines rather than *several* truths in *many*? Although the five Ultra-Orthodox Jewish students mentioned above turn their backs on active proselytizing, and, in fact, merely want to be left alone to practice their faith in their own ways, the educational questions they pose—by implication—are nonetheless daunting.

The issues become even more complex when aggressive believers (in anything) on a college campus go on the offensive, bent on preaching, converting, and imposing their unimpeachable truths on others. Any claim to a right to a laissez-faire, religious separatism in an academic environment, as in the case of the Yale *haredi* students mentioned above, is complicated and ominous enough to be sure. However, a claim to religious exceptionalism and aggressive proselytizing can easily become a destructive force in any open-ended inquiry community. Are college and university officials obliged, therefore, to "tolerate those who, if they prevailed, would destroy the practice of tolerance?"—to repeat the words of J. L. Sullivan et al. in the epigraph that introduces this chapter.

It is my position that students in a university ought to be encouraged to wrestle with the possibility of multiple theological truths in the company of their peers, and to come to terms with the prospect of multiplicity in a way that is both self- and other-respecting. Whether one is a true believing atheist, Christian, Muslim, Pagan, or *haredi* Jew, if one's mind is closed a priori to another point of view, there is a major risk that the cross-campus dialogue on religion and spirituality will be terminated before it ever gets started. Unfortunately, some students who hold their beliefs as invariant religious truths often prefer the monologue to the dialogue, and preaching to persuasion.

In academia, however, at least in theory, everything ought to begin and end with dialogue, and the endpoint of dialogue is always up for grabs. Thus, the mission of higher education is to open up minds rather than shut them down. How, then, do we get students in a university to wrestle with the enigmas of contrasting religious truth claims in the company of their peers, if some students believe that the very principle of pluralism is the enemy to be vanquished? Why, in these cases, should the *secular* ever be put in the position of accommodating the *sacred*, if the secular is considered the enemy? These are some of the thornier issues raised by the paradox of religious pluralism.

I deeply respect the insight of Alan Peshkin, an educational anthropologist who spent over a year engaged in a participant-observation study of a self-proclaimed Christian fundamentalist school. In the excerpt at the beginning of this chapter, Peshkin talks about the "paradox of pluralism" that confronted him throughout his study. He was a Jew living among very orthodox Christian educators who were convinced beyond any doubt that not only was he the biblical "enemy" of Christianity, but that he would go to hell unless he "asked Jesus to come into [his] life." In spite of his fears that to many Christians Jews were the killers of Christ and that schools like the one he was studying were considered by some Christians to be beacons of light simply because they were repositories of implacable religious truth, Peshkin asserted their right to survive in a pluralistic democracy. His words are trenchant:

> [such schools] may indeed become a "clear and present danger" to our open society, but until that time has been judged to exist, we must abide by the paradoxes. Their right to thrive is inviolable, at least until they overstep the line between safe and unsafe—an extraordinarily difficult issue to decide—and thereby signal that it is time for intolerance to replace tolerance. (p. 299)

Peshkin's observation is vital: Pluralism in a democracy will always create difficulties, because in the interest of consistency and fairness, even those who would seek to destroy the notion of pluralism, and democracy along with it, have an "inviolable" right to exist. Even though it is my personal conviction that absolute religious belief of any kind in a democracy, as on a college campus, sometimes promotes more darkness than light, I for one will strenuously resist any effort to suppress or curtail its expression. I also hold, however, that religious absolutists reach *the limits of this expression* whenever they seek to suppress or curtail the rights of others to speak their own religious truths, no matter how heretical or out-of-step with the majority. Prudence will always be necessary whenever we begin to define these limits, of course. However, until these boundaries are reached, educators must remain committed to the paradoxical educational principle that the very best way to teach students how to deal intelligently with religious dissent and compromise is to expose students to as much intense, divergent belief as possible. This includes those *intolerant* belief systems that, on principle, forbid religious compromise and dissent.

One way for educators in the university to expose students to real religious diversity is to declare the following for all to hear: Religious narratives that represent a closed and final revelation, whether they come from prophets who claim to *possess* the truth, or from those who claim they *are* the truth, are more than welcome in the campus-wide dialogue! Closed religious narratives have an equal right to coexist with those religious narratives that remain forever open and in flux. This is the essence of the paradox of religious pluralism, and it calls to mind something Niels Bohr, the Nobel physicist, once said: "The opposite of a true statement is a false statement, but the opposite of a profound truth can be another profound truth" (cited in Palmer, 1998, p. 62).

Like it or not, there are no definitive empirical tests that can determine once and for all whether particular claims to religious truth are true or false, in the same way that there might be in some areas of science. (Even the notion of "definitive" scientific proof is up for grabs, however, according to at least one historian of science. See, for example, Fuller, 1988, 2000.) One of the implications for religious pluralism in Bohr's insight is that, in the end, when all the multifaith conversation has stopped, and whether we agree or disagree with one or another contrasting points of view, opposing religious claims will always remain profound mysteries. They will need to be understood and appreciated on their own terms *before* they are refuted and dismissed on our own terms. It is my experience that, even though we in the university understand all too well the *downside* of closed and final religious revelations on a college campus, we make very little effort to understand their *upside*. A commitment to religious pluralism demands that we make an all-out effort to identify the upside—the potential "profound truth"—before we launch into a critique of the downside, no matter how valid and necessary.

Among the upsides are the following: To my mind, those believers who claim to possess the final and closed truth have something that they can believe in with all their hearts, minds, and wills. They are able to locate comforting, soul-sustaining answers to life's very difficult questions in one or another revered Sacred Book. Many believers study their Books carefully. They are secure in the knowledge that their sense of right and wrong begins and ends with these Holy Books. Very little about morality is left up in the air. The Words in these Books are both authoritative and prescriptive, absolute and universal. In spite of the countless, internal tensions and contradictions in these Books, they are able to give believers a source of hope to which they can return every day of their lives. Often in these pages, believers are able to find the love, morality, redemption, gratitude, faith, and, above all, renewal that they so desperately seek, but fail to find, in the secular world.

In a secular world of shallow and broken relationships foundering on the shoals of noncommitment, the Book is a rock of stability. In a world of trendy and vapid, self-help advice that goes nowhere because it is so superficial and self-serving, the Book is a source of enduring wisdom. In a world dominated by high-tech jobs whose satisfactions can be measured mainly by whether they provide adequate health care, generous stock options, and excellent pension benefits, the Book offers believers the genuine vocation of helping to create a new social order rich in compassion, justice, and love. In a world of higher education that, as it becomes more and more specialized and careerist, renders students perennial *sophomores* (a Greek word that means "wise morons"), the Book offers genuine wisdom, a Lasting Truth that will set students free.

Without putting too fine a sarcastic point on it, I ask educators to consider seriously the manner in which many of us read and teach our own "sacred" books. Too many of us secular academicians, if we are honest, choose to read and teach our books in order to be informed, entertained, aroused, and confirmed, or else we prefer to tear them apart. It is rare indeed, according to those critics who claim that postmodern literary theorists in the academy have corrupted the humanities, that intellectuals will ever read, or teach, a book for the express purpose of living their lives by it (Ellis, 1997; Hanson & Heath, 1998). For believers, in contrast, their books are soothing: They represent the "good news" of forgiveness, peace, justice, reconciliation, enlightenment, hope, love, compassion, and immortality. Too often for us academicians, our books represent the opportunity to debunk and dismantle their content, in the interest of "critical reading" or "deconstruction." This is a way of reading that even the postmodern philosopher, Richard Rorty, has recently come to call "mean . . . adversarial and argumentative. . . ." (1998, p. 130).

Despite the upside of absolute religious belief, however, and in the interests of fairness and intellectual honesty, educators need to remind students that throughout history, whenever absolute religious belief has been carried to an extreme, ugliness has often replaced beauty. Even though no one can doubt that religious faith has provided incomparable comfort to millions, even billions, who have been the victims of life's crushing blows, the dark side of religion has also cursed humanity from the very earliest times. Nietzsche once said somewhere that the bloodiest record of human history has been written at the "butchers' benches" of religious leaders. The maddening enigma of religious faith is that there is no Final Court of Divine Opinion that will ever certify one faith as the True Faith, in such a way as to secure universal agreement. Thus, to some historical observers, the major faith-based religions appear destined to exist in perpetual conflict, each triumphantly declaring their objective and absolute validity, while engendering suspicion and hostility among all the opposing groups (see, for example, Kurtz, 1986; Schwartz, 1997).

In this respect, I remember a very conservative Catholic Charismatic student (a religious movement that stresses direct divine inspiration, often taking the form of speaking in tongues, healing, and prophesying) who entered my office one day early in the semester to express her grave misgivings about the religion-and-education course she was taking with me. She called me an "anti-Catholic" and a "proabortionist" and then went on to read me several proofs for these charges that she had recorded in her notebook during the first few weeks of the course. During our conversation, it became clear to me that whenever I made comments in class about the comparative strengths of various religious perspectives on such issues as abortion, capital punishment, and euthanasia, she interpreted these as being *ipso facto* anti-Catholic. To her, religion was a zero-sum game; a word of praise for one belief system was an implicit word of condemnation for another. What she did not like was the even-handed manner in which I tried to guide discussion on the several religions we studied. As she said: "Don't you see that impartiality on matters of religion favors non-Catholics, atheists, agnostics, and wishy-washy liberal believers, and, at least implicitly, condemns those of us who are partial to the one true religion called Catholicism? Unless you are clearly *for* the Church, you are clearly *against* it."

As I got to know this student better over the course of the semester, we developed a mutual, yet cautious, trust. She began to see that, despite what she considered my "hidden postmodern biases" (I never make any attempt to conceal them, but I do work very hard to keep them in check) in leading discussions, I was indeed trying to give all religions, including Catholicism, their rightful due. Although she promised to "pray for the day that [I] might reclaim [my] own lapsed Catholicism," she "prayerfully retracted" many of her accusations against me in her journal at semester's end. I quote at length from her final journal entry.

> At the beginning of class, and at times throughout the course, I've been concerned that you would think that I hadn't grown or been enlightened, if I didn't become more open-minded in my faith. I thought that you would be proud of me if I became *less* of a Catholic. I have found instead that you have tried to respect my faith and value me as a person. This safe feeling helped me to share more of myself with the class and to experience their acceptance and understanding. I want people to know the Church, because I know what a peace the Church provides and that It alone is Truth (I simply cannot add the phrase "for me"). But now I value people who don't know the glory of Catholicism, because they are unique and special and on their own journeys. Even though I have all the Truth I need, as a result of this course I will ponder the "existential questions" from the "multiple perspectives" of others, to use your words. I want to grow and to challenge myself. In fact, I am going to start a discovery type of Catechism Study for my Catholic Youth Group, where respect for different points of view on Papal teachings will be the norm. I think you will be pleased with this. And I will continue to pray that you, too, might embrace your church once again, and that you might openly acknowledge the evil of abortion and euthanasia.

Despite her newfound openness to different perspectives, this believer raises troubling questions for religious pluralists. Personally, I shuddered at what some tortured crackpot—who believed with all of his heart in the validity of my student's earlier accusation that I was a "proabortionist"— might have done to me in a moment of blind, self-righteous, religious rage. Generally, pluralists might ask: Are perpetual suspicion and conflict inevitable among the more absolutist of the faith-based religions? Does the paradox in religious belief reside in the fact that for every light side there exists a dark side striving to be victorious? Will beauty and ugliness always be in a precarious relationship in the world's greater and lesser religions, with ugliness a looming threat to win the day? Is every religious blessing destined to be overridden by a curse? On my most hopeful days, I do not believe so. On my worst days, I am filled with doubt.

My one constant as an educator, however, is my conviction that in dialoguing about religion across campus, both my hopes and my doubts about the success of the venture, and about religion and spirituality in general, are worth sharing with students and colleagues, and theirs with me. Hope and doubt in matters of faith exist in a dialectical relationship, whereby the former can sometimes check the bitter cynicism of the latter, just as the latter can often check the wide-eyed naivete of the former. One of the paradoxes of religious belief is that no hope is realistic without an honest doubt to temper it; while no doubt can sustain the human spirit unless there is hope to transform it. It is my experience that conversations across the university about hope and doubt, and about a number of related religio-spiritual topics as well, are bound to be both nourishing and vigorous, as long as they remain "unbounded." This is a concept I discuss in the sections that follow.

Bounded Versus Unbounded Discourse

Before the pluralistic dialogue can begin in earnest, on a college campus it must become "unbounded." Stephen Carter (1998) introduces a concept he calls "bounded discourse" in *Civility: Manners, Morals, and the Etiquette of Democracy.* Bounded discourse—"[deliberately constructing] an arena in which some ideas can be debated and others cannot" (p. 134)—systematically excludes religious ideas not only from higher education administration programs, among others, but also from cross-university dialogue. Our benevolent, liberal understanding that students' religious and spiritual inclinations are best left to the private sphere of life automatically rules out of bounds any public conversation about these issues that makes us feel uncomfortable.

While I certainly concur with Carter's insights regarding "bounded discourse," I myself prefer the term *dialogue* to *discourse.* Dialogue, according to *Webster's New World College Dictionary,* 3rd edition, means having a conversation that is open and frank with the goal of seeking mutual understanding. Dialogue, like Socrates' dialectic, though not as formally, suggests a going back and forth in frank discussion and interchange, asking questions and searching for the nugget of truth in each other's ideas. It connotes a genuine conversational encounter. Discourse, on the other hand, according to *Webster's,* is less to and fro, and more of a straightforward presentation of ideas in a discussion. In spite of recent postmodern reformulations of the term to give it political overtones, discourse still connotes a long, formal treatment of an issue, mainly in the form of a lecture, treatise, or dissertation. In principle, I have nothing against this usage, but, for my purposes in trying to encourage open and honest, dialectical conversations about religion on a college campus, I like the notion of dialogue as opposed to discourse. Having said this, however, I will respect Carter's use of the word by using it in this chapter whenever I refer to his concept of bounded and unbounded *discourse.*

Thus, what Carter is charging, is that whether in the classroom, counseling center, campus coffeehouse, advising office, or residence hall, we "take off the table" what truly matters to many students: *their heartfelt search for religious and spiritual meaning.* The unintended, but no less tragic, result is that in our calculated efforts to "bound discourse" about religion, we severely narrow our mission, along with our effectiveness, as higher education leaders. Worse, we relegate religion to the nether regions of the private realm where it is not allowed to enter the public arena in any full, rich way. Consequently, the religious voices of our students disappear from public view. Furthermore, Callahan's (2000) concerns in the excerpt that introduces this chapter notwithstanding, the prospects for "harmonization" of what is *particular* and what is *universal* in religious experience grows more and more unlikely. The robust, pluralistic dialogue necessary to examine and understand religious difference and commonality never gets off the ground.

Daniel Callahan wonders how a community can respect genuine differences in values and moral perspectives and still find a way to transcend those differences in order to reach consensus on "some matters of common human welfare." The dilemma for any community, in his view, is to find a way to resolve the conflict between "particularism" and "universalism," a "fight" he wants to end in a "draw." So do I. This has been the pivotal challenge for college and university communities, of course, in matters of race, class, gender, and sexual orientation. However, the religious implications of this challenge have gone largely unexplored as yet. Callahan ends up where I do, even though he is talking mainly about moral philosophy and bioethics. While he is not directly concerned about *religious* difference, and though he does not talk about how to address the challenge of pluralism and universalism in a *university* setting, nevertheless I find his overall approach to pluralistic dialogue resonant with my own.

Here is Callahan (2000) on the central problems of "harmonizing universalism and particularism":

> No society can be utterly multicultural: it must share some common values to even be a functioning, minimally humane society. Nor should any society be monolithic in its values, simply pushing aside cultural differences: those differences are not necessarily incompatible with a functioning society and are often an enrichment to it. . . . I contend that it is perfectly appropriate in a pluralistic society for the various cultures within it to comment on and criticize each other—and where necessary to attempt to change by persuasion each other's values when they seem harmful or mistaken. . . . Criticism and persuasion, yes; coercion, no. [Pluralistic discourse] may sometimes bring peace, but often it must disturb the peace. . . . All cultures deserve our presumptive respect, but none can claim a moral exemption from scrutiny and evaluation. (p. 44)

Where the topic of religion is concerne
Callahan's two "rules" for pluralistic dialogu
will elaborate on these guidelines in the ne
the final chapter):

versity, for
and it is
diffe

- First, insist on granting all participar
  tory, presumptive respect.
- Second, display empathy and underst
- Third, whenever appropriate, encoura̠_ _. _._._._._._, ._...._....
  ate, and critical commentary from all sides. *Proceed with utmost
  caution at all times.*
- Fourth, when necessary, help participants to identify, and possibly
  transform, particular religious beliefs that appear to be harmful,
  mistaken, or coercive. *Proceed with utmost caution at all times.*
- Fifth, be crystal clear as to the reasonable limits of religious dialogue by establishing (ideally by consensus) strict guidelines for avoid-
  ing psychological or physical harm to each and every participant.
  Proceed with utmost caution at all times.

As if to buttress Callahan's worst fears regarding the danger of particularism taken to an extreme, a campus minister at another college confided
to me recently that she has become an avid proponent of "parallelism"
among religious groups (Wolfe, 1999). Parallelism for her is an approach
to religious diversity that encourages a variety of religious groups on campus to exist on parallel tracks, each self-sufficient, hermetically autonomous, and anti-secularist. In my opinion, this campus minister's policy of
"parallelism" is simply another way to practice Carter's "bounded discourse," and with the same, disastrous results mentioned above. Parallelism does have the virtue of allowing different religious groups to be *a part
of* American higher education while still being *apart from* that same
system. However, the glaring disadvantage of an officially endorsed, religious apartheid is the further marginalization of diverse religious voices
on campus.

Worse, and I echo Diana Eck (1993) here, the existence of a simple
religious *diversity* in the university does not guarantee the full-bodied
educational encounters that a vigorous religious *pluralism* requires. Religious diversity, according to Eck, expresses a *fact*: It recognizes the presence on campus of a number of religio-spiritual groups, each requiring
our tolerance, in the name of such ethical principles as respect for autonomy and nonmaleficence (doing no harm). Respect for religious di-

Eck, is a minimalist moral obligation on a university campus, unsatisfactory because it does not go far enough. It tolerates ence, to be sure, but it too often leaves intact a "retreat into a volun-y isolation" (p. 43). It opts in favor of a laissez-faire religious particular-ism and against a religious universalism, a universalism that respects, but in some instances transcends, difference.

In contrast, religious *pluralism*, according to Eck, necessitates "a posi-tive and interactive interpretation of plurality" (p. 43). It requires direct, give-and-take participation with the "other." At times, it stirs up the "hor-nets' nest." It insists that we allow the "other" to get under our skins, to engage with us, to disturb us, even, if the circumstances warrant, to change us. Simple tolerance, respect, and celebration of difference must always give way to the active seeking of understanding, and a willingness to consider transforming or modifying our previous religious views. This is both the burden and the opportunity of pluralism. People need to take an active initiative, says Eck, to "build bridges of exchange and dialogue . . . and this must include constant communication—meeting, exchange, traffic, criticism, reflection, reparation, and renewal" (pp. 197–198).

Absent these critical face-to-face, to-and-fro encounters between and among the various religious groups on a campus, all sides suffer. It soon becomes obvious that we do not take each other seriously enough, nor do we trust each other, to ask the respectful yet hard questions about the things that truly give our lives meaning. In place of "bridges of exchange and dialogue," we substitute gratuitous head-nodding and a folklore ap-proach to religious difference. We become religio-spiritual sight-seers and tourists. We might even attend a few "exotic" religious services, sing some "lovely" religious songs, listen to some interesting spiritual stories, per-haps even engage in a little harmless liturgical experimentation. However, at the level of real give-and-take dialogue, nothing has really touched us at our core. We emerge religiously and spiritually unscathed.

When bounded discourse prevails in academia, each religious group becomes what Wolfe (1999) calls tragically "another subculture within an alien system of learning [rather] than an integral part of that system" (p. B7). Whenever this happens, everyone loses. I have in mind particularly those devout religious students who find themselves in the classrooms of certain types of professors—secularist despisers of religion—who have very large, anti-religious axes to grind. Whether or not they intend to, these professors stifle explicit religious dialogue by dismissing it as either irrelevant or anti-intellectual. A few openly mock religious believers (par-ticularly Christian conservatives) in a way that would bring a lawsuit, or at least a public rebuke, if the same were done to members of ethnic or racial groups. According to at least two highly respected observers (Marsden, 1997; Nussbaum, 1997), outright religious bigotry has become so obstinately and fashionably normative in the humanities, social sciences, and natural sciences today that the academy's vaunted ideals of intellectual pluralism and academic freedom remain largely a sham.

Frank McCourt, the Pulitzer Prize-winning author of *Angela's Ashes*, comments poignantly on the kind of professorial religious bigotry he experienced while a student at New York University. In *'Tis* (1999), he describes what for him was a common, but still memorably painful, personal incident:

> Whenever an Irish writer is mentioned, or anything Irish, everyone turns to me as if I'm the authority. It's the same with Catholicism. If I answer a question they hear my accent and that means I'm a Catholic and ready to defend Mother Church to the last drop of my blood. Some professors like to taunt me by sneering at the Virgin Birth, the Holy Trinity, the celibacy of St. Joseph, the Inquisition, the priest-ridden people of Ireland. When they talk like that I don't know what to say because they have the power to lower my grade and damage my average. . . . I fear professors with their high degrees and the way they might make me look foolish before the other students, especially the girls. (pp. 179–180)

In my own professorial experience, I cannot begin to recount the number of orthodox Christian students—fundamentalists, Pentecostalists, evangelicals, and charismatics—who have complained to me over the years of the derision and sarcasm they experience both in the classroom and in the residence hall. For them, there is neither intellectual nor religious freedom at their universities; there is only the open disdain aimed at their religiosity that forces them to retreat even further into their sectarian groups. It is mainly there that they are able to seek the consolation and strength they need to sustain them in the battles ahead.

Unhappily, I have heard a plethora of such horror stories from undergraduates and graduate students in my own university and throughout the country. Many have seriously considered leaving higher education due to the searing religious ridicule they believe they have received. Even sadder, few have had the courage to take their complaints to a higher university authority, for fear that they would not be taken seriously. One woman on my own campus, a born-again Baptist, who did manage to graduate *summa cum laude*, tearfully recounted to me that in a large science lecture hall during her first year on campus, a professor, who imperiously introduced himself to the class as a "scientist " and an "evolutionist," proceeded throughout the semester to make snide comments about "dumbamentalist [sic] Christians." Frequently in his lectures, this professor stereotyped all fundamentalists as "Creationists," "zealots," and "intellectual imposters." When in private she confronted him with these cruel and mistaken epithets, he told her he was only "teasing" and said to "lighten up" because he was not referring to her.

It is certainly true that liberal fears of a resurgent, authoritarian Christian right, or any religious right (or left) for that matter, are justifiable. Some orthodox groups, if their dogmatic rhetoric is to be taken at face value, want to dominate the public dialogue and repress dissent (Bawer, 1997). This is unacceptable behavior in any secular university that sees itself, at least in theory, as promoting heresy (from the Greek, *hairein*, ability to choose) in all things intellectual. The academy's classical commitment to heresy goes by the name of academic freedom—the unconstrained right to pursue truth wherever it might lead, and regardless of how many chips must fall—so that students might choose for themselves a set of defensible truths to live by. In fact, the founders of many of the world's major religions were heretics in their own right. Whether Jesus or Mohammed, Lao Tzu or Buddha, each was a rebel who flouted the religious traditions of the time. The history of religion can be read as a history of heresy, a chronicle of defiance against religious conformity and compliance.

However, as Marsden (1997) points out, "the vast majority of religious conservatives do not speak in this imperialistic way" (p. 33). Actually, the majority of Protestant fundamentalists are not publicly dogmatic on political issues. They support principles of tolerance, civility, and separation of church and state. Moreover, Christian fundamentalists, like Islamic and Jewish fundamentalists, include within their ranks reactionary, moderate, and even progressive voices (Cox, 1995). Among the religious right, for example, there are diverse groups like African-American Baptists and Mennonites that avoid the extremes. Not all embrace the doctrinal or political positions of the Christian Coalition (Marsden, 1997). The reality of religious pluralism, adroitly ignored by so many critics of religion, is that pluralism is a fact even among so-called monistic religious groups.

I always urge that my more orthodox Christian students read George M. Marsden's (1997) ironically titled *The Outrageous Idea of Christian Scholarship*, a book I have referenced before in this chapter. Marsden, an evangelical Christian scholar of international renown, makes the convincing argument that instead of a feared "establishment" of religious belief in higher education, what we now have, owing to the hegemony of secularists and ideological religious nay-sayers, is a "virtual establishment of nonbelief." Marsden fears that when students are told to leave their religious convictions at the door of their classrooms the "result is not diversity, but rather a dreary [academic] uniformity" (p. 35). For Marsden, religious faith and intellectual scholarship are not mutually contradictory. In fact, religious scholars can do the academy a genuine service by dismantling such prevailing secular dogmatisms as naturalistic reductionism, moral relativism, and the espousal of a rigid line of separation between church and state.

When Should Intolerance Replace Tolerance?

Notwithstanding Marsden's sensible rejoinders to one-sided, secularist intellectuals, Peshkin's (1988) observation, which I cited earlier, is still critical. Whenever groups or individuals, in the name of religious absolutism, "overstep the line between safe and unsafe," then "intolerance must replace tolerance" (p. 299) *in order to preserve the principle of tolerance.* This is the most difficult challenge regarding the paradox of religious pluralism on college campuses. Who decides what is "safe and unsafe"? What are the acceptable limits of tolerance and intolerance of strongly held (and expressed) religious views? Again, who decides? What do we do when two or more implacable belief systems collide, and when all the learned conversation has led to one stalemated result? This is the unyielding conviction that the Full Truth resides in only *one* point of view and, therefore, all competing truths are lies, heresies, or apostasies that must be repudiated and expunged, regrettably by any means necessary.

Is Richard Rorty (1999) right when he says that we must always use "persuasion rather than force" to deal with "people whose convictions are archaic and ingenerate"? Who determines the guidelines for what beliefs are "archaic and ingenerate"? More importantly, what do we do when all the civil dialogue and attempts at persuasion end and the shouting (or worse) begins? Unfortunately, I have no answers to such daunting questions that will please everyone. And neither does anyone else, including Richard Rorty. Thus, I can only respond to the paradox of religious pluralism with humility, cautious conviction, and a real-world incident.

The state where I live has been locked for many months in an extraordinarily heated debate. This debate has polarized proponents and opponents of Vermont's new (2000) civil unions law for gay and lesbian couples. The civil unions law gives Vermont same-sex couples all the legal rights and benefits as married couples. For months, letters and op-ed pieces from politically conservative and progressive forces have appeared in the state's largest newspaper, *The Burlington Free Press*. The correspondence has been contentious, and much of it has been downright nasty. The state's Christian Right, along with its Christian and Jewish Left, also entered the debate very early, and, at times, they too were often guilty of self-righteous mudslinging.

Despite the state legislature's well-intended efforts to hold mutually respectful, open hearings on the civil-unions bill before its eventual passage, people took irreconcilable positions. Where Vermonters stood on the civil unions legislation ultimately defined them to their neighbors and loved ones as being either bigots or anti-bigots, pro-Christian or anti-Christian, prosocial justice or antisocial justice, promarriage or anti-marriage, procivil rights or anti-civil rights, profamily values or anti-family values, prochildren or anti-children. In the fall of 2000, a number of politicians were voted in or out of office depending on their positions on this piece of very controversial, nationally unprecedented legislation.

Early in the debate, representatives from the Westboro Baptist Church in Topeka, Kansas, visited Vermont's state capital, Montpelier, to register their disapproval of the same-sex civil unions legislation. Members of the Westboro Church are so sure that their God hates homosexuals that they travel the country picketing liberal churches and statehouses that might potentially support same-sex marriages. These are the same churchgoing Christians who picketed St. Mark's Episcopal Church in Casper, Wyoming, where Matthew Shepard's funeral was held in 1998. Shepard, a University of Wyoming college student, was savagely beaten and left alone to die—tied to a fence post on the Wyoming prairie—simply because he was a homosexual.

The Christian picketers protested at his funeral with signs that said "God hates fags—Matthew is in hell." In the Montpelier, Vermont, demonstration in 1999 against gay marriage, Sara Phelps, the granddaughter of the church leader, the Reverend Fred Phelps Sr., told a newspaper reporter, Tamara Lush (1999), that "God hates fags. They hate us. So they hate God. There is more hate in the Bible than love. God will send all the fags to hell" (p. 1B). For good measure, the Westboro Baptist Church's web site address for all the world to see is www.godhatesfags.com.

The troubling question for religious pluralists in such a case is this: Does a Sara Phelps, either as a student or as a visitor, have a rightful role to play in any religious dialogue on a secular (or even sectarian) college campus? If she does, where, if at all, does the university draw the line on her freedom of expression? If she does not, what, if any, are the reasonable guidelines that would justify her exclusion from the campus conversation? What does an institution of higher learning do when the rights of a pluralistic majority collide with the rights of a monistic religious minority, and vice versa?

To state the controversy somewhat differently: Because Sara Phelps asserts a "truth" about the "sinfulness" of homosexuality and same-sex civil unions that is radically incompatible with the "truth" the other side asserts; and because locating the common ground between the two drastically polarized positions appears unlikely, is a resolution possible or even desirable? According to James Davison Hunter (1994), the "difference" that a Sara Phelps represents is "irreducible and irreconcilable," not one "that can easily be 'appreciated,' 'validated,' 'accepted,' or 'celebrated'" by her opponents, or theirs by her (p. 209).

If Hunter is right, then short of repressing a Sara Phelps's right to express her belief that some questions are biblically settled once and for all, and are, therefore, beyond the pale of open-ended, critical inquiry, then we need to ask ourselves a number of questions: What is going on here that we find troubling? What can we learn from each other, if anything, regarding our differences? What needs to be transformed, both in others and in ourselves, so that we might avoid potentially destructive conflicts? Where is the point when we give up and rule the Sara Phelpses of the world out of bounds in higher education? When and how do we make the decision to marginalize or eliminate them from the conversation?

There is a far more nuanced and conciliatory, yet still traditional, religious position on same-sex civil unions than the one Sara Phelps holds, this one advanced by the very liberal *Commonweal Magazine* for Catholic laypersons. I maintain that this view also deserves equal airtime in the cross-campus dialogue on this issue. The official *Commonweal* (Steinfels, 2000) editorial position is this:

> Reasoned resistance to same-sex unions and to teaching children that homosexual and heterosexual sex are equivalent deserves equal regard as we consider how to order our common life. This resistance often rests on religious beliefs and moral views that tie procreation and the care of children to the building of families. It rests as well on deeply embedded ideas about men and women, sex and the family. Is this simply prejudice hallowed by religion and history, as some might argue, or is it religion and history reminding us that these customs and social forms are deeply congruent with the human ability to survive and flourish? (p. 6)

The editors at *Commonweal* opt for an all-out national conversation about the religious, moral, political, and legal implications for sanctioning same-sex civil unions, and possibly same-sex marriages sometime in the future. The editors' position seems to be that the issue is not one of civil rights alone. It is also "social experimentation on an unprecedented scale," and, therefore, it deserves to be debated throughout the United States, both in and out of the courts. Anytime one group of Americans wants to transform what another group thinks and values, say the editors, by "radically rearranging social institutions and moral norms," then genuine, prolonged democratic debate must be the major tool for change. Change in the laws governing marriage should not become the sole responsibility of the courts, as it was in the Vermont case. In my estimation, proponents of same-sex civil unions must also find a way to engage in dialogue with the *Commonweal* view without stigmatizing it as religious zealotry covered over by a phony liberal "happy face," a denial of basic civil rights, or homophobia.

A series of related questions around the issue of homosexuality actually came up in the spring of 2000 at Tufts University in Massachusetts, and Middlebury College in Vermont, where nondiscrimination policies collided with religious-freedom rights (McMurtrie, 2000). On each campus, the InterVarsity Christian Fellowship/USA chapters banned gay leaders, because their lifestyle was thought to be in direct opposition to the Christian belief that homosexuality was sinful. This action raised the spectre of religious organizations discriminating on the basis of sexual orientation. The InterVarsity Christian Fellowship claimed a right to hold religious views no matter how "politically incorrect," along with the right to elect its own leaders consistent with those views. The gay students claimed the right to nondiscrimination, in the sense that civil rights must always trump religious-freedom rights whenever the two are in conflict.

To complicate matters, Tufts University stripped the InterVarsity chapter's funding and "derecognized" it as an official university organization (a decision it later rescinded). Middlebury decided to move more slowly. Ironically, the Tufts University chaplain, a very liberal Unitarian Universalist, defended the InterVarsity chapter on the grounds that the matter was one of religious freedom rather than discrimination. While admittedly the legal issues in these cases were complex, and while each side believed it alone inhabited the moral high ground, in my opinion, something important was missing in the debate on these campuses. The respective institutions failed to seize the opportunity to promote a vigorous cross-campus dialogue on all the religious, moral, political, and legal issues that were at stake. A genuine educational moment for discussing the dilemmas of real religious pluralism slipped away.

For my part, a Sara Phelps has a moral right to be in my classroom. I believe she should be accepted on college campuses everywhere in the

United States. While, personally, I find her hatred of homosexuals to be ignorant and dangerous, and her peculiar interpretation of Christianity to be vindictive, constrictive, and mistaken, I welcome the opportunity to get her to air her views in an educational setting where she might learn something about the rules of civil dialogue. I also want others in the dialogue, including atheists, civil libertarians, social justice advocates, and gays and lesbians, to get a firsthand sense of how a Sara Phelps's religious, moral, and political convictions can exist on such an entirely different plane from theirs. Her beliefs are real, intransigent, and deep-seated—so much so that they become a matter of moral life and death to her, and to others who might also hold them. The same is true for those members who belong to the InterVarsity Christian Fellowship at Middlebury and Tufts, as well as for those gays and lesbians who feel victimized by Phelps's over-the-top Christian beliefs.

Here is Walter Lippman, writing in 1955, on a guideline for pluralistic dialogue in a democracy that I find compelling even today:

> If there is a dividing line between liberty and license, it is where freedom of speech is no longer respected as a procedure of the truth and becomes the unrestricted right to exploit the ignorance, and to incite the passions, of the people. . . . What has been lost in the tumult is the meaning of the obligation which is involved in the right to speak freely. It is the obligation to subject the utterance to criticism and debate. Because the dialectical debate is a procedure for attaining moral and political truth, the right to speak is protected by a willingness to debate. (cited in Hunter, 1994, pp. 238–239)

Although I prefer the word *dialogue* to *debate*, because it is less adversarial and dichotomous—guided more by a wish to reconcile and integrate than by a need to fight and win—I agree essentially with Lippman. I believe that, in a democracy and on a college campus, Sara Phelps has a right to speak freely on the issues she cares so deeply about. However, this right carries with it the corollary obligation to allow others to dialogue, and to disagree, with her, and vice versa. Moreover, her right also entails that she speak about her beliefs in a way that engages rather than enrages, so that others might hear her rather than fear her, and vice versa. The vice versa is essential, because it means that no single voice is granted special a priori moral privileges in the pluralistic conversation. All participants possess the same rights and must exercise the same responsibilities. The outcome of this type of conversation should always rest on the merits of the views expressed.

A Sara Phelps must learn the fundamental rule of courteous pluralistic dialogue: Impute the best motive by giving others the benefit of the doubt, at least initially. This means: *Stop* the name-calling; *listen* to others; *question* others; *learn* from others; then and only then *proclaim* (with as much personal conviction and passion as desired) the "truth" to others. Furthermore, Sara Phelps, like her adversaries, must be prepared to repeat this *dialogical* (a way of talking that seeks mutual understanding, but not necessarily agreement) process over and over, as often as necessary. If she, or anyone else, refuses to accept mutually agreed upon rules of civil dialogue on a college campus, then, sad to say, Sara Phelps must be sent into exile. She has freely chosen to forfeit her right to be part of the ongoing conversation about religio-spirituality on a pluralistic college campus. From this moment on, she can no longer be considered a fully functioning, rights-exercising member of a community of peaceful seekers.

Toward Unbounded Dialogue

By way of summary, how then should college and university administrators and educators respond to what is a long-overdue need for us to learn how to talk openly and honestly about religion and spirituality in the academy? How do we begin to participate in "unbounded" religious dialogue? Or is it more desirable for us to relinquish any responsibility by asserting that these "sectarian" matters be contained strictly within the provinces of the human wellness center, the counseling center, campus ministry, the religious studies department, or Christian InterVarsity, Hillel, and the Newman Center?

For starters, I assiduously reject the suggestion that we ought to relegate religious dialogue to any number of isolated sectarian enclaves. I believe it is precisely during those times when students pursue meaning outside of religiously designated safety zones that they experience the most compelling learnings, as do others who might initially have been critics or skeptics. We must be willing and able to let students know that whenever and wherever issues of religious and spiritual meaning arise for them, we are ready to respond thoughtfully and knowledgeably, just as we would when racial, gender, and sexual-orientation issues arise. We will never arbitrarily rule these questions out of bounds just because they make us nervous, or because we claim to know little about them, or because we ourselves might be harboring stubborn, anti-religious stereotypes that embarrass us.

Moreover, fearless, open-ended, intellectually stimulating, cross-campus dialogue about religio-spirituality is what liberal education ought to be about. Religion has been such a fundamental component of life in all cultures and times that students cannot understand the history, politics, or art of most societies, including the United States, without examining religion's central role in producing both good and evil during the last three millennia. Also, a genuine liberal education requires an in-depth study of religious influences on all the major university disciplines, including the humanities, social sciences, and sciences. Absent this study, students get only half the story of human knowledge, thereby rendering their education as decidedly illiberal.

Finally, because the study of religion is one of the primary tools for making meaning, perforce it must play a key role in any examination of morality, ethics, and the formation of character. Despite claims to the contrary, certain traditional religious virtues (e.g., faith, hope, love, piety, compassion, sacrifice, forgiveness, obedience, self-respect) still have considerable value in secular pluralist societies. As I will point out in chapter 5, many students consider a purely secularized morality to be foundationless and arbitrary, hence relativistic. Thus, to confine the dialogue on religio-spirituality either to the religious-studies department or to designated safety zones is not only to favor (and to protect) secular moral standpoints in the university; it is to prevent all students from coming to terms with the tensions in their lives between "tradition and modernity, community and individualism, consensus and pluralism, faith and reason, and religion and secularity" (Nord, 1995, p. 380).

The first step in opening the dialogue is for us to listen intently and nondefensively and to respond in a spirit of active engagement whenever the topic of religion comes up. This approach conveys the unmistakable message to the entire campus that students, faculty, and staff have a right to be heard on religious matters. They do not need to restrict the pursuit of meaning to the goings-on in churches, synagogues, mosques, shrines, temples, or meditation rooms. Free speech on a college campus should be alive and well in all areas of human interest and conviction, including the religious. We should encourage, and respond to it, anywhere and everywhere.

The second step, in Eck's view (1993), and my own as well, is that all of us have a mutual obligation, in the interests of academic integrity, to listen critically and, whenever appropriate, to change or modify our own, previous positions on these topics, given the intellectual and emotional force of what we hear. We expect this outcome, for example, in political, economic, philosophical, and educational conversations in the seminar and lecture hall. Why not in religio-spiritual conversations? Anything less than this potentially self-transforming response on our part trivializes, and, worse, consigns to the outer regions of academic dialogue the deep-est convictions that indelibly shape the lives of millions of students every-where.

It goes without saying that this kind of unbounded religious dialogue throughout the academy will be very difficult to achieve. I offer no simplis-tic answers. In fact, I readily acknowledge that such a dialogue might finally be unachievable, although I will not stop my efforts to encourage it. While, at times, the subject matter may indeed be too hot to handle, given the long history in this culture of maintaining an unbridgeable wall of separation between church and state, I am optimistic. Furthermore, even though my own pedagogical failures in mastering this kind of unbounded religious dialogue both in and outside the classroom are legion, I am continuing to learn how to do it better. I am working hard to locate the religio-spiritual common ground that we all share in class, without being reluctant also to identify the irreconcilable differences that separate us.

I am striving diligently to encourage open, candid, considerate, and critical dialogue among the believers and disbelievers in my classroom and throughout the campus. I am struggling to do this in a way that recognizes the irreducible diversity of each of these, at times cacopho-nous, religious voices. In addition, I am trying to do this without inadvert-ently imposing an intellectual uniformity or, worse, a religiously correct blandness on my students. This imposition only guarantees the mind-numbing, soul-killing repression that I find intellectually unacceptable in so many politically correct universities and colleges. I am convinced that consideration for others and passionate conviction are not mutually ex-clusive. In fact, the former makes it safe to express the latter. I think of myself as both a particularist and a universalist, and, like Daniel Callahan (2000), I want all sides in the religious conversation to get their due, with none being privileged as the a priori victor.

The third step is to construct what Nicholas Wolterstorff (cited by John Wilson, 1999) calls an "ethics" of dialogue:

> Thou must not take cheap shots. Thou must not sit in judgment until thou hast done thy best to understand. Thou must earn thy right to disagree. Thou must conduct thyself as if [Moses, Buddha, Confucius, Jesus, Mohammed, Pope John Paul II, Bishop John Shelby Spong, or Pat Robertson (brackets added)] were sitting across the table—the point being that it is much more difficult (I don't say impossible) to dishonor someone to his face. (p. 3)

If Wolterstorff is right, then ethical dialogue on religion needs to be grounded in the virtues of compassion, generosity, candor, and intellectual integrity. An ethic of religious dialogue ought to begin with the principle that, at all times, one needs to refrain from going on the attack. It must proceed to the principle that a genuine attempt to understand another's religious views must always be a prerequisite for critique and judgment of those views. Honest disagreement is a right to be earned, rather than an entitlement to be expected; and one earns this right by demonstrating the capacity to honor, rather than dishonor, a competing point of view, even while challenging it.

The hardest task for me as a teacher is to enlarge the conversational space—to construct an unbounded-dialogue region—about religion in and out of the classroom without asking adherents of the various religious and nonreligious narratives to bracket their own strong beliefs. The most devastating criticism from students that I sometimes hear is the one that accuses me of enticing them to engage in a "postmodern" dialogue about religion that (wittingly or unwittingly) forces them to voluntarily annihilate a significant piece of themselves in the search for common religious ground—absent all the sectarian particulars.

These students resent what they consider to be my transparent attempts to smuggle my own postmodern preferences for plurality, tolerance, religious equivalence, and what one student called my "narrative-reductionism" into my teaching. They want me to be more honest and up-front about my biases. They demand that I include a personal truth-in-packaging statement in my syllabus at the beginning of my course. They want this in the interests of candor and fairness, so that they are better able to give full, informed consent to taking my course at the very outset. I am only too happy to oblige them.

The fourth step, therefore, in encouraging unbounded religious dialogue on college campuses is to start the conversation with candid, personal disclosures on everybody's part concerning where they currently stand on their religio-spiritual journeys and where they would like to end up. Putting our religio-spiritual cards on the table early is a good way to set the stage for enlarging the conversational space for everyone. By way of personal example, the gist of what I reveal early in my courses and consultancies is as follows:

> Each of us lives in a religious narrative that is cultural and historical in origin. As yet, I have no Final Answer as to whether the Ultimate Truth of any or all of these narratives exist outside of a humanly constructed culture. The reason I teach the courses I do, visit the universities that call me, and engage in formal and informal conversations with people who are in the process of finding and making meaning, is simple. While the metaphysical itch to locate a Final Answer is important

to me, what is more important at this stage of my life is to engage in an ongoing, vibrant conversation with others about just this sort of question.

I do know, however, that if our individual religious narratives were indeed connected to some Transcendent or Divine Reality outside of us, it is highly unlikely that we could formulate a universally accepted method of determining which religious story was the True Account of meaning-making. I do not deny the possibility of Ultimate Transcendence, Objective Religious Truth, or Universal Spirituality. I only assert that, in my experience in particular, and in the historical record in general, it appears unlikely that anyone is able to construct or discover Ultimate Religious Meaning *except through interpretation or mediation.* And this, in turn, is irrevocably blurred by the *personal, historical, and cultural contingencies which shape our humanness.*

In William Butler Yeats's words, we can never escape the "rag and bone shop of our messy lives" (cited in Natoli, 1997). I know of no religio-spiritual story that definitively transcends the "rags and bones" of particular times, places, and psyches. And so, in the end we are left with two options: telling our "rags and bones" stories to others, and listening to theirs as well; or keeping our stories to ourselves. I for one believe that the former is the best educational choice for those who choose to spend their time together in a learning community.

At this point it is up to the individual participants in the dialogue to decide whether or not the "rags and bones" of my particular perspective on religio-spiritual matters will be a help or a hindrance in furthering their own searches for meaning. Because they know what to expect from me, they will be able to make a more informed decision about whether to remain in, or to leave, my groups. In the next two chapters, I discuss six representative religious narratives that those students and colleagues who have elected to stay in my groups have shared with me during the last 32 years.

Chapter 3

Religions as Narratives (I): Three Mainstream Stories

As an evangelical Christian, the Bible serves as the source that instructs, enlightens, and guides all my convictions. I accept and believe by faith that the scriptures—each and every line—are the inspired Word of God. My faith is firm and unwavering. Revelation is absolute, finished, and universal.

—Jack, an evangelical Christian,
an undergraduate English major, and an Orthodox Believer

If there is a God, why has there been so much unbearable pain in my life? Can you help me to figure this out? Why does this God permit so much suffering? He is either a monster, inept, or a figment of our imaginations. I want so much to believe in the traditional Christian God, the one who cares for me and watches over me, but I no longer trust this God. I have suffered too much in his name.

—Jane, a graduate student, a public school teacher, and a Wounded Believer

I was raised in a very moderate Episcopalian church, and I have stayed loyal to it up to this day. The community is wonderful, and people feel tremendously grounded. They never ask the questions about religion that we do in the university. Why can't I just take for granted that God exists, that God is good, and that God will reward or punish me according to my lights. Why do professors make it all so complicated?

—Helen, a social work major, and a Mainliner

The Indispensability of Stories

What is it about stories that is indispensable, that rarely fails to rivet our attention? According to Sallie TeSelle (1975):

We all love a good story because of the basic narrative quality of human experience; in a sense, any story is about ourselves, and a *good* story is good precisely because somehow it rings true to human life. . . . We recognize our own pilgrimages from here to there in a good story; we feel its movement in our bones and know it is "right." We love stories, then, because our lives are stories and in the attempts of others to move, temporally and painfully, we recognize our own story. (pp. 159–160)

TeSelle is suggesting that the "real" truth of any theology, religion, or spirituality can be found in the power of the story each tells. To what extent do we find ourselves there? Do we recognize, in Anne Lamott's (1994) words, that "stories are the way to the truth," because we can only get to the bottom of our own "anger and damage and grief" in the religious stories that we construct and/or adapt for our own? Do we, in Neil Postman's (1996) view, "use the word *narrative* as a synonym for *god*, with a small *g*" (p. 5)? He goes on to say that "god . . . is the name of a great narrative, one that has sufficient credibility, complexity, and symbolic power to enable one to organize our lives around it" (p. 5). Do we agree with Stanley Hauerwas (1977) that "the true stories we learn of God are those that help us best to know what story we are and should be, what gives us "the courage to go on" (p. 80)?

If Lamott is right that "stories are the way to truth," what story do we tell about ourselves that best describes our "pilgrimage" from "here to there" and perhaps back again, in our quest for a sustainable spiritual truth? Does our story help us to understand our history, shape our destiny, develop a moral imagination, and give us something worth living and dying for? What story are we currently living in, and how does it help us to get to those defining truths that we need to order our lives?

More than one postmodern philosopher has remarked that behind every theory is an autobiography. If this is true, and I think to some extent it is, then religion and theology contain inescapable elements of the autobiograpical. Religion is a highly personal narrative that the believer creates in order to evoke, and to answer, the most confounding existential questions, the ones that defy easy scientific, political, or technological answers. In fact, I believe that science, politics, stock markets, and even technology are also stories in their own right, stories that scholars, nations, corporations, and special interest groups construct in order to serve their purposes. Whenever I read narrative theologians like the sociologist-novelist-Catholic priest, Andrew Greeley (1990), I realize why my own childhood Catholicism continues to have such a strong hold on me even today, long after I have formally abandoned it.

When I was a child, the Catholic version of Christianity totally captured my imagination, not with its authoritative dogmas and doctrines, its magisterium and moral teachings, but with its compelling and memorable stories. These were stories about Mary and Jesus, the crucifixion and the resurrection, the saints and the popes, martyrs and heretics, the local church pastor and the ladies sodality, the Jesuits and the Sisters of Mercy, the Catholic elementary school and Notre Dame University, and, of course, the Irish and the English, the Catholics and the Protestants. The stories inspired and edified me. The official church teachings only induced guilt, boredom, and rebellion.

I believe that for religion to work well on a *personal* level, it must first be born in narrative before it grows into creed, rite, and institution. It must be profoundly autobiographical and appeal to the narrative imagination long before it can convince the discursive intellect. Even today, often in spite of myself, I am living out the story of a *Catholic* agnostic, a *Catholic* educator, a *Catholic* philosopher, in short, a *Catholic* anomaly through and through. Because the Catholic story has defined so much of me, for better or worse it will remain with me forever. It has given my life "form, order, point, and direction," in the language of the anthropologist, Clifford Geertz (1973, p. 52), even though I have long since formally renounced it.

At the institutional level, the most captivating religious narratives—e.g., Taoism, Buddhism, Hinduism, Christianity, Judaism, Islam—are those that feature unforgettable characters, momentous events, magnetic ideals, and sonorous and seductive languages. It is my contention that the real power of Christianity lies mainly in the simple *allegories* that Jesus taught rather than in the theological *algorithms* that scholars construct. We also tend to remember the story of Jesus's life—his birth, his virgin mother and carpenter father, his peripatetic missionary activity, his camaraderie with his disciples, the people he met and helped along the way, his cruel persecution and tragic death, his resurrection—*before* we recall his specific teachings. Who Jesus was, and the story he lived, sets the stage for our hearing his message. The same is true for the Eastern religions.

For example, Lao Tzu (604 B.C.E.), the "grand old master" of Taoism, was a fascinating and enigmatic figure. Upset by his people's refusal to heed his message of goodness and simplicity, and seeking solitude for the remaining years of his life, Lao Tzu rode westward on a water buffalo toward what is now called Tibet. Stopped at the Hankao Pass by a gatekeeper, and refusing to heed the warning to turn back, Lao Tzu sat down for three days and composed a slim volume of five thousand characters. He presented this to the gatekeeper as a kind of bribe to let him pass through. The volume was called *Tao Te Ching* (*The Way and Its Power*). To this day, it tells a story of spontaneity, naturalness, yin and yang, and creative quietude that satisfies the spiritual hunger of millions throughout the world (Smith, 1991).

One more example of a compelling religious story: Most Western observers do not know that Islam has always had a strong mystical tradition, beginning with Muhammad (570–632), the religion's chief prophet and "proclaimer." His Hadiths (prophetic sayings), though not part of the *Qur'an*, speak everywhere of the incredible mystery of God's transformative love. Rabi'a (717–801), the esteemed Sufi mystic poetess, was once a slave but later freed because of her profound spirituality. Her complete surrender to Allah attracted many students who wanted to learn how to follow her simple path of resignation. Later Al-Hallaj (858–922), the founder of Sufism and its first martyr, was hung, drawn, and quartered for referring to himself as the "Supreme Reality," an insight he received while in a mystical trance. Ibn Arabi (1165–1240), the most famous of all Sufi philosophers, claimed to write "at the command of God," transmitted to him directly through periods of ecstatic mystical revelation.

Rumi (1207–1273), the chief character in the story I wish to tell here, was perhaps the greatest Sufi mystic of all. A Sufi is a "man of wool" who, through joyful witness and ecstatic experience, seeks to uncover the living presence of Allah the Beloved. Born in Afghanistan, Rumi spent the first half of his life as a highly respected Islamic scholar and theologian. His existence was soon to undergo a major mystical transformation, however.

In December 1244, Rumi met a dervish (a whirling, chanting beggar dedicated to a life of poverty and chastity) named Shams I Tabriz who changed his life. Rumi grew to love him, and the man who was once a reclusive, Islamic scholar now became a poet and a romantic who danced all day and sang all night. When his soulmate, Tabriz, was murdered two years later, Rumi used his grief to explore the mystery of divine love. He devoted the rest of his life to describing in luminous verse how everything in the world is a magnificent manifestation of the divine. Rumi's poetry has extraordinary appeal today to many Westerners, because it combines in one narrative themes of joy, caritas, and service in behalf of what he called the "Divine Flame of Love" (Harvey, 1996).

I would argue that the brilliance of all the religions and spiritualities the world has ever known lies in their peculiar narrative power. Taoism and Sufism, without minimizing the perennial wisdom of their teachings, tell wonderful stories. Their major figures, Lao Tzu and Rumi, are the characters of exciting and inspiring fiction, and the adventure in their spiritual awakenings draws us in. If, as I contend, religion is basically a story lived out by people to give meaning to their lives in a particular place and time, as it was for Jesus, Lao Tzu, and Rumi, then we must continually ask whether a particular narrative still speaks to our needs today. Does the story of Jesus, Buddha, Confucius, or Solomon continue to help us understand who we are, whom we belong to, how we should behave, and how we might come to grips with the mystery of our existence?

Narrative Construals of Reality

I treat each of the nonfiction readings I assign in my courses, along with the personal accounts I hear from students and colleagues, as important religious stories, or in the psychologist Jerome Bruner's (1996) words, as unique "narrative construals of reality." Each religious construal of reality has a particular assemblage of characters—heroes and villains—as well as a characteristic history, plot, and setting. Each construal poses questions about the meaning of existence and proposes its own special solutions. Each construal, in turn, features a specialized language including many technical concepts. Some narrative construals are philosophical, some theological, some poetical, and some a creative combination of each. Furthermore, each construal presents a specific point of view—one often ardently held, fiercely defended, and zealously propagated.

I want my students and colleagues to understand that, for most of us, religious truth lies in the eye of the storyteller, and that two storytellers can often see the same ineffable "realities" in startlingly contrasting ways. Thus, the truth of any single religious story is frequently a matter of interpretation emanating from the perspectives of opposing, sometimes overlapping, religious stories. In my estimation, the pedagogical value of getting students and colleagues to think about religion as contrasting "narrative construals of reality" is, in Jerome Bruner's words, "the itch it creates to know 'why' a story is being told now under 'these' circumstances by 'this' narrator. . . . Narrative construals of reality lead us to look for a 'voice'—despite authorial efforts to seem objective and dispassionate, like the omniscient narrator" (p. 138).

Truth be told, this approach to look for the "voice" and the "story," rather than the Truth, in what we read and hear from others, has its problems. Some formerly devout believers react to my narrative construal of religion with disillusionment, even sadness, and then they proceed to reject *all* religious stories, including their own, as nothing more than comforting fictions meant to soothe the weak-minded. Some "heretics" use my narrative approach to reinforce their previously held cynicism about religion. They continue even more vigorously to repudiate any idea of an Objective Truth that might transcend a particular story. Others turn hungrily to the secular narratives of business, science, education, or politics as substitutes for the religious dogmas they gleefully discard. Still others manage to cling even more tenaciously to the belief that *their* religious story is "obviously" superior to all the rest, on the grounds that it alone contains Inerrantly Revealed Truths. Lastly, there are always those who lash out furiously at me for dismissing their religious beliefs as "mere stories." As a workshop attendee once charged: "You yourself believe in nothing Absolute, so you trivialize all the things we would die for by calling them fantasies. What makes you think *your* 'story' is so great? What 'story' would *you* ever die for?"

Notwithstanding these risks, however, most students and colleagues, I am relieved to report, appreciate the opportunity to understand that they live in a religious world constructed according to the guidelines of particular narratives. Furthermore, while some may not always like it, they accept that I, for one, am unable to teach a course, or lead a campus-wide dialogue, on religion and spirituality with any kind of intellectual honesty or fairness, unless I can put the various narrative construals of reality in conversation with each other. Despite the shortcomings of my method, I can do this best by examining a religion's *narrative* power instead of pointing out the superiority or weakness of its *revelational, propositional,* or *ecclesiastical* claims. More to the point, I want to know how their religious stories, or lack of them, help to shape the overall stories that students and colleagues tell about themselves.

Six Types of Religious Stories That College Students Tell

For the rest of this chapter and all of the next, I will present six types of religious stories that students and colleagues frequently tell about themselves in my courses and workshops. *I call these the narratives of orthodoxy, wounded belief, mainline belief, activism, exploration, and secular humanism.* These narratives speak less about the content of specific religions and spiritualities and more about personal journeys and discoveries. They describe what Wade Clark Roof (1999) calls "varieties of spiritual quest." Like Roof, I find that many young people today are less likely to tell their religio-spiritual stories in strictly denominational terms; although, in my experience, more college students do than I think Roof acknowledges, particularly the groups I will be calling the orthodox believers and the mainliners. I agree with Roof, however, that there has been a drastic shift among people of all ages from identification with traditional faith communities toward "inwardness, subjectivity, the experiential, the expressive, and the spiritual" (p. 7). I will discuss these types of narratives in greater depth in the chapter to follow.

My hope is to sketch miniature portraits for each of these narratives that will not end up as stereotypes. I believe that the six portraits I draw in this chapter and the next capture a set of characteristics that university leaders will find helpful in understanding the vast range of religious experience that exists among college youths and adults today. I have found these religious narratives among every age-, gender-, racial-, ethnic-, and socioeconomic group on all the campuses I visit, including, most notably, my own. I also find that most students only need a little encouragement, the right questions, and a supportive dialogue space to tell their stories to others.

No single narrative exists as a pure type, of course, and, at least in theory, none need be mutually exclusive. I for one find something personally resonant in several of them. Although my six narrative types bear some similarity to Roof's (1999) "five major subcultures," their differences are substantial. For starters, our labels are dissimilar. Also, I treat each type as a story that today's college students tell about their religio-spirituality; Roof presents them as "maps and terrains" (pp. 3–15) in order to understand the religious experiences of post–World War II baby-boomers. While I greatly appreciate Roof's research, particularly his earlier *A Generation of Seekers* (1993), my own methodological take on religious narratives is educational, philosophical, and theological; his is sociological, based on hundreds of life histories and surveys, carried out over several years. Moreover, I am mainly interested in how these narratives get represented on today's college and university campuses. His concerns are more societal and large-scale.

Finally, I must mention *what I will intentionally be omitting* in these six narratives. I will not be discussing the history or theology of any of the world's major or minor religions. This is a comparative-religion task far beyond the scope of my goals or abilities for this particular project; also this work has been done many times by scholars far more qualified than I, and I recommend two excellent readings in this area in chapter 5.

Also, while I am an ardent admirer of non-Western religions, and while I recognize the growing presence of such belief systems as Buddhism, Confucianism, Hinduism, Islam, Sikhism, Taoism, and so forth, on college campuses throughout the United States, I will not be constructing a *specific* non-Western religious narrative in these pages. First of all I would not know where to start, so numerous and complex are these accounts. Second, the dominant religio-spiritual orientation on most college campuses that I know is still Judeo-Christian, and variations of this account are what I hear from students throughout the United States. Hence, the sub-title of this chapter—"three *mainstream* stories"—refers to Christian and Jewish organizations, particularly the Catholic Church, the major Protes-tant denominations, and Ultra-Orthodox, Orthodox, Conservative, and Reform Judaism. Gallup surveys show that while the number of non-Western believers in this country is growing each decade, less than one percent of the current population is Islamic, Buddhist, or Hindu, about the same percentage of those who profess these faiths on college campuses.

However, it is important for me to acknowledge immediately that this number is bound to change dramatically by 2050 or much sooner, if the U.S. Census Bureau is correct. White people of European ancestry will constitute less than half the population in the United States, with much of this predicted growth occurring among Latinos, Middle Easterners, and Asians (all data cited in Gallagher, 1999, p. 147). All of these groups will bring their religious narratives with them, as they are now doing in small, but impressively incremental numbers. What is considered "mainstream" religion today will undergo radical change tomorrow. I fully expect in the years to come that several non-Western religious narratives will take shape among college students and become part of the mainstream, and I hope that I will be here to write about them.

In the next chapter, I do present the expanding influence of non-West-ern religio-spiritualities on American belief systems in what I refer to as the exploration narrative. Also, I would argue that the six narratives I describe in these two chapters each have their parallels in the non-West-ern religions. Because Islam, Buddhism, and Hinduism, for example, are themselves pluralistic narratives, each will have its fair share of orthodox, wounded, mainline, and activist believers, as well as its prototypal explorers.

The main reason I construct the six narratives that follow, however, is that not only is selection unavoidable, given space and focus parameters, but these stories are the ones that I typically and persistently hear on college campuses everywhere. If the narratives reveal a Western, Judeo-Christian bias, it is because between 80% and 90% of college students come out of this particular narrative background. As I will argue in the final chapter, religious socialization, like any kind of socialization, does indeed go all the way down, and, like it or not, the Judeo-Christian story is still the way that most college students construe religion and spirituality. In reaction to this understandable narrative myopia, one of the main rea-sons why I have written this book is to argue that the mainstream Western religious narratives need the enrichment—the stretching and deepening—that non-Western and alternative religious stories can provide.

They need this, if they are to continue to survive in the face of an escalating religious skepticism and pluralism both in this country and throughout the world. If my argument is valid, even now the mainstream religions in America are undergoing substantial philosophical and theological changes due to reform efforts from within as well as from without. Contact with other faith traditions makes transformation—no matter how subtle—inevitable. I believe that such reconstruction is both valuable and necessary.

Three Mainstream Stories

The Orthodoxy Narrative
My Faith in the Absolute Truth of the Bible is Firm and Unwavering!

The narrative I describe in this section is that of the orthodox, evangelical Christian. The central theme of this story is unwavering faith in God, along with an ironclad conviction that the Bible is the sole repository of God's absolute truth. The purpose of the story is to bring as many people to this truth as possible, mainly through active proselytizing and role modeling. I choose this particular story to tell, because most of the orthodox believers I see in my classes and workshops tend to be theologically conservative Christians. Also, their influence appears to be spreading on college campuses throughout America.

> Why do I get the sense I am being attacked in this course, whenever I open my mouth to declare my belief in Jesus Christ? Why do I feel that both the professor and my peers want me to forsake my faith? As an evangelical Christian, the Bible serves as the source that instructs, enlightens, and guides my convictions. I accept and believe by faith that the scriptures—each and every line—are the inspired Word of God. This is my conviction. It is firm and unwavering. Although, at times, I can honestly respect the convictions of others, I will never forsake what I have come to define as my personal religious conviction. Only I can live inside my truth, and I know my truth to be right, not just for me but for others as well—after all, Revelation is absolute and finished and universal. I only want others to open their hearts, and listen, and accept, and rejoice in the Word of the Lord. And if they can't or won't, I will still love them and pray for them.

These words were written for me in a journal entry by "Jack," an undergraduate English major, and they were meant to send me a message: Whether or not I knew it, I was upsetting him with what he called my "liberal" animus against the more "conservative" religious believers in class, in spite of my self-declared efforts to be evenhanded toward religious differences.

During the semester he took my course in religion, spirituality, and education, I remember that Jack sat in silence for much of the first half of the term—sometimes staring fretfully at the rest of us while gently shaking his head over some point being made in class, sometimes looking distractedly into space during discussion of a difficult text, and sometimes quietly reading his Bible whenever heated dialogue, and the discord that accompanied it, threatened to disrupt the well-being of our seminar. About halfway into the course, Jack came to my office one day in a highly agitated state. Not only was he having great difficulty with all of the texts I had up to this point assigned for the course—he felt that I had purposely chosen "postmodern" and "relativist" authors who were critical of what he called "true-blue Christian believers" like himself—but he persistently questioned the basic value of my offering such a course to education majors in the first place. He wondered whether he should drop the course, because he felt like a "fish out of water."

Again, in his words:

> I don't think we can ever teach students about religion in public schools, because few teachers are equipped to know how to pick up the shattered pieces of students' beliefs and values that would result from an open-ended analysis of what is sacred to them. Isn't it better to believe in *something* rather than doubt *everything*? I think the teaching of religion should be left to the home, church, or private religious school, but never to secular institutions. No student who is a Christian should ever be required to question such fundamentally unassailable beliefs as sin, redemption, Jesus Christ our Savior, and biblical inerrancy. I know I will never question them, either for myself or for my students. So, tell me, why am I here in your course?

I have heard complaints like these before from students, of course, and so they do not surprise me. I remember a well-meaning colleague once saying to me that he did not know why in the world I wanted to offer a course on religion and education to teachers and teachers-to-be, because, as far as he was concerned, it was an open invitation to all the "religious nuts" in the community to "sell their wares" in an academically sanctioned, college classroom. To make matters worse, they would have a "chance to earn professional credits as well." My colleague envisioned a group of obnoxious "Christian fanatics" trooping into my seminar each semester, constantly forcing their "fantasies" about miracles, angels, weeping Madonnas, the "sweet love" of Jesus, sin, redemption, grace, and carefully selected biblical passages on the rest of us. I can honestly say that in over three decades of teaching I have met only a few so-called "Christian fanatics" who even come close to matching his stereotype.

Jack, I soon discovered, was actually less interested in imposing his beliefs on us than he was in making sure that I, and others, were not foisting our "anti-Christian, secular humanism" on him. Jack was a strong believer, certainly, but he was no unreasonable fanatic. He was what I would call an orthodox evangelical believer—whose Truth happened to find expression in converting the world to Jesus Christ. My use of the term *orthodox* (from the Greek meaning "right or straight opinion") follows James Davison Hunter's (1991). Orthodox belief "is the total commitment on the part of adherents to an external, definable, and transcendent authority" (p. 44). It is an authority that is unchangeable, final, right, and absolute.

Orthodox Jews surrender to the authority of Torah and the religio-cultural community that lives by it. Orthodox Catholics defer to the authority of the papacy, the Roman Magisterium, and to fixed church traditions. Orthodox Protestants devote themselves to the inerrant authority of Scripture. Orthodox Muslims (Islam literally means "submission") submit themselves to the authority of Allah's will, as interpreted by Muhammad in the *Qur'an* (a series of readings or recitations that consist of 114 chapters).

In my experience, orthodox believers actually come in all ideological shapes and sizes. Pluralism is evident everywhere. Some are stridently religious, others moderately so; some are anti-intellectual and self-righteous, whereas others are reasonable, charming, even modest in their claims. In fact, the tone in which orthodox believers express their heartfelt convictions can range all the way from placid to stormy. Orthodox believers can be Shiite fundamentalists or Zionist Jews, evangelical Reaganite conservatives or liberation-theology liberals; or even scientific skeptics or flat earthers. No single religious, political, economic, or educational ideology has a corner on the market of the orthodoxy narrative, if its beliefs are nailed firmly in place, and its access to certainty unquestioned.

Jack, however, was neither a stormy nor arrogant orthodox believer. He was earnest, personable, and disarmingly insightful. Every so often during class discussion he would become the bright English major, calling our attention to the hidden authorial biases we might be missing in the assigned readings, as well as to the *nonsequiturs* and question-begging in the self-serving arguments some of us were making. He had recently joined a strict, bible-based, evangelical Christian church group in my state, and, unlike the more liberal, Episcopalian church of his youth, this community offered him and his fiancée something very precious. This was the confident assurance that they had found the Truth and, along with it, Eternal Life—not to mention supportive, like-minded friends here on earth. Many students in our seminar envied Jack his involvement with a close community that he could trust and turn to in times of personal strife.

When Jack finally began to open up in class, he impressed all of us with his sincerity, warmth, and strong conviction, even though many remained suspicious of his views and politely kept him at arm's length. He won no converts, nor do I think this was ever his intention. However, Jack did leave the course no less convinced that, in the best of all possible universes, the one where God is in His place and all is right with the world, his Christian beliefs would eventually become normative for everyone.

There is much for us to learn from orthodox Christians like Jack on a college campus. Orthodox believers of all stripes, but particularly theologically conservative Christians, are clamoring for attention and respect like never before in the secular academy. They are here to stay, and they want to be a transformative presence. Survey reports indicate that among Christians, orthodox Protestants and Catholics comprise upwards of 30 to 40 percent of the United States population (Carpenter, 1998; Miller, 1995). Similarly, their numbers are growing at a very fast rate on college campuses throughout the country (Marsden, 1997).

Although some orthodox Christians, by and large, are far more tolerant and heterodox than press stereotypes tend to depict them, they do hold some beliefs in common. Like Jack, most think that the United States is experiencing a major moral crisis, and the liberal elites in the universities, government, and media are the chief culprits. Many also hold that because this country is a Christian nation, a constitutional amendment ought to permit prayer in the nation's classrooms (Miller, 2000). The majority also feels that abortion and homosexuality are major sins against God's absolute moral law (Wolfe, 1998). The difficult task for all of us in the academy will be to learn how to address fairly, yet honestly, the strengths as well as the weaknesses in the orthodoxy narrative, without censoring, ridiculing, or ignoring views like Jack's in the cross-campus religious dialogue that I am encouraging.

The orthodoxy narrative is an understandable reaction to the excesses of liberalism and modernism during the twentieth and now the twenty-first centuries. Orthodox believers see themselves as engaged in a cosmic battle between the forces of conservatism and liberalism, religion and secularism, good and evil. For the orthodox believer—whether Hindu, Jewish, Muslim, or Christian—godless secularism has won the day. Individualism, skepticism, and hedonism have become the dominant values of secular pluralist societies. Family structures and sex roles have undergone major upheaval. Absolute moral standards have eroded beyond the point of no return, and this includes a respect for the dignity of *all* human life, both born and unborn.

Moreover, postmodern academics and Generation-X youths seem to challenge all types of authority on the principle that it is *ipso facto* "oppressive" and "reactionary." Technology, science, and bureaucratic rationality have become the only reasonable way to understand, and organize, the confounding realities of everyday life. In a high-tech age, religion increasingly gets buried in the catacombs of home and church, a decaying corpse that ought to be heard from no more in public life. It is my contention that those of us in higher education need to understand the seriousness of the cry of many young people on campus for a set of moral and spiritual truths that are enduring. These are truths that might fortify them against the personal uncertainties of human finitude. They ask: Is there some incontrovertible, transcendent meaning in chronic unhappiness and dissatisfaction, catastrophic accidents and illnesses, disheartening personal failure in work, love, and learning, lingering anxiety, and in the crushing finality of death?

The core of the orthodoxy story, whether religious or otherwise, is the principle that *Truth is unimpeachable, absolute, and final.* For Jack, this Truth is embodied in his inexorable conviction that God's power can direct lives and history; moreover, it can heal imperfection and overcome evil. Best of all, it can lead people toward biblical righteousness. This narrative finds its *extreme religious* expression in the two-and-a-half-million-dollar *fatwah* (a final legal decision by an Islamic leader) that the Ayatollah Khomeini issued against the life of the writer, Salman Rushdie. Khomeini, the theocratic leader of Iran, decreed the death of Rushdie in 1989 because, in *The Satanic Verses*, he depicted Muhammad as deluded and taking down dictation for the *Qur'an*, not from Allah, but from a devil in disguise.

Another extreme, less lethal example (although some might argue that this signals the death of the ecumenical movement in the Catholic Church) can be found in the 2000 Vatican's Congregation for the Doctrine of the Faith (CDF) declaration, *Dominus Iesus: On the Unicity and Salvific Universality of Jesus Christ and the Church.* This is a papal document highly critical of what it calls the "so-called theology of religious pluralism." The statement says that only faithful Catholics loyal to Rome are able to attain divine salvation. All other faiths, including Protestant

Christianity, Buddhism, Hinduism, and Islam are "gravely deficient" because they contain "defects" that render them inferior (Smith, 2000).

Intellectually, these radical positions ought to trouble those of us who want the search for truth in the academy to be both unending and open-ended. Orthodoxy, taken to the limit, in Rauch's (1993) words, "is the strong disinclination to take seriously the notion that you might be wrong" (p. 89). Orthodox believers like the Ayatollah Khomeini and Sara Phelps make up their minds once and for all because they think they have found a transcendent stamp of approval for the things they believe to be true. They also know without a doubt that the rest of us can find this definitive (and certifiable) Truth, if only we are willing to read *their* "right" books, listen to *their* "right" speakers, discern *their* "right" transcendent signals in everyday life, and open up our minds and hearts to receive *their* Final Revelation.

As an educator, I fear the imperialism of some orthodox narratives, because I am well aware of the disastrous consequences in people's lives whenever these narratives are carried to an absolutist extreme (Lawrence, 1989; Ulstein, 1995). In my classes and workshops, for example, I have had numerous students through the years lament to me that their rigid, religious upbringings—sometimes fundamentalist Christian, sometimes traditional Catholic, and sometimes Orthodox Jewish—had ruptured relationships in their families beyond the point of no return. Once these students had rebelled against the religious faiths of their youth, more orthodox family members—along with some church and temple leaders—summarily branded them as "heretics," "turncoats," and "sinners," and banished them from the community. Sadly, many of these students ultimately became wounded believers, who would go on to spend a troubled adulthood mourning the loss of parental and sibling approval. More tragically, they would blame themselves for blindly refusing to accept a faith that made no rational or emotional sense to them.

I have also had a few students, who, after identifying themselves in class as Christian fundamentalists, evangelicals, or Pentecostalists, went on in a patronizing manner to write off the rest of us as lacking any kind of "moral" credibility because we did not hold the same beliefs as they. They lost patience with us because we dared to *question* their interpretation of "God's Word" when we should have *acquiesced* to it. They grew angry because we might have pushed a little too hard at times to get them to explain the inconsistencies in their understanding of absolute biblical Truth, particularly when some passages appeared to contradict other passages.

In my own teaching, I continue to struggle, sometimes in vain, to make a connection with the more zealous types of orthodox students. For my taste, they are too quick to close their minds to alternative views. They too frequently grow impatient, often angry, with those of us who genuinely wonder why a superior and final Truth is said to exist in one holy book or in one holy figure rather than all the others. I want desperately to follow orthodox believers' reasoning, to understand in some small way their godly zeal. While I admit, at times, I do not know what to do with the more overbearing orthodox believers, the ones who want to *convert* me rather than *converse* with me, I am also strangely attracted to them. So too are many of their peers. We want to know what makes them tick, what makes them so sure that the search for truth and meaning stops abruptly with key biblical proof-texts, church creeds, and charismatic preachers. I find that it is often as instructive for us to interact with them in stimulating conversation as it is for them to dialogue with us, provided all the participants fastidiously follow the guidelines for pluralistic conversation that I have been proposing throughout this book.

At times during my classes and cross-campus conversations, I must report that it is the *Christian* orthodox believers in particular who provoke the wounded believers, explorers, and secular humanists (see the sections to follow), because of the unyielding certitude of their religious convictions. They often display an irritating tendency to cite slanted, biblical proof-texts in their public conversations, as if these alone are enough to settle any conversation—once and for all—on the difficult religious questions that come up in a seminar or a colloquium. Nevertheless, even though I say this, some otherwise skeptical students are drawn to orthodox believers' genuine theological innocence; to their modest, unquestioning faith in a devoted, compassionate, biblical God, waiting to embrace all of us in truth and in love, if only we are willing to make ourselves vulnerable to His merciful and solicitous entreaties.

I make it a point to ask deliberately evocative questions of all orthodoxy narratives, religious, political, or otherwise, whenever I enter into conversation with those who swear by their inerrant truths. I find that, in most cases, these types of questions, while discomforting, tend to promote rather than obstruct dialogue. They help to teach students to *dialogue with* one another rather than to *pontificate at* one another. They precipitate much honest soul-searching on everyone's part. It is my view, contrary to my colleague's warning that my new course would attract only "religious nuts" and "Christian fanatics," that the vast majority of orthodox believers who do find their way to my classes, workshops, and colloquia are far more subtle and thoughtful, even though certain, in their beliefs than he might think. Most welcome the opportunity to address my leading questions, because they take me at my word that I am not interested in disparaging either them or their beliefs. I genuinely and humbly want to understand them, even learn from them, although I do not have to be like them. This needs to be the message that we send to all orthodox believers in our cross-campus conversations.

My primary aim in asking the questions that I do is to stir up some conversational enthusiasm (from the Greek, *enthousiasmos*, inspired or possessed by God). Religio-spiritual conversations are best when they are both empathic and spirited. While the questions below might seem somewhat provocative, they do manage to evoke both compassion and passion. The Sara Phelpses of orthodox belief, who harbor such unshakable convictions as "God hates fags," have as yet to make an appearance in any of my groups, and for this I am grateful. However, in the interest of encouraging genuine narrative diversity, and in eliciting their responses to my questions, I would gladly receive them in the event that they did show up someday. The types of questions I ask are as follows:

- Is it possible that while there indeed may be one Truth, there might also be many ways to get there, each equally valid and valuable, depending on the religio-spiritual narrative that makes the most sense to the believer? Or am I diluting the idea of Truth?
- Must finding the Ultimate Religious Truth always be a zero-sum game? If you and I come up with different answers to our honest religio-spiritual questions, does it mean, therefore, that one of us is wrong and the other right? In order to secure my salvation (or peace of mind), why must I be forced to ignore, demean, convert, or destroy you, and vice versa? Are there no other alternatives? Or am I naive in thinking that there is no absolute wrong or right?
- Why do you think that exclusive claims to Ultimate Religious Truth through the ages have resulted in so much "holy horror"? How do you suppose it is possible for such wonderful religious virtues as service, repentance, compassion, love, goodness, and hope to get transmuted into their ugly opposites? Why do you think that orthodox religious belief so often becomes the spark that fuels conflict, hatred, suffering, and even death? Conversely, should I be putting more emphasis on the "holy joy" than the "holy horror" that orthodox religious belief has brought to the world?

- What do you think of this assertion of mine? "No God, or sacred book, or church teaching, or religious practice, or prophet must ever be presented as greater than the love that we ought to have for one another, *despite our many differences*." Isn't this conviction the crowning point of all that is good in the world's major religions, including, most definitely, Christianity, at least as Jesus himself construed it? Or am I reading my own secular humanistic biases into the world's major religions?
- Do you think it is possible to secure the consolations and assurances that the orthodoxy narrative confers on its exponents without the guilt, shame, and arrogance that sometimes accompany it? Or is the latter to be expected whenever flawed human beings try to live up to the ideals and expectations of the former?
- Is it possible that God is far too big for any single orthodoxy narrative to contain? Or is this just another way of relativizing all religiospiritual narratives by claiming that one take on God's Truth is as good as any other, because who really knows for sure?

The Wounded Belief Narrative
If There Is a God, Why Has There Been So Much Unbearable Pain in My Life?

The particular story that follows is graphic, and it is painful for me to recount. I have heard other versions of it many times in the years that I have taught. I could have sanitized it, in order to make it appear less judgmental, but the tragedy for so many in the wounded belief narrative lies precisely in its starkness and its cruelty. Thus, I will leave the essential elements of this story intact. Because I have heard stories like this mostly from students in the more conservative Christian denominations, I will not gloss over this fact. Obviously, however, Christianity is not the only religion that wounds some of its believers. Mark Juergensmeyer (2000) documents a variety of cruelties perpetrated on both believers and nonbelievers by representatives of some of the other major world religions— Messianic Zionism, Hamas Islam, Sikhism, Hinduism, Buddhism—in his extraordinary *Terror in the Mind of God*. His focus is on "global violence." Mine is on the psychological and physical violence done in the spurious name of religion against college students. I can only write about the students I have known, and so I will try to construct a narrative about wounded belief that is at once credible and sensitive. The chief theme in the wounded belief narrative is suffering. Its objective is to understand

and overcome the pain in such a way that the sufferer is able to find a transcendent meaning worth living and holding onto.

> I want so badly to believe in God, but I can't. When I was younger, I was taught by my church pastor not to question his authority, to obey him even when I disagreed with his teachings, because he was speaking as "God's Chosen Messenger." Later, throughout my early adolescence, whenever my father would enter my bedroom at night to rape me, he would ask me over and over: "Do you love God? Do you love me? If you love us both, then you must obey me." I was held a captive by his questions and his threats. I was told that I would lose his love *plus* my eternal soul, if I questioned his authority. I hated reading Alan Peshkin's *God's Choice* during our course, not because I disagreed with what he said about the absolute mind control of many Christian Fundamentalist schools, but because he was actually describing the way I was raised, both in my Catholic church community and at home. If there is a God, why has there been so much unbearable pain in my life? Can you help me to figure this out?

These are the distressing words of "Jane," a wounded believer. Because of a strong recommendation by a faculty advisor she trusted, Jane, a graduate student, found her way, somewhat cautiously, into my course one fall semester. I find that Jane represents a particular type of religious seeker who is showing up more and more frequently in my classes. Although severely injured in the name of religion, and understandably bitter, the wounded believer has, for a variety of complex reasons, refused to give up completely on religion. In fact, most wounded believers, even though gravely suspicious of organized religion and its official hierarchies, and profoundly damaged (psychologically, intellectually, and/or physically) by the abuse that authority figures of one kind or another have imposed on them, want desperately to understand what might have gone wrong in the religions of their youth. They also want to know how they might be able to make things right. More women than men in my courses and workshops are likely to identify themselves as wounded believers, although, when feeling supported and ready, the men have touching stories of their own to tell.

Wounded believers appear to be the direct antithesis of many orthodox believers, although some might very well have identified with this narrative at an earlier point in their lives. Unlike the majority of orthodox believers, wounded believers are highly tentative in their religious views, extremely self-effacing, fearful, genuinely ambivalent, and almost obstinately anti-authoritarian. They can also be very angry or very resigned, depending on their individual temperaments and the severity of their earlier experiences. All of them have wretchedly sad stories to tell, however.

I think it safe to say that it is highly unlikely many will go on to become orthodox believers, if and when they "heal" from their religious injuries.

Jane, in her mid-40s, was a third-grade, elementary-school teacher. Raised a life-long Catholic, she belonged to a parish noted for its very conservative forms of worship, as well as for its near-literal understanding of both the Christian Bible and many of the official documents of the Church. The *Catechism of the Catholic Church* was one of the major sources for her pastor's homilies during Sunday mass. To Jane's chagrin, these homilies always emphasized the importance of personal piety, obedience to authority, church dogma, an angry God, an apocalyptic future, and a literal reading of the most conservative Papal encyclicals and other pronouncements.

Jane's most frequent entries in her journal during the semester recounted the anger, anxiety, and self-doubt she experienced while growing up as a member of this church. Both her mother and father were staunch supporters of the presiding pastor and enthusiastic advocates of his teachings. Jane often wrote that she felt the entire church edifice, including her family, was aligned against her whenever she chose to express her individuality. She spoke incessantly in our seminar about how powerless she felt while growing up. Her persistent question, in one form or another throughout the 15 weeks we spent together in the seminar was: "If there is a God, why has there been such unbearable pain in my life?"

More technically, wounded believers in my classes and workshops share a common dilemma: *They struggle to understand the problem of theodicy.* Some approach the issue theologically and philosophically; others, like Jane, far more emotionally and personally. Theodicy (this word in Greek means God and justice) is the problem that arises when the suffering of innocent people is set against the Western belief in an all-loving, all-knowing, and all-powerful, monotheistic God. How do we justify God given the near-ubiquity of unspeakable evil? The pivotal challenge in theodicy, at least since the seventeenth-century philosopher Gottfried Leibniz coined the term, is the effort to come to terms with the following types of questions:

- Why do the innocent suffer?
- Why do bad things happen to good people?
- How can an absolutely just God allow injustice?
- Why can't an omnipotent God prevent the occurrence of natural and human tragedies?
- Why does an all-loving God allow hate-filled people to harm His creatures?

- If God knows beforehand that evil will happen, why doesn't He do everything in His power to stop evil?
- In what ways, if any, are God's power and goodness compatible with the fact of suffering?
- Why does God give people free will, if He knows in advance the evil they will do?
- Why didn't God create people who would never harm others? What is the point?
- If God is to be praised for all the *good* in His creation, shouldn't He also be rebuked for all the *evil* in His creation?
- Why does God allow the problem of theodicy to remain a mystery to human beings, given the indisputable fact that, through the centuries, more religious faith has been shattered over the problem of good and evil than for any other reason? Again, what is the point?

Here is the Christian apologist, C. S. Lewis (1962), on theodicy: "If God were good, He would wish to make His creatures perfectly happy, and if God were almighty, He would be able to do what He wished. But the creatures are not happy. Therefore, God lacks either goodness, or power, or both. This is the problem of pain, in its simplest forms" (p. 75). In her own language, Jane is asking for answers to many of these questions in order to make some sense of the pain she experienced throughout her adolescence at the hands of her father. To put a human face on the abstractions of theodicy, Jane represents the type of wounded believer in my courses and workshops who has suffered unspeakable sexual abuse by a friend or close relative.

Often these malefactors defend their atrocities with loathsome, self-serving references to God. I have also had students come into my course who have been sexually abused by clergy, and these victims are, without question, the most broken (and often the most bitter) exbelievers I see. Their sense of personal betrayal is nearly total. Stefan Ulstein (1995), a researcher who interviewed dozens of exfundamentalist Christians (both men and women) whose faith had been irreparably damaged by predatory clergy who molested and raped them, makes this razor-sharp observation:

> As the dark secrets of childhood sexual abuse entered the public dialogue, too many respected churchmen were revealed as pedophiles and pederasts. Many young adults who came forward for healing and justice were further humiliated by a patriarchal structure that stressed obedience to authority and silence for the sake of the church's reputation. Churches struggled to keep their secrets and their leaders' prerogatives rather than seeking justice for their children. The millstone

might have been a good replacement for the necktie in many congregations. (p. 19)

It took Jane the better part of an entire semester to disclose the "dark secrets of her childhood" to her classmates. I recall vividly the day she decided to go public toward the end of our seminar, and my heart pounded when she did. Encouraged by reading Stefan Ulstein's (1995) accounts of Christian fundamentalists who experienced similar sexual calamities at the hands of relatives professing a strong belief in God and church, Jane blurted out the following at our final class meeting:

> I want to tell you how important this course has been for me in so many ways. The other day I was talking to a friend who still practices Catholicism. She constantly peppered me with questions about my lack of faith. She tried to convince me that I do not exist by some accident, that there is a Supreme Being, that God still cares for me, and though I am born into an imperfect world where evil does exist, Jesus will always fix the brokenness. Do you know what I said to her? "Your caring God turned His head during the countless times my father beat and raped me throughout my teenage years. My father told me to accept what he was doing because it was God's wish that I give him pleasure. I hate my father with a passion, and I would kill him today if I knew where he was. I turned my back on my family 15 years ago, the same time I turned my back on my church. This is the same church where the pastor told me that my father was really a good man who got caught at a weak moment. He simply lost control and stumbled into sin, and it was my responsibility to comfort and protect him by not hating him, by forgiving him. Your God and your church stripped me of all my power and control and sapped my inner strength. I am only now beginning the long journey back." I want to thank all of you in this class for helping me face the challenge of reconciling my past with a healthy vision for my future.

Jane's stunning revelation drew audible gasps from her classmates. One of the great difficulties I have found as a teacher in dealing with wounded believers in my classes and dialogue groups is in knowing how to respond to them during such moments of dramatic self-disclosure. Because I am not trained as a therapist, I do my best to listen, affirm, and, when appropriate, I try to relate the self-disclosure to the formal course content and readings—in a manner that I hope is both prudent and sensitive. However, a few wounded believers come into my course experiencing such extreme psychopathology in all aspects of their lives that it is difficult for me, a layman, to separate out cause from effect in the matter of their religious suffering. Thus, I try always to hold to one pedagogical principle: *My seminar is not a therapy group, and I am not a therapist.* My interaction with wounded believers in class and outside always involves very difficult judgment calls requiring exquisite sensitivity. I am never completely sure whether I and the group are actually helping or harming these troubled students. However, these students are real, and they show up everywhere I teach and visit. Their presence on a college campus, and in a classroom such as mine, demands some kind of academic response.

My heart aches for students like Jane, and, although her case is particularly melodramatic and gut-wrenching, other wounded believers in my classes and workshops will often talk about their less sensational cases with the same kind of intense feeling. Each semester I can count on an impassioned group of wounded believers describing the varieties of injustices they have experienced in their churches as the result of *rigid religious doctrines* and their damaging personal consequences. For example, ex-Roman Catholics will complain about the Church's intractable positions on such issues as abortion, birth control, homosexuality, and divorce, and how they have been stigmatized and punished as a result of their dissent on one or more of these disputes. Ex-Protestant fundamentalists will recount lurid tales of being exiled from their families and communities whenever they dared to challenge the near-divine authority of church leaders on matters of biblical literalism or puritanical moral conduct. Jews, who have been forced out of their orthodox temples for raising pointed questions about the oppression of women, homosexuals, and those who intermarry, will lament their marginalization by traditional Jewish religious leaders and their congregations. I have also heard similar complaints on several of these issues from the few Muslim students I have had who were former adherents of Shii Islam (a minority form of Islam, whose adherents believe that a direct descendant of the Prophet Muhammad should lead the Muslim community).

In addition to the above, wounded believers will talk about the following issues:

- broken church promises
- a profound sense of religious betrayal
- unfulfilled spiritual expectations
- unrealistic and hidebound church dogmas
- a guilt- and anxiety-inducing set of moral teachings that brook no exceptions
- in the case of physical and mental abuse, an official church stance that frequently blames the victim and excuses the victimizer
- an intellectually, theologically, and emotionally disappointing rationale for human suffering

For her part, however, Jane was still searching desperately for answers as the course came to an end. During the horrible years of her adolescence, her church and parochial school had chosen to ignore her failing grades, her apathy, and her unbearable loneliness and guilt. Furthermore, because her father was such a highly respected member of the community, with an impeccable reputation for generosity and integrity, the hierarchy told her a number of times to forgive, forget, and keep the family intact—even if this meant maintaining a strict code of silence regarding her abuse. Thus, Jane walked away for good from the formal Catholic structures that had been the defining narrative for so much of her life.

What is Jane's state of mind now as she thinks about the future? In her own words:

> I managed to escape from a church that refused to accept responsibility to care for the emotional needs of all its flock. I walked away from a family that excused or denied my father's conduct right up to the end. Since then, opportunities have been abundant in my adult life to deal with the past—my career choice to teach, my marriage to a wonderful man, and the birth and rearing of my son. Each crossroad at times recreates the tension and angst I once experienced on a daily basis. My decision to become a teacher seemed a natural option for someone who wanted other children to grow up healthy and strong. But, at this juncture in my life, I want a spirituality I can believe in. I want a faith I can stand by. I want to commit myself to some religious community greater than I without constantly wondering when that community will betray me again.

> Christianity, and especially Catholicism, leave me cold. But I want to be able to talk about religion with my students and son without always living on the edge of anger, fear, and guilt. I am a prisoner of my awful story, and although I know I have the key within me to escape, for the life of me I can't seem to find the way. But, anyway, thank you so much for listening, encouraging me, and, most of all, for helping me to get a little closer to the emptiness and resentment that still eat away at the center of my being.

I suggest that we in higher education can respond best to the plight of wounded believers by listening compassionately to them, and, when necessary, by directing them to the appropriate mental health professionals for psychological assistance. As educators, we are better equipped to help them look philosophically and theologically at the larger problem of theodicy. It was during one of my visits to another campus in 1999, while we were discussing the random, senseless shootings at several public schools around the country, that a devout Christian student offered the following narrative on suffering:

I think I know why millions turn to Christianity, Judaism, and Islam for comfort, despite their many internal contradictions. I believe that these religions make a noble effort, each in their own ways, to speak to the *evil of meaninglessness*. This, to my mind, is the most devastating evil of all. These faith systems give us a hopeful reason for persevering, an answer to the bewildering riddle of why we are born and raised in love, yet spend a lifetime suffering and dying. Why is life so bittersweet? These religions offer us stories that are consoling, that explain why bad things happen to good human beings, and these accounts somehow make the tragedy of existence bearable for many. I know my Christianity gives me a spiritual *terra firma* on which to stand when everything is collapsing around me. This is enough for me.

This student offered a particular narrative approach to the problem of evil that others in her group, including myself, found salient. Viktor E. Frankl, the Jewish logotherapist who survived six years in the Auschwitz death camp, said as much: "Suffering ceases to be suffering in some way the moment it finds meaning" (quoted in Willimon, 1985, p. 166). Christianity, for example, answers the difficult questions of theodicy with a central symbol, the cross, by giving us a man-God who hangs there and suffers with us. It also rewards us with another pivotal symbol, the empty tomb, by giving us a man-God who survives His bodily death through Resurrection. The question for Jane, and others like her, however, is this: Does the Christian account—the cross, the empty grave, and the promise of eternal life—help her to put her suffering into some kind of perspective? Jane has decided that, in her case, the answer is no, and so she will need to seek elsewhere for the solace she failed to get from her Catholicism.

The following are some starter questions I ask students that get them talking about the problem of evil in relation to their religio-spiritual narratives:

- Why is it that certain groups through time have been stigmatized as evil?
- Why do you suppose there is so much hate in the world?
- Why has the presence of evil been so persistent throughout history?
- Why are certain people, more than others, prone to commit evil deeds?
- Why are some cultures more prone to violence than others?
- Do you think that some religious narratives are more likely to provoke or promote violence, in spite of their professed beliefs to the contrary? Why?

- Do you think that some religious narratives are more likely to prevent violence? Why?
- Why do you think that some people suffer, while others appear to prosper?
- Is pacifism a viable alternative to the culture of violence in the United States?
- Is war ever justifiable? Which religions support war? Why? Which condemn it? Why?
- Why do we have to get sick, be injured, or die in accidents?
- Why is nature at once so kind and yet so cruel?
- What in your religio-spiritual view is the meaning in loss, suffering, dying, and death, particularly when these are untimely events in people's lives?
- How do we teach love, compassion, responsibility, responsiveness, respect, and generosity without inadvertently turning these qualities into their opposites?
- What concrete strategies in families, churches, synagogues, mosques, temples, governments, and the schools are most likely to prevent or minimize violence between and among human beings?
- What counternarratives do you think we ought to construct in order to alleviate the epidemic of violence throughout the world?

I cannot emphasize enough that we must always ask questions like these about students' belief systems with respect and humility, but also with integrity and unflinching honesty. At all times, we need to think of students' responses to such hard questions as their way of telling a particular story about theodicy. While I personally believe that a Final Account of good and evil—one that achieves a Universal Relevance—is lost and gone forever, I make it a point never to dismiss the value of such an account for those who might believe with all their hearts in its cogency. I do try to stress, however, that Grand Accounts of suffering work only for some but not for others.

The Mainline Narrative
I Am Very Comfortable with my Religion. Why Is This So Threatening to Academia?

I can't understand why we haven't studied the mainline churches in this course. In my opinion, you've asked us to examine religious narratives that are way out of the mainstream. Do you have an ulterior motive for doing this? Also, your approach to the material in this course is way too intellectual and critical for me. I don't know how you can claim to deal impartially with religion and then criticize it in the process. This is elitist and dismissive. I was raised in a very moderate Episcopalian church, and I have stayed loyal to it up to this day. I belong to a wonderful church community, and people feel tremendously grounded. These people go about the business of their lives day after day never asking the questions about religion that we've asked throughout the semester. They take for granted that there is a God, that God is merciful and just, that we are responsible for helping each other, and that in the next life people will get pretty much what they deserve. Isn't this what the world's major religions believe? Why do you and the others in this class have to make it all sound so complicated? I'm beginning to think that people like me threaten people like you in academia, because we are so comfortable with our beliefs. I for one don't like to be disrespected, and so I'm dropping the course.

These are the words that Helen, a senior social work major, unleashed at me during an upsetting conversation I had with her after class one afternoon. Helen represents a growing number of students who enroll in my religion classes and workshops mainly because they want to learn something about other religious narratives. However, they stipulate one condition: They do not want these narratives to pose any discernible threat to their own mainline religious beliefs. Helen is liberal, open-minded, and multicultural on social issues, but traditionalist on religious matters. She is entirely comfortable with the faith of her parents, which, in turn, was the faith of their parents, back through many generations.

Helen is a good American individualist who believes in the principles "to each her own" and "live and let live" where different people's religions are concerned. She is also a "universalist," to use Callahan's term in an earlier chapter, in the sense that she is intellectually interested in other religions primarily for what they might share in common. This common ground is a way for Helen to confirm what might be universal and true in her own religion.

As a liberal, Helen is more than willing, even eager, to display a respect for religious difference. On one occasion, when she was out of town with a Jewish girlfriend, she even attended a temple service and ate kosher food. At another time, she visited a Zen Buddhist meditation center in her college town in order to do firsthand research for a paper she was writing for a multicultural education course. However, Helen draws the line at Eck's "active encounter" between and among the different religions. She does not want to ask too many questions about her own faith, nor get too close to other faiths, for fear of losing confidence in the personal security that her own church membership brings her.

Alan Wolfe (1998) refers to churchgoing Americans like Helen as people of "quiet faith" (pp. 39–87). These believers want the United States to be religiously capacious: open to, and uncritical of, people of different faiths. But they also want to be left alone to practice their own faiths quietly, in their own ways, without the threat of dilution or influence from other religions. Unlike Helen, many college students today tend to be free-agent, unchurched seekers, eager to try out and discard a variety of religions and spiritualities until they find the one(s) that will enhance their personal well-being. They are the explorers whom I will be discussing in a subsequent section, and, for the most part, they are religiously rootless. They are engaged in what Robert Wuthnow (1998) calls spiritualities of "seeking" and "practice," not tied down to any particular doctrines, places, or denominations. Explorer spirituality is fluid, private, diverse, and, most of all, nonaffiliative.

People like Helen, in contrast, steadfastly hold onto the organized religions into which they were born, the ones they have practiced most of their lives. The mainline religions best meet their need for what Wuthnow (1998) calls a "spirituality of dwelling." The difference between *mainline* and *mainstream* religions is subtle but important; the former is a normative term, the latter a descriptive term. *Mainline* is a word used by sociologists to denote a particular religious perspective that is moderate and traditional (e.g., Bellah et al., 1985). *Mainstream* religion is simply an empirical designation referring to those groups that exist in the middle of a "stream" where the "current" is strongest. Mainstream religions refer to the most common religions in a culture. Mainline religions, on the other hand, refer to the most conventional and long-established religions, those that emphasize the need for a permanent sacred space in which to worship God in traditional (but not necessarily orthodox) ways. This sacred space provides clear boundaries between the sacred and the profane, a stable support community, a sense of order, and a moral bulwark against the excesses of secularism (Wuthnow, 1998, pp. 1–18).

Here is Jack Miles (1997) on the reason why people like Helen remain in the mainline churches:

> Organized religion typically provides for the seasons of life: for birth, childhood and coming-of-age; for marriage and other forms of life companionship; for old age and death, bereavement and remembrance; and even for a harmonious division of the calendar year into seasons of mourning and joy; repentance and triumph. . . . [many people] find [the mainline churches] calming and attractive. (Miles, p. 59)

Helen was upset with me because she believed that I was being indirectly critical of a major thematic leitmotif in the mainline narrative: *the church as familiar and consoling place of refuge*, particularly during the storm and stress of life's more upsetting developmental events. The mainline narrative's central purpose is to provide the comforts and justifications, the rituals, teachings, and social gatherings, of organized religion. These, according to Miles, are what people require as they move through the turbulent "seasons" of their lives. I was a menace to Helen at a particular time in her life when she sought *confirmation* of her mainline beliefs instead of the intellectual *provocation* that she had come to expect from detached academicians like me. It was clear to her that my seminar narrative and her church narrative were on a collision course, and so she made the decision to leave before the impending crash.

Educators need to understand that somewhere between the religio-spiritual narratives of orthodoxy, wounded belief, and exploration is a narrative that is enormously appealing to a particular group of college students. These students are neither excessively conservative or avant-garde. They dislike authoritarianism in religion as much as they dislike faddism. They prefer a life of worship that balances traditions, standards, self-discipline, and moral conscience with a degree of personal freedom, biblical latitude, and the *joie de vivre* of close community life. They are the "salt of the earth" religious types on any college campus, solidly committed to their beliefs but not triumphalistic, quiet not noisy, and civil not contentious. I especially appreciate the Helens whom I see in my cross-campus dialogue- and seminar-groups, because they remind me of two important truths that secular academicians like myself tend to forget. It is possible for students to believe strongly in a particular *religion* without succumbing to the lures of *religiosity*. Moreover, in the words of Robert N. Bellah et al. (1985), "[spiritual] solitude without community is merely loneliness" (p. 248).

As strange as it might seem to many skeptics in the postmodern university, the traditionalist mainliners are here to stay. They are the hold-outs against postmodernity and the religious experimentation and deconstruction that so often accompany it. Less dogmatic, conservative, and evangelical than most orthodox believers, and far less harmed by their religious experiences than wounded believers, mainliners happily, almost defiantly, retain membership in the churches and temples of their youth. They remain at least moderately comfortable with the doctrines, rituals, and practices that are so familiar and satisfying to them. Mainliners in my classes and workshops tend to be from Catholic, Protestant, Jewish, and, in a few cases, Islamic backgrounds. They come to my courses and workshops, not to question their religious beliefs, but to enrich and deepen them. Frequently, they must face some hard challenges by the explorers, activists, and secular humanists who, in the heat of encounter, misinterpret mainliner church satisfaction as simply another form of anti-intellectual, bourgeois complacency.

Mainline religious believers still constitute a large numerical force in the United States. According to recent data, about 87% of Americans consider themselves conventional, churchgoing Christians, at least some of the time (41% attend church once a week). While a few of the mainline Protestant churches have lost huge percentages of their members to evangelical and Pentecostal churches, some of the more conservative ones have not. The Episcopal and Methodist churches have suffered the severest losses (a collective 82% in the last 30 years). However, the Southern Baptist, Mormon, Jehovah's Witnesses, Assemblies of God, and Church of God in Christ denominations have grown exponentially over the last 30 years. The last three denominations, for example, have increased their collective membership over 1000% since 1970. As an aside, in certain parts of the country, moderate evangelicals worship in megachurches where as many as 10,000 people attend a single service (all data compiled by Shorto, 1997).

Also, there is some evidence that people who once left are now returning to the mainline churches in greater numbers than ever before. Cimino and Lattin (1998), editors of a newsletter, *Religion Watch,* that monitors trends in contemporary religion, point out that Eastern Orthodoxy and Roman Catholicism have experienced a tidal wave of new converts over the last decade. Nonethnic conversions to Eastern Orthodoxy are growing in number due to its rich liturgy and sense of mystery. Roman Catholicism has been increasingly attractive to Latin American immigrants because of its colorful rituals, its sacramental character, and its teachings on social justice. Moreover, a number of young and middle-aged Jews are returning to their synagogues, particularly to the reform and orthodox communions. They do this in order to discover, and in some cases to reestablish, their identities as cultural and religious Jews. Lutherans and Presbyterians appear to be holding their own in membership as they schedule more frequent communion services and follow a stricter church calendar.

The mainline black churches in America, as different as they are from each other, still form the heart of many African-American communities. Some are middle-class and suburban, while others are politically liberationist in tone and mission (Cone, 1997), responding to the needs of the working poor, the out-of-work poor, and the welfare-dependent poor in the urban centers. The latter groups, who are the most socially alienated, are leaving the black churches in alarming numbers in the urban areas. Some of the larger black "megachurches" still claim a loyal following in the inner city, particularly among suburban blacks who have moved away from those locales but who return regularly for Sunday services. The mainline black churches manage to survive and, in some locations, prosper throughout the United States because their ministries work hard to bind communities together in hope, love, discipline, and racial pride (Bellah et al., 1991).

From the vantage point of history, the mainline Protestant churches in general have formed a "religious center" for American life. According to Bellah et al. (1985):

> They have offered a conception of God as neither wholly other nor a higher self, but rather as involved in time and history. . . . They have sought to be communities of memory, to keep in touch with biblical sources and historical traditions not with literalist obedience but through an intelligent reappropriation illuminated by historical and theological reflection. They have tried to relate biblical faith and practice to the whole of contemporary life—cultural, social, political, economic— not just to personal and family morality. They have tried to steer a middle course between mystical fusion with the world and sectarian withdrawal from it. (p. 237)

Helen and other mainliners like her call the academy's attention to the fact that the denominational churches in this country have an important *public* function to serve. They are America's "communities of memory." The mainline churches provide what George Washington in his Farewell Address called the "indispensable supports of political prosperity . . . religion and morality" (cited in Bellah et al., 1985, p. 222). De Tocqueville, observed in the 1830s that the American mainline churches were actually political institutions that supported the moral principles undergirding democracy. He also claimed that the churches cultivated an ethic of service to others, communitarianism, and self-sacrifice (see Bellah et al., 1985).

These are qualities that any public social order needs in order to survive. When a society isolates its churches by privatizing and marginalizing them, then it loses a critical moral compass. I find that in my classes, some mainliners, when they are willing to come out of their polite shells, assume the role of the "moral compass" in religio-spiritual discussions. What is more, their peers are likely to listen to them. There is rarely a hint of religious zealotry in the mainline message because it so often comes packaged in the language of such benevolent American values as moderation, neighborliness, public service, and community volunteerism.

The mainline religious narrative is not without its serious difficulties and challenges, however. Internationally, although Catholicism has grown by 400% in Africa, and even though it remains attractive to certain immigrant groups, it has fallen to 22% of the total mainline population in the United States. Furthermore, although 41% of Americans attend church weekly, in Canada, the number is 38%, in once-Catholic Spain and France, it is 25% and 21%, respectively, and in Austria, it is 16%. The American Jewish population is the same size today as in 1960, about 5.5 million, with 50% of those Jews who marry each year doing so outside their religion. Many of these Jews go on to reject their religion altogether. Furthermore, there are more Muslims in the United States than there are Presbyterians. And Buddhism claims more converts each year (100,000) than Episcopalians and Methodists combined, thanks mainly to celebrity conversions by Hollywood movie stars like Richard Gere and Steven Seagal (Shorto, 1997).

Although annual polls continue to show that Americans believe in a God (nine out of ten adults), seven out of ten believe in an afterlife, eight out of ten want religious training for their children, and eight out of ten believe that Jesus is God, there are glaring contradictions, nevertheless (data cited in Reeves, 1996). Almost 10% of the population claims to be agnostics, atheists, or humanists, and this group is growing each year, albeit at a very small percentage (data cited in Lewy, 1996). Increased education usually correlates with a radical falloff in religious belief and observance, particularly among young college and graduate students, professional scientists, and academicians (see Lewy, 1996, pp. 77–80; also E. J. Larson, 1997).

What is more paradoxical, however, is that 64% of Americans who profess to be mainline churchgoers do not believe in moral absolutes; 44% believe that people can be religious even though they do not attend churches or synagogues, and 54% express little or no confidence in their clergy. A 1993 sociological study reports that actual church or temple attendance each Saturday or Sunday during the course of a year, in spite of claims to the contrary, is only 26.7% (all the data are reported in Reeves, 1996). Moreover, whereas 93% of American homes contain at least one Bible, very few mainliners actually read it. Fifty-four percent have no idea who the authors of the four Gospels were. Sixty-three percent do not even know what a Gospel is. Fifty-eight percent could not name five of the ten Commandments. Thirty-nine percent of mainline Christians do not believe in the Resurrection of Jesus. Eighty-two percent of Catholics disagree strongly with the Church's position on birth control, the ban against women priests, and divorce. Finally, 62% of Conservative Jews believe they do not have to be observant in order to be religious (all the data compiled by Shorto, 1997).

What these data suggest is that much mainline religious commitment in the United States is ambiguous at best. At times it can be superficial, conformist, highly individualistic, ambivalent, and materialistic. In Reeves's words (1996), "Pious rhetoric is not necessarily an indication of a deep-seated, life-changing commitment . . . We . . . go about our lives pretty much the same as those who have no faith at all" (pp. 20–21).

Therefore, even though mainline religion appears to be alive and well in the United States, it is clear from the data that many of its proponents take what they need from it while remaining thoroughly secular. It is my opinion that these kinds of contradictions and compromises ought to be the stuff of cross-campus dialogue, because they raise several compelling questions about the differences between the ideal and the real functions of religion in a secular pluralist society. Some of these questions follow:

- To what extent will the mainline denominations need to become more eclectic in order to survive in a culture that some describe as a gigantic "spiritual supermarket"?
- Is it likely that mainline denominations have already made too many compromises with their religious heritages, ending up with diluted theologies, liturgies, and values?
- Is it possible that new conflicts will arise between those mainline congregations that are more traditional and those that are more experimental?
- What are some dangers in the return to tradition that face those mainline congregations that are becoming more conservative?
- What are some dangers in the turn to "designer churches" that change according to the latest innovations in worship, teachings, and spiritual practices?
- When does the need for religious stability and rootedness turn into a denial of those changes that any denomination needs in order to remain vital, responsive, and pastoral?
- Is it possible for the mainline denominations to make reasoned compromises with the world without the cooptations and dilutions that often accompany those compromises?

Here is what I wrote in a letter that I sent to Helen at the end of the semester, something I do for all my students as my way of bringing closure to my courses:

I truly understand your frustration with our not spending time on what you call the "mainline" religions. I wish I had the time in one semester to cover all the religions of humankind, including the mainline Christian religions. I do not, and so I choose the narratives that I think students know little or nothing about. I make the assumption that most of my students have been raised in the "mainline" faith traditions. (Whether or not they remain in these is another question, of course.) I made my pedagogical approach very clear at the beginning of the course, and I can only wonder why you decided to stay in the course knowing that I would not be covering the mainline religious narratives in any systematic way. Please know, though, that I am glad you decided to stay with us for as long as you did. Know, too, that your presence was greatly missed during the last third of the course.

I would like to respond to your charge that "mainline religion must be too passe for academia." In *my* academia, mainline religion is important, and a narrative that I greatly respect. I understand your frustration with the lack of airtime that your narrative received during the semester. But you made it sound as if I and the class were deliberately downplaying some religio-spiritual narratives in favor of others that I considered superior. I would make the case that several of the books we read in the course were written by "mainline" Protestant Christians (two of the authors were practicing Episcopalians). Their views very much set the tone for the entire course. Also, you should understand that what constitutes an appropriate definition of "mainline" is very controversial in the religious studies literature. The term itself is considered "elitist and dismissive," to use your language. Wittingly or unwittingly, the term marginalizes other religious narratives by pushing them away from the center of religio-spiritual dialogue and onto the periphery. This makes them look merely inferior or supplemental.

I know that your use of the word "mainline" doesn't intentionally subordinate the other narratives. But the more you played this particular theme during the semester, the more I wondered why you refused to talk with the rest of us about the things you believed. I am sorry that you felt your mainline religious convictions were "disrespected." I only wish you had summoned up the courage to express your beliefs freely (as most others in the class did), trusted the group to truly hear you and learn from your disclosures, and, failing this, let the proverbial chips fall wherever. To sit in silence week after week leaves too many words unsaid and too much feeling unvented. I for one know that you could have enriched my own religio-spiritual narrative, if you had given me a chance. Nevertheless, I wish you well, and I hope that you find a congenial and helpful way to use some of the content that you took away from the course.

In the next chapter, I will examine three alternative religious narratives that depart in some significant ways from the three narratives I have highlighted in this chapter.

Chapter 4

Religions as Narratives (II): Three Alternative Stories

I love my new church, and I have decided to become a Unitarian-Universalist minister. This church answers my need to be whole. I can be both religious and activistic. In fact, I now realize that I am religious only to the degree that I am actively involved in social justice projects. I am putting my deeds before my creeds.
—Jason, a student affairs professional, and an activist

I am at peace with the awareness that no particular religion or spirituality will ever completely define me. I am a seeker and a finder, a pluralist and a monist, a relativist and a universalist, a Westerner and an Easterner, a Jew and a Muslim, a feminist and a humanist, an Old-Ager and a New-Ager, a believer and a doubter. Who I am changes in every moment that I connect with God and with others.
—Anne, a junior faculty member, and an explorer

I do know, however, that, for now, I am able to find the meaning and the morality I seek in the work that I do, in the opportunity to learn something new every day of my life, in the people that I meet and in those I love, and in the joy that I find in the simple things I take for granted. I am willing to admit that, in many ways, I am a thorough-going, here-and-now secularist. But why am I so restless?
—Robert, a senior faculty member, and a secular humanist

Three Alternative Stories That Students Tell

What I am calling "alternative stories" describes an overall religio-spiritual view that intentionally integrates a number of beliefs and practices from a variety of sources into new expressions. I mean for the term "alternative" to be descriptive without being pejorative; I use it neither to marginalize or to subordinate these narratives to mainstream stories. The alternative view goes way beyond traditional and modernistic understandings of Christianity and Judaism. Many alternative religious adherents whom I meet on college campuses are not necessarily lapsed Christians or Jews, because they have never been raised conventional believers in the first place. Their boomer parents, if Roof (1999) is correct, probably mixed and matched beliefs and practices from a number of religio-spiritual systems, thereby rendering more traditional forms of Christianity and Judaism almost unrecognizable.

Those alternative believers who do manage to hold onto some Christian and Jewish beliefs frequently blend them with imaginative combinations of New Age spirituality, Eastern mysticism, alternative orientations such as Native American spirituality, gaia and goddess worship, and other possibilities that are virtually limitless. Some alternative adherents have given up altogether on any kind of spirituality, blended or otherwise, because they cannot square the findings of science, or common sense, with the revelations of religion. Others look to create a new synthesis of science and religion that transforms the more traditional theologies into an exciting new mythos of creation and redemption (see biologist Kenneth R. Miller's 1999 argument that evolution actually offers a powerful logic for a divinely created world).

As I will show in this chapter, alternative students, staff, and faculty are complex bricoleurs, assemblers who construct belief systems from the bits and pieces of traditional, modern, and postmodern religions and spiritualities. Many are postdoctrinal, postinstitutional, and postbiblical. Some are atheists and agnostics. Others, however, struggle to remain in the churches of their youth. As alternative bricoleurs, they work from within to transform these structures by making them more personal, more inwardly spiritual, and, for some, more committed to outreach and social justice efforts.

Alternative religious groups have doubled in number in the United States in the last 20 years. According to one source, the latest edition of the *Encyclopedia of American Religions*, there are now over 2,100 religious groups in America that do not call themselves Christian, Jewish, or Islamic (cited in Creedon, 1998). Many, however, combine at least some nominal mainline beliefs with their own, ending up with what Jeremiah Creedon approvingly calls a "pastiche spirituality." He says:

> New hybrid modes of worship are constantly appearing, from the new Christian megachurches, whose mammoth services can resemble arena rock, to tiny garage religions hardly bigger than the average band. . . . We are living in what observers call an age of extreme "religious pluralism." . . . We are transitioning from a Christian nation to a syncretistic, spiritually diverse society . . . [where expressions of faith] bear little resemblance to the "pure" form of any of the world's major religions. (p. 45)

What I will describe below are three of the alternative narratives that I hear most often in my work with students and colleagues: the activism, exploration, and secular humanism narratives. They serve as excellent examples of stories that are truly "spiritually diverse," and "syncretistic," to use Creedon's language.

The Activism Narrative

My church answers my need to be whole. In fact in my church, I am religious only to the degree that I am actively involved in social justice projects.

I was not raised in any mainline church. I do not consider myself a true believer, and I have certainly never been wounded by organized religion. When I was young, my parents took me to Quaker meetings for about two years, and I remember being ambivalent about these services. Not much seemed to be happening, as people sat around in silence most of the time. They spoke only when they felt prompted by something called the "Inner Light." I loved Quaker teachings on pacificism and equality, but, overall, the particular group I knew seemed a little too passive and isolated for my tastes. Later, when I was a sophomore in college, I attended a Reform Jewish temple with my girlfriend over the course of a year. While I liked the people I met there, I could never fully identify with the community because I wasn't Jewish. I knew little or nothing about their culture, and I had no firsthand sense of their history. I always felt like a visitor not a member. At times I even felt like a voyeur.

When I graduated from college, I stayed away from any kind of organized form of worship for a number of years. I guess you could say I was a spiritual shopper, someone you would call an explorer, one time flirting with Buddhism, and another time going to Ethical Culture meetings. [The Ethical Culture Society is a religious association founded in 1876 by Felix Adler in New York City. The focus in this religion is on ethical development. It eschews the supernaturalism of the monotheistic religions, opting instead for social work and education. See David S. Muzzey's *Ethical Religion*, 1943.] Two years ago, having taken a new job at an urban university, and because I was feeling lonely in a strange city and on a whim, I attended a Unitarian-Universalist service downtown. I can tell you that it not only changed the way I thought about religion; it also changed my life.

The church I belong to on the West Coast has rejected a Christian, even a theistic, identity. It is liberal, all-inclusive in its membership, welcoming even atheists, and, most importantly, it is socially active. I am now working on weekends in my church as the peace-and-justice professional, helping to organize workers in the inner city. I also deliver the homily once a month, because the pastor wants my point of view represented during services. I am thinking seriously about quitting my university job, as much as I love it, in order to go back to graduate school for a master's degree in divinity. You see, I want to become a Unitarian-Universalist minister. For the first time in my life, I feel spiritually and politically fulfilled. My church answers my need to be whole. I can be both religious and activistic. In fact, in my church, I am only religious to the degree that I am actively involved in social justice projects. As my church says: I must put my deeds before my creeds. If I didn't know better, I would say that I've died and gone to some kind of heaven, which I don't even believe in. Why didn't I know about churches like this when I was in college?

These are the reflections of "Jason," a student affairs professional at a large urban university. He was present at one of my "ally" workshops (a group of religiously diverse participants that included students, university leaders, and off-campus clergy) during a visit I made to another campus far from my own. Jason is a self-proclaimed social-justice activist, and he has finally found a church community that more than satisfies his need to be both "spiritually and politically fulfilled."

The activist religious narrative is an appealing one to Jason, and to a particular coterie of students whom I frequently meet on campuses and in my classes. This narrative tells a story about making a better world that emphasizes what theologians call the "already," as opposed to the "not yet." Jason, and others like him, believe that we must be responsible for building the Kingdom of God in the here-and-now, rather than waiting for some distant paradise to come. They advocate an energetic faith dedicated to the liberation of oppressed peoples, equal rights for all, and radical social transformation marked by full democratic participation in decision-making. Theirs is a story that judges religious leaders to be effective according to their commitments to inclusiveness, and to bringing about social reform in behalf of the least among us.

On the one hand, the activist story has the disadvantage of leaving many students in my classes who hear it with a disquieting and immobilizing sense of guilt regarding what they come to see as the self-seeking narrowness of their own lives. Also, some students reject this story outright because to them it appears to repeat the same old political-correctness cliches, only this time with an added religious fillip. On the other hand, the activist story has the advantage of moving some students like Jason to consider belonging to those religious communities where they are encouraged to make firm commitments to serve others, and to carry through with them, as a public expression of their faith. Among those I have known, some activists can be explorers, secular humanists, and even mainliners; but few tend to be orthodox believers or wounded believers.

I have decided to tell the story of the politically liberal social-justice activist at this point rather than the politically conservative true-believer activist, the type who is cast in the mold of a Phyllis Schlafly, a Jerry Falwell, a Ralph Reed, or a James Dobson. The political activism associated with such conservative Christian groups as the Moral Majority, Campus Crusade for Christ, the Christian Coalition, the Eagle Forum, Promise Keepers, and the Christian Men's Movement is aimed less at social justice, and more at the evils of modernism and postmodernism. These are the targets of the orthodox believers I have already covered in a previous section, and they include secularism, pluralism, relativism, egalitarianism, feminism, hedonism, and nihilism. (See Linda Kintz's *Between Jesus and the Market*, 1997, for an extensive, very impartial discussion of activists working in behalf of the conservative Christian agenda in contemporary American politics and culture.)

Moreover, I will talk here about Unitarian Universalism as one particular liberal incarnation of the activist narrative. I find in my own college town, and others I visit, that a steady number of young social-justice activists, disillusioned by the politically ineffective mainline churches, are joining this association. Some of these students and young professionals count themselves as environmentalist, anti-corporation members of Ralph Nader's Green Party; others see themselves as anti-racists in the image of the Reverend Martin Luther King, Jr., or the Reverend Jessie Jackson; and still others think of themselves as feminists in the ilk of Margaret Sanger, the founder of Planned Parenthood, or bell hooks, the African-American "insurgent intellectual" (hooks, 1994).

While the students and professionals who are attracted to this church are largely middle class, white, and well educated, they have at least one thing in common: They do not wish to jettison the mainline religious project entirely. A few even remain Christian, at least nominally. All feel the need to belong to some type of religio-spiritual association, congregation, fellowship, church, or society that is collectively dedicated to improving the human condition in this life rather than waiting for the next. In addition, some join because they appreciate the Unitarian Universalist encouragement to explore a number of spiritualities as a way of finding truth. Some cherish a congregation that promotes open, non-punitive dialogue on questions of faith. Some want a religion that genuinely respects difference and individualism. The group that I am calling the social justice activists, like Jason, join the fellowship because it "acts locally and thinks globally on the great issues of our time—homelessness; gay, lesbian, bisexual, and transgender rights; and protection of the environment" (Flanagan, 1999, n. p.).

The Unitarian-Universalist church in North America has a comparatively small membership, around 200,000 by one count, and less than 300,000 worldwide (Buehrens & Church, 1998, p. 76). However, it makes an appeal to certain religious dissidents and liberal egalitarians in the United States that is virtually irresistible. This has been the case throughout the church's history. (I am indebted to such authors as Buehrens & Church, 1998; Marshall, 1999; and Mendelsohn, 1995, for the brief history that follows.) Unitarian Universalism is a church that has often attracted doctrinal outcasts from other churches, as well as many religious and political antinomians, who also happen to be deeply humanitarian. Throughout its history, the church has been the object of cruel persecution by the dominant Catholic and Protestant powers.

For example, Michael Servetus (1511–1553), a dynamic, Spanish religious reformer and physician, who discovered the pulmonary circulation of blood, was also the founder of Unitarianism. He rejected the Christian belief in the Trinity because it was not bible-based. For this, John Calvin had him arrested in Geneva, tried for heresy, and burned at the stake with his books tied to his waist. Also, a contemporary of Servetus, Faustus Socinus, a Northern Italian, openly defied Calvin by denying the doctrine of the Trinity, the divinity of Jesus, the existence of hell, the salvation of the elect, and the depravity of humanity. He later established 300 Unitarian Churches in Poland. For all of this, he was arrested, tried, and his books were burned in the public square of Cracow. He managed to escape death, however, thanks to the help of two heroic Jesuits.

Some of the West's greatest thinkers were Unitarian Universalists. For example, John Milton, author of the *Areopagitica*, was a Unitarian, as were the authors Charles Dickens and Samuel Coleridge. So too was Florence Nightingale, who organized a nursing corps in the Crimean War, resulting in the creation of the nursing profession. The discoverer of oxygen, nitric and nitrous oxides, and carbon dioxide, Joseph Priestly, was an active member of the Unitarian Church. In the United States, the first Unitarian Universalist Church was John Murray's, in Gloucester, Massachusetts, formed in 1779. Later, Ethan Allen, the Revolutionary war hero of the Green Mountain Boys in Vermont became a Unitarian Universalist. Both Thomas Paine and Thomas Jefferson expressed a deep affection for Unitarian Universalism in their writings, particularly in their letters. Some historians claim that Jefferson was at least a "closet" member of the church (Marshall, 1999).

Other great names associated with this church are William Ellery Channing, Theodore Parker, Ralph Waldo Emerson, a transcendentalist writer, poet, and minister of the Second Church in Boston, Henry David Thoreau, Susan B. Anthony, Elizabeth Cady Stanton, Horace Mann, Leland Stanford, William Lloyd Garrison, and Clara Barton. American Presidents John Adams, John Quincy Adams, Millard Fillmore, and William H. Taft were Unitarian Universalists. More contemporary members include Adlai Stevenson, Albert Schweitzer, Dr. Benjamin Spock, Linus Pauling, and the Unitarian Universalist minister and popular author, Robert Fulghum.

The Unitarian Universalists founded a number of American colleges and universities including St. Lawrence University in New York, Tufts University in Massachusetts, Meadville Theological School in Chicago, Goddard College in Vermont, and the California Institute of Technology in Pasadena. None of these colleges are under denominational control today because this would be an egregious contradiction, given the noted Unitarian Universalist repudiation of sectarianism, religious party lines, and proselytism of all kinds.

What Unitarian Universalists believe can be summed up in a nutshell: *Do not come to a Unitarian Universalist church to be given a religion; come to develop your own religion.* Unitarian Universalists learn to construct their own religio-spiritual narratives because they do not expect, or want, anybody else to do it for them. They look to no inerrant catechisms or bibles for ultimate truth, or to no infallible teaching magisteria. Thomas Paine once proclaimed that he looked with special affection on Unitarian Universalism, because it came closest to his own philosophy of religion: "My own mind is my own church" (quoted in Marshall, 1999, p. 100). Similarly, church member Clara Barton, founder of the American Red Cross, declared: "I defy the tyranny of precedent. I cannot afford the luxury of a closed mind" (quoted in Buehrens & Church, 1998). Many members I know, but not all, would wholeheartedly agree with Paine and Barton.

Unitarian Universalists, despite the diversity of their religious beliefs, tend to be this-worldly, humanitarian, anti-creedal, inclusive, and politically progressive. They see their major religious function as going on the offensive to solve the problems of injustice, cruelty, and discrimination. They are committed to rationality, real-world problem-solving, the dignity and worth of all human beings, a human rights ethic, and, above all, service and social action. If any church in the Western hemisphere can be said to be a paradigmatic activist church, it is the church of Unitarian Universalists. It is for this reason that liberal students like Jason, who still have a need to be church-affiliated, find this particular fellowship to be highly compatible with their political views.

The Unitarian Universalist church is attractive to some university students, faculty, and staff precisely because it is a public church, one that is conspicuously and proudly anti-racist, anti-sexist, pro-gay and lesbian, pro-environment, multicultural to the core, and feminist. Moreover, it is not afraid to be openly critical of any given political or social system that fails to live up to its highest moral ideals. For example, during the public brouhaha over same-sex civil unions in the state of Vermont (that I mentioned in chapter 2), many members of the local Unitarian Universalist church in Burlington were actively involved in the movement to get the state legislature to pass this bill. Some of these members were students of mine (heterosexual, bisexual, and homosexual) whose eyes lit up with passion and conviction when they began to talk at a public colloquium about their religious witness. They delighted in showing how their religio-spiritual beliefs had actually made a real-world difference to them but, more importantly, to others.

Scotty McLennan, the Unitarian Universalist Chaplain at Tufts University, describes this type of activist student in a best-selling, personal narrative called *Finding Your Religion: When the Faith You Grew Up with Has Lost Its Meaning* (1999). His narrative emphasizes, above all, the intimate connections that cohere between political activism and religion, between inspired community service and an enlivened spiritual faith. Jason would find McLennan's book to be spiritually affirming. McLennan narrates a series of personal stories told by Tufts' students that illustrate, among other things, how many of the world's great religions are openly activistic in promoting social justice for the marginalized and oppressed. Many of these students were able to find meaning in social outreach when they joined a group of what McLennan calls "spiritual traveling companions" representing different religious traditions. Through direct, sustained contact with "companions" from other religions, they were able to demolish the shallow stereotypes of these traditions so often promulgated by a lazy, ill-informed American media, as well as by their own churches.

For example, some students discovered through their new "spiritual companions" that one of the "Five Pillars" of Islam is giving charity to the needy, as a way of acknowledging the intrinsic worth and equality of every human being. This is a public manifestation of the Islamic obligation to honor all of Allah's creatures, particularly the destitute. (The other "Pillars" include reciting the creed "There is no god but Allah, and Muhammad is his chief prophet"; praying five times a day; fasting during daylight hours in the lunar month of Ramadan; and making one pilgrimage to Mecca.) Also, some students learned that many meditating Buddhists belong to a type of *sangha* (Sanskrit for a monastic group or community) that urges them to go out into the world to perform a ministry of social service outreach. For example, two recipients of the Nobel Peace Prize, the Dalai Lama of Tibet and Aung San Suu Kyi of Burma, chose to forgo the isolation of monastic communities in order to spend their lives working in behalf of the powerless and the marginalized *outside* the *sangha*. Moreover, some students came to understand that Judaism has a long tradition of respect for social justice, dating back to the Exodus story of the ancient Hebrews' liberation from Egyptian slavery. In fact, Jewish feminism today, as embodied in some Jewish Women's Collectives on campuses throughout the United States, is rooted in the basic liberation theme of Passover.

Those non-Catholic students at Tufts University, who thought of the Roman Catholic Church as hierarchical, dogmatic, and elitist, discovered, much to their surprise, that Catholicism has its own social justice component in the liberation theology movement in South and Central America, as well as in a number of Papal Encyclicals since 1931. The *communidades cristianas de bases* (Christian base communities), established by the church thirty years ago in Latin America, consist of hundreds of groups of fifteen to twenty people who get together for literacy training. They spend their time organizing for social justice within the context of Bible reading, prayers for liberation, and mutual assistance.

McLennan himself finds religious meaning in a small activist community—the Holy Spirit Group—of four Unitarian Universalist Christian ministers. They meet every other week to "share their lives," but, more importantly, to "go out into the community to try to serve and make a difference . . ." (p. 111). One of the Holy Spirit Group's political achievements was working successfully for the passage of two laws in the state of Massachusetts,

> providing for home visitation and parenting education for mothers under twenty-one, and ensuring summer food service for hungry children to supplement the term-time School Breakfast Program . . . It means a lot to roll up our sleeves and work publicly for social change together, and then to return to a private space where together we contemplatively experience how compassion flows directly out of the heart of God. (p. 112)

McLennan's major insight for those of us in the academy is a simple one: Religio-spirituality makes the most sense to a particular group of students *whenever it tells a story of human rights and social transformation; whenever it invites believers to criticize existing structures of power and privilege such as the wealthy, white, male hierarchies in the churches, universities, businesses, media, and government.* Some students want a religion that is not afraid to name the suffering of all social classes, including the middle-class whose human spirit is being broken and narrowed by status-seeking and competition, whose sole meaning in life seems to be vested in an endless spiral of consumption and waste, hedonism and ennui. One of my activist students calls this middle-class phenomenon of meaninglessness the "poverty of affluence." Another calls it the "worm in the apple of corporate capitalism." This downward trajectory, in the words of Bellah et al. (1991) "kills the soul. . . . It deadens our consciousness and thickens our senses. Drug and alcohol addiction are leading symptoms of this" (p. 211).

I have the greatest respect for the activism narrative, as I do all the others, but there are still serious questions that need to be asked of students like Jason, and that he needs to ask of us in return. No narrative is to be granted an a priori immunity to sincere points of contention in the cross-campus dialogue. Questions like the ones below allow all participants in the cross-campus conversation to engage in a dialogue of "mutual truth-seeking critique." This is a dialogue that Diana Eck (1993) believes will open us up to both the strengths and the weaknesses in other religious points of view. The result, for Eck, is genuine interfaith "encounter," because it asks the hard questions that promote constructive self-criticism, real pluralism, and mutual transformation. Obviously, before we raise these challenging questions, we must work very hard to establish a cross-campus ethos that radiates trust, compassion, understanding, and support. Some of these questions are:

- Why do you suppose that the Unitarian Universalist church remains predominantly a white, upper-middle-class, highly educated group of people, in spite of its professed mission to help and to attract people of other classes who are most vulnerable to injustice and human cruelty? What is the lesson here for other churches?
- On the one hand, how does the Unitarian Universalist church avoid the temptation to universalize the truths of its own group? How does it avoid reducing (and thereby dismissing) the diversity of religious truths in other churches to a single common denominator, e.g., all religions teach compassion or social justice or the Golden Rule, under the banner of universalism?
- Conversely, how does the Unitarian Universalist church calculate the risk of respecting, indeed celebrating, the uniqueness and the distinctiveness of truths in other religions—under the banner of particularism—so much so that they are never able to meet with those religions on any common ground? In Callahan's (2000) terms,

mentioned in a previous chapter, neither universalism nor particularism ought to be declared the eventual winner in a religio-spiritual sweepstakes. It is up to the Unitarian Universalist church to declare a draw, if it is to be true to its principles. How does the church do this with any kind of intellectual or moral consistency? How does any church?

- How does the Unitarian Universalist church remain humble and open to the possibility of inspired biblical truths of many orthodox or conservative mainline denominations, particularly when those truths might be in direct conflict with the signature Unitarian Universalist belief that there are no all-illuminating, inspired truths that are authoritative for everyone? How does the church come to terms with this example of what I have earlier called the paradox of religious pluralism?

- How exactly is the Unitarian Universalist church a *religious* entity rather than merely a *partisan, liberal-leaning political caucus*? Is there room in this inclusive church for anti-liberals? Would Rush Limbaugh's, Sara Phelps's, or anti-abortionist Ralph Terry's presence at a Sunday service be celebrated, particularly if they came to question, proclaim, convert, or scoff? Why should the Unitarian Universalist church bother tolerating these people who are more than likely to be intolerant of the church's beliefs?

- Might some people find the activist narrative to be spiritually vacuous and religiously unfulfilling because it places so much of its emphasis on political deeds rather than on religious creeds, rituals, or traditions? Where is the religious "beef" in this story, the sense of mystery and transcendent meaning? Is religion in the service of a political agenda a sufficient response to young people's cry for meaning on college campuses? Is there a way that deeds can replace creeds that edifies and inspires, rather than secularizes and neutralizes?

- Why must the secular principle of social justice in the activist narrative be elevated above other, more traditional religious principles such as faith, hope, love, obedience, humility, reconciliation, holiness, resignation, sacrifice, self-discipline, prudence, self-denial, and patriotism? Is the activist narrative only a one-note religious symphony? How might the activist narrative add more "notes" to its religio-spiritual repertoire?

- Does the activist narrative offer a false promise that the "already" can become the "not yet," that the current social and political system can become a social justice utopia if only we are willing to roll

up our sleeves and work hard to achieve this outcome? Is this naive, given the ubiquity of war, injustice, violations of human rights,
persecution, suffering, and dying throughout history and throughout the contemporary world (see Jonathan Glover's *Humanity: A
Moral History of the Twentieth Century*, 1999, for a view of the
dark and destructive side of human nature)? Or is this promise the
only hope that we have to improve the human condition here and
now? Is it religion's role to transform the here-and-now into the
kingdom of God, or is it to help us survive, and possibly improve,
the here-and-now as a prelude for the real kingdom to come in
another life? Is this dichotomy too sharp?

The Exploration Narrative

*I am dancing the never-ending, sacred dance of someone who is a spiritual
being learning how to be human and a human being learning how to be
spiritual. I am, and always will be, an explorer.*

All my life it seems as if I have engaged in what I think of as a "sacred dance." You
asked us once in the group to free associate answers to the question "Who are
you as a religio-spiritual being?" Well here is my response. I am an Old Age
mystic and a New Age Jew. I am a Unitarian Universalist and a neo-pagan. I am
a spiritual being learning how to be human and a human being learning how to be
spiritual. I believe everything is interconnected and I touch God in each moment
of connection. I believe in magic and in miracles. I started my life as a Jew and I
have danced my way to a kind of all-embracing post-Judaism. I have danced
joyously through Unitarian Universalism, Hinduism, Buddhism, eco-feminism,
mysticism, Vipassana (Insight) meditation, astrology, reincarnation, Native American shamanism, Goddess spiritualities, New Age Wisdom, mindfulness, crystals,
and Jungian psychology. During my sacred dance, I have been to Mexico, Peru,
Greece, India, Pakistan, Rome, California, and Alaska seeking enlightenment.

Where have I ended up? I am now dancing the dance of nature, as depicted in the
religions of Native Americans, Celts, and goddess worshippers. In fact, I have
come full circle in a sense. My present religious narrative is actually not very far
from the practice of my reformist Jewish childhood. How different after all is
reveling in the God of Judaism from channeling a spiritual entity? How different
is Jewish prophecy from New Age divination? Aren't ritual and mystery in one
religious form more similar than different in another religious form? Isn't the
practice of my daily divinations and meditations similar to saying my daily prayers
when I was a child? Who I am as a religio-spiritual being depends on where I am
at any given time in my sacred dance. I am both body and spirit, being and doing,
unity and diversity.

What have I learned in your religious dialogue group this semester? I have learned
how important it is for me to become more whole as an integrated human being.
In my work as a college professor, I want to work with love in my quest to end

discrimination. I want to be even more relational than I am. I learned that I am a religio-spiritual explorer, an activist, and a humanist. I love both my humanity and my divinity. I learned that the religion of my childhood and my youth is more a part of me than I thought possible. I learned that I have a lot more in common with orthodox believers and mainline believers than I thought. I learned that I am both a pluralist and a relativist, a monist and a universalist. I don't think, though, that I am an absolutist. I'm just not strong or sure enough yet in my sacred dance ever to be in this place. I learned most of all, however, that who I am changes in every moment that I connect with God and others in my sacred dance. I have been privileged and graced to be part of your wonderful religious dialogue group for three months. Thank you so much. I thank myself so much. I thank my dialogue mates so much.

"Anne," a junior faculty member, wrote these reflections in a personal letter, after spending a month with me and other young faculty talking about ways to create a more holistic pedagogy in the American university. This is an approach to teaching that speaks to students as people with souls as well as bodies, and with feelings as well as intellects. While Anne's "sacred dance" is obviously unique to her situation, maturity, intelligence, and experience, it nicely captures the general tone of the exploration narrative. I hear versions of it all the time in my encounters with students, staff, and faculty. Throughout the 1990s and, now, in the twenty-first century, the exploration narrative has been the single, most popular story of religion and spirituality that my undergraduate and graduate students like to tell.

The narrative's episodic permutations are limitless. No two "dances" or "journeys" (another word I often hear to describe this narrative) are exactly the same, although the questions and themes tend to be universal. Immanuel Kant (1724–1804) summed up these questions in his own way in the *Critique of Pure Reason*: "What can I know? What ought I to do? What may I hope?" I would add to Kant's questions this one: "What can I believe in?" I sometimes think of an exploration narrative like Anne's as a rolling account of an unfinished spiritual odyssey, a "quest" to answer Kant's perennial questions—the climax and denouement yet to be determined. At times, I find these accounts to be maddeningly vague and intellectually self-indulgent; at other times, I find them to be incredibly inspiring, candid, and loving. Always, I take them to be a very serious, and defensible, response to the cry for meaning on college campuses that I discussed in the first chapter.

I am always touched that people like Anne are willing to share the content of their "sacred dances" so openly with the rest of us. I never take this openness for granted in any of my groups. Anne's willingness to be so vulnerable and honest about her story helped to establish a level of trust in her particular group that I find to be fairly common in the work I do. Once group members relax and realize that they have religious stories to tell, journeys and "dances" to narrate, that others genuinely want to hear and understand—no matter how challenging or awkward their questions—then the conversation flows freely. People make a commitment to work very hard together in order to understand each other's narrative constructions, because they rarely have the opportunity in the everyday world to engage in heartfelt discussions about transcendent or immanent meaning. In fact, many students have told me that they have never had these kinds of conversations with their families, or even, surprisingly, in their churches, synagogues, or temples. In my opinion, this is a missed opportunity for cooperative meaning-making. I can only hope that it is not fatal.

Just who are these explorers who increasingly make their way to university campuses throughout the United States? The majority whom I know are white, more often women than men, middle-class, mostly unchurched from birth or else lapsed, and deeply reflective. Many have grown terminally disillusioned with the mainline religions for a variety of alleged reasons. Among these are the churches' centralization of authority; rigidity of traditional doctrines, creeds, scriptures, and boring, unimaginative liturgies; loss of intimacy and a sense of mystery; and, as one of my explorers said, "too much bureaucracy and hierarchy and not enough soul." Explorers like Anne look mainly toward alternative monotheistic and polytheistic religions other than Christianity and Judaism for meaning.

One fast-growing group of explorers on college campuses throughout the United States is the Neo-Pagans (currently comprising 113 college groups, according to their world wide web site), a religious movement that includes more than 100,000 adherents in this country and Canada. They are an excellent example of what religious-studies scholars call *syncretism* (from the Greek *synkratizein*, to combine, mix, or blend). Neo-Pagans combine elements of diverse spiritualities and religions into a uniquely eclectic, decentralized movement. They borrow from Egyptian, Celtic, Norse, and Greek paganism, as well as from neopagan witchcraft (Wicca) and a number of goddess religions. I have met many Neo-Pagans during the last few years, some of whom were greatly disenchanted with what they perceived to be the sexism, dogmatism, and collectivist tendencies of the mainline religions.

Neo-Pagans are intensely individualistic, many are environmentalists and feminists, and some are Wiccans. Neo-Pagans frighten more conventional believers on college campuses because of their unorthodox spirituality and colorful religious rituals; thus, they often find themselves to be the targets of evangelical Christians who see them as advocating witchcraft, satanic rituals, and animal sacrifice. These stereotypes bear little resemblance to what it is that Neo-Pagans actually believe and practice. Even though it is very difficult to identify exactly what Neo-Pagans have in common, because they are such a diverse, almost anarchistic group, most revere nature and ritual. Most subscribe to a genuine religious pluralism wherein many spiritual paths are seen as leading to the divine.

Moreover, most are polytheistic, pantheistic, experiential, nondogmatic, and non-creedal. Some believe in reincarnation and in goddesses. Others draw their spirituality from science fiction and fantasy. Furthermore, some Wiccans practice magic, often casting good spells on people and using candles and crystals in their meditations. The Wiccans' code of ethics, known as the "Wiccan Rede," emphasizes autonomy and not harming others: "An ye harm none, do what ye will." Also, "What ye send forth comes back to thee, so ever mind the Rule of Three [good and bad actions return threefold]." It is interesting to note that a number of neopagan congregations have chosen to become members of the Unitarian Universalist church (see Reisberg, 2000, pp. A49–A50; Smith, 1995, pp. 765–766).

Some explorers do decide to stay in their mainline Christian churches, trying to make them more participatory and individualistic by introducing social-outreach initiatives and meditation activities, and even sacred labyrinth walks (Bell, 1993; Graham, 1997). During the last decade, explorers have introduced such alternative spiritual expressions as Zen and Eastern mysticism in some Reform and Reconstructionist branches of Judaism. A growing number of explorers, though, abandoning Western religions entirely, prefer to look exclusively in an Eastern direction, spending much of their time cultivating what Robert Wuthnow (1998) calls a "spirituality of the inner self." This spirituality includes such contemplative practices as Transcendental Meditation, Zen, vipassana (a form of Buddhist meditation where one gains insight by looking deeply into things), mindfulness training (being fully in the present, and witnessing deeply to everything that is happening in the moment), and *samadhi* (strict concentration).

The ultimate goal of a spirituality of the inner self is to achieve a detachment from Western ways of thinking and perceiving, and to gain what Buddhists call *samatha*—a state of being typified by a calmness, tranquility, and equanimity. In this regard, two hundred years ago, Friedrich Schleiermacher (1768–1834), the founder of liberal Protestantism, made the following salient point, one that rings true for many explorers even today:

The capacity for joy and meaning are crushed out of children in the course of their education by the modern rage for calculating and explaining under the leadership of the discreet and practical men who dominate society. In everything there must be design and aim; something has always to be performed, and if the spirit can no more serve, the body must be exercised. Work and play, but no quiet, submissive contemplation. (quoted in Rockefeller, 1996, p. 4)

In the light of my experiences, I have to acknowledge that there is no single type of explorer among college students. This is a difficult narrative to pin down, because explorers are generally so restless and mobile. I find that in some ways the exploration narrative is the most pluralistic religio-spiritual story of all, because there are so many variations. Some explorers, it is true, are strong individualists who tend to choose and switch their denominational allegiances according to what they believe will make them happiest in the present moment. Others are far less fluid than this. Some value direct experience over doctrine and theology. Others find at least some meaning in church teachings and theological traditions, particularly in their efforts to reinterpret them in light of their personal needs.

Some explorers distrust churches. Others are more willing to take religious institutions as they find them, because they understand that churches are human, hence predictably flawed, constructions. Some are private and isolated. Others are wary of privatizing their faith and, hoping to influence public policy, become members of activist churches. They might join a variety of mutual-support religious groups, including evangelical congregations, in order to create richer, more intimate forms of community life. Some explorers are believers; others are disbelievers. Some just keep their beliefs to themselves, wondering what all the fuss is about.

What explorers whom I have met do share in common, however, is an infectious sense of wonder, and, in religious matters, they exude a spirit of adventure and experimentation. The vast majority of them tend to be informed "shoppers," moving around, always on the lookout for the best value in the religio-spiritual "supermarket." Furthermore, in William James's (1961) term, explorers are usually "healthy-minded": optimistic, happy, innocent, mystical, liberal, emotional, and enthusiastic. James describes them in this way: "[They] have an intuitive belief in the all-saving power of healthy-minded attitudes as such, in the conquering efficacy of courage, hope, and trust, and a correlative contempt for doubt, fear, worry, and all nervously precautionary states of mind" (p. 90).

There are significant exceptions, of course, to these generalizations about "healthy-mindedness," as well as a dark side that James identifies, and I will raise questions about these at the end of this section.

I find, too, that most explorers are extremely reluctant to label them-selves either denominationally or theologically. They do like to refer to themselves as "seekers" or "travelers," though. They are wary of such ambiguous characterizations as theist, agnostic, or atheist, because they believe it is important to keep an open mind regarding the truth claims of the various religions and spiritualities. Generally, it is the explorers, of all those students, faculty, and administrators who come to my classes and dialogue groups, who are the most responsive to the *emotional and aesthetic components* of religion. For them, spirituality must first make a direct impact on their hearts before it can find its way to their heads. In addition, their religions and spiritualities must tell transformative personal stories, if they are to have any staying power or aesthetic appeal.

Most explorers harbor at least a vague suspicion of what theologians and philosophers call the noetic (from the Greek *noetikos* meaning to perceive with the mind) properties of religion—those that can only be understood intellectually and rationally. Non-noetic explorers like Anne participate in a never-ending sacred dance looking for belief systems, leaders, and a series of spiritual practices that best capture the *ineffable sense of sacredness* that lies at the core of human existence. Anne knows that there are some things that cannot be put into words, some things that are just so overwhelming that they can only be felt.

Here again is William James (1961), this time on the "ineffability" of what he calls the "mystical" experience:

> It defies expression, that no adequate report of its contents can be given in words. It follows from this that its quality must be directly experienced; it cannot be imparted or transferred to others. In this peculiarity, mystical states are more like states of feeling than like states of intellect. No one can make clear to another who has never had a certain feeling, in what the quality or worth of it consists. (p. 300)

Explorers like Anne avidly traverse the theological landscape, and they keep their spiritual options open, in the genuine hope that someday they will find a faith, either institutional or private, that best suits their particu-lar tastes and temperaments. Many spend the major portion of their lives traversing rather than arriving, sometimes leaving behind everything they know. For them, the adventure, and the spirituality, lie in the process of exploring rather than in the act of foreclosing. There are some explorers, however, who, sooner or later, will decide on a particular belief system, and they will go on to raise their children in this tradition. I have known only a few of these people who have become orthodox believers, though, because their spiritual commitments still remain much too fluid for this to happen—even after they have ostensibly settled down.

Rabbi Rami M. Shapiro, director of the Rasheit Institute for Jewish Spirituality in Miami, Florida, believes that each of us, in order to find enlightenment, must become genuine spiritual travelers and leave home for the unknown, as often as it takes. This is something Anne has frequently done during the course of her adult life. Shapiro (1998) says:

> God said to Abraham, "Leave your country, your family, your father's house, and walk inward to the land I will show you." This is what true spirituality demands: to leave everything we know; to relinquish everything we are; to wander without a goal, path, teacher, or teaching, simply trusting that when we get "there," we will know. Buddha did that. So did Lao Tzu, Jesus, and Mohammed. They all left home. (p. 47)

The central leitmotif in the exploration narrative, then, is the unceasing search to find something to believe in, something to love, something that will tie together the tag-ends of people's chaotic lives. This is true even for persons like Anne for whom this "something" is the spiritual journey itself and not the destination. In this regard, an undergraduate business major once remarked in one of my dialogue groups:

> I'm getting the feeling that learning in my major how to make a lot of money seems trivial compared to what we've been talking about the last three days. My restlessness, my need to find something passionate in my life, and later in my work, is really a search for God, isn't it? But why is it the deeper I go, and the more I look, the further away I get? Will I ever find something that satisfies my yearning, that helps me to make sense of my life? Or should I stop all the navel-gazing and get real, that is get wealthy and be happy?

My best response to this business student's questions was that, for those explorers of an Eastern bent, qualities such as *prajna* (Sanskrit for understanding and wisdom), *maitri* (Sanskrit for bringing love and joy to others), mindfulness, truthfulness, *karuna* (Sanskrit for compassion toward those who are suffering), *dana* (Sanskrit for generosity and giving), courage, and balance are the real "wealth" in life. Not only are they pivotal to gaining success in business, but they are even more necessary for living a life of decency and goodness, and, yes, finding real happiness. I told this student that just one hour spent reading such Buddhist authors as Thich Nhat Hanh (1995), The Dalai Lama (1999), or Robert A. F. Thurman (1998) would forcefully bring this point home to him.

These writers believe that true happiness can be achieved only if someone strives to live a reflective, generous, and compassionate life. One of their primary teachings is that the paradox of happiness lies in the fact that happiness is, at best, an accidental by-product of living in the world with love, compassion, dignity, moderation, serenity, and grace. Happiness is not a state that we can intentionally will to happen. Americans too often make themselves very unhappy by striving so desperately to be happy, as the bored facial expressions of many vacationers and tourists so sadly demonstrate.

However, I also reminded my business student that I think the most important quality of all is *faith*—being willing to make the leap into the unknown, embarking on a journey that will change us, with no preconceptions or expectations of what that change might be. I quoted him Fenton Johnson's (1998) insight about faith and fear: "Faith is first among the cardinal virtues because everything proceeds from it including and especially love. Faith is the leap into the unknown—the entering into an action or a person knowing only that you will emerge changed, with no preconceptions of what that change will be. Its antonym is fear" (p. 54).

Because the opposite of faith is fear, not disbelief, my business student must continue to search for the meaning that eludes him, even though the deeper he goes, the further away he seems to get. Like most explorers, he must dance the dance of discovery for its own sake, with passion, in order to find some unifying purpose he can give his heart and mind to. I find that among many explorers I meet, I see far less fear than I do love and joy, because explorers are more apt to make Johnson's "leap of faith into the unknown" many times throughout their lives.

I generally value the presence of explorers in my courses and dialogue groups because they like to tell stories, particularly stories about their own faith journeys. They also like to hear them, because they appreciate a religious text that weaves a good tale, or a fellow traveler who regales the group with an enthralling spiritual anecdote or parable. Here is Wade Clark Roof (1993) on storytellers:

> [Explorers] are deeply enmeshed in the narrative tradition—for at heart they are storytellers, and like all storytellers, they know that life is an open-ended plot. They have a narrative perspective on commitment, which locates its meaning in their unfolding lives. As long as there are years to live, their narrative of life will continue to evolve, open always to reinterpretation and emendation at each stage along the way. (p. 261)

I am convinced that explorers will continue to be a forceful presence in the American university. It is worth our while to try to understand them, even though, for many academicians, they can often be exasperatingly nebulous about what they believe. Most explorers are eclectic in their tastes, thinking of religion as an abundance of riches, ripe for the spiritual picking. Eclectics like Anne will continue to dance their "sacred dances." They will "choreograph and improvise" spiritual insights gained from their travels, readings, practices, and gurus. Often they will end up with a very creative, spiritual reconfiguration. In Anne's case, she has fashioned a "post-Judaism," an intriguing melange of Reformist Judaism, New-Age paranormal psychology, Buddhist mindfulness, a Celtic and Native American love of the earth, and Goddess forms of worship. She believes that she has achieved the ideal East-West snythesis of *yin* and *yang*, and theism and pantheism.

Some explorers will be more mystical in their approach, expressing a love for mystery, stillness, and attunement that frankly elude too many of us who fit the ugly stereotype of the distracted and hard-driving Westerner. Mystics believe, in contrast, that the way to hear God's call is simply by shutting their mouths and listening, something few of us in the university know how to do very well. We miss what is most sacred because we have not learned how to transcend the sounds of our own voices or the incessant chatterings of our own minds. For the mystic, spirituality is to be found mainly in a series of private moments, perhaps communing with nature, or simply contemplating the ups and downs of life, or trying to be mindful of what might be precious and enduring in the ordinariness of day-to-day living.

Despite its many strengths and insights, however, we in the university need to ask serious questions about the exploration narrative. The issues I raise below have frequently ignited many conversations in my seminars and dialogue groups. Most explorers understand that, if they are to make a real difference in the world, a difference that reaches beyond the spirituality of their inner lives, then they need to make connections to those of us who wonder about the things that they believe with all their hearts—but sometimes have difficulty explaining with their mouths.

- How can explorers maintain a serious presence in the religious dialogue on American campuses without being dismissed by academicians as wooly-minded New-Agers or religio-spiritual dilettantes? Or do these perceptions not matter?
- Is a private, highly syncretic, noninstitutional, decentralized, and interiorized faith one that is substantive or long-lasting? To what extent is there validity to the charge that the exploration religious narrative is actually a story of white, middle-class self-indulgence? Further, as they age and confront life's realities, will explorers' ex-

perimentations disappear into a stolid middle-class conformity, along with all the other extravagances of youth? Conversely, is it a more valid thesis that an emphasis on the "spirituality of the inner self" will be what ultimately saves the mainline churches if these churches are smart enough to see the potential? Is Wade Clark Roof (1999) right when he says that as nests empty at home, former explorers who returned are once again dropping out of mainline churches to find more depth and meaning?

- Does the popularity of the exploration narrative among the Baby Boomers, Generation-Xrs, and now the Millennials (Howe & Strauss, 2000) signal the end of the mainline churches as we know them? Will one cosmic system fit all some day? Phyllis Tickle, in *God-Talk in America* (1997), estimates that by 2010 over 20 percent of all adult Americans will worship, pray, and receive spiritual instruction exclusively over the Internet. Will churches, synagogues, mosques, and temples, therefore, soon become quaint anachronisms?

- Is Diana Eck (1993) right when she claims that a believer cannot be "seriously committed to multiple centers" of religio-spiritual meaning? Is it true that believers must "give their hearts" (the literal meaning of the Latin, *credo*) to one, and only one, religious commitment, before they can become genuine pluralists (p. 95)? Is Eck possibly speaking from an older generation's narrative of faith that it must first be grounded in a single tradition in order for it to expand? Is it possible that explorers are actually anticipating the future of all religious faiths as a kind of multiple membership in a plurality of faith communities without exclusive affiliation with any single one?

- To what extent does the exploration narrative directly confront the plight of wounded believers and the presence of "radical evil" in the world? Does the narrative ever come to terms with the concerns of activists to build a more socially just world? Is the exploration narrative, particularly in its Eastern embodiment, right when it says that social justice must begin first with the presence of compassion in individual hearts?

- Diane Winston (1998), a religious studies scholar, contends that words like "syncretism," "cafeteria-style" religion, perhaps even "explorer" narratives, are derogatory, because they trivialize and demean Third-World, and alternative-American religions. Rarely are these terms used to describe Christianity. Winston prefers a term like *trans-religiosity* to describe "an individual's participation in different traditions without feeling any contradictions" (p. A60). Is Winston's criticism an accurate one? If so, what are some better ways to describe the construction of those spiritual paths that obviously represent a creative blending of religio-spiritual beliefs, mythologies, rituals, and practices?

The Secular Humanism Narrative

I am able to find the meaning and the morality I seek in the work that I do, the people I love, the simple pleasures that life gives as a gift to me, and in the opportunity to learn from, and to help, others. Why is it, then, that I still think I need something more than this?

I am a restless humanist. At one time in my life, I was in search of a meaning beyond meaning. Gregory of Nyssa, the 4th century theologian, used a perfect word to express what I was looking for—*epektasis*. This is a "straining forward" toward mystery, toward a "luminous darkness," toward an "unsatiated desire" to find the elusive biblical peace that "surpasses worldly understanding." I wanted to discover the stillness in the center of it all that is Taoistic. I wanted the compassion and the quieting of my voracious worldly cravings that are Buddhist. I never found any of this, and I do not know if I ever will.

I have always been profoundly troubled by the presence of evil in the world. I am, for example, unable to explain the darkness that has enveloped the twentieth century—arguably the most bloody of a long line of very bloody centuries. This is a century that has produced 100 million casualites throughout the world as a result of wars alone. I want to make sense of war, cruelty, natural disasters, injustice, grinding poverty, slavery, suffering, and the very real personal death—most likely the extinction—that awaits me and all those I love. I want to unravel the impossible dilemma of why upwards of 80 billion people have been born, lived, and died since the beginning of human life on earth. I wonder: to what end? At whose pleasure or will? Or is it all a matter of blind, evolutionary chance, a cosmic roll of the dice, a monumental coincidence?

At an early point in my life, I was a totally conventional, churchgoing, Christian believer. Later, during my college years, I became an unconventional, church-disparaging, disbeliever. Throughout most of my professorial career, I have retained a studied, intellectual skepticism toward the things I can not see, touch, taste, or submit to the test of reason. Today, I am relatively comfortable in what for me is an honest and respectful religious doubt—a kind of existential agnosticism. My "faith," if this is what I can call it, is in line with Niels Bohr's who once said about science and theology: "Every sentence I utter should be regarded by you not as an assertion but as a question."

I find much to admire in the humanistic faith of ethics scholar and theologian, Sharon Welch. For Welch, religious faith is less about God and more about intellectual curiosity, teaching, writing, service, political activism in behalf of social justice, and "meditative awareness." Her test of her own faith is always to ask how, and in what tangible ways, it continues to transform her life, how it functions to make her a better human being, willing to act courageously on her highest ethical ideals. In fact, at one point, Welch, the Harvard-trained theologian and religious studies scholar, says that she can serve God without believing in God.

I can honestly say that I too, at this stage of my life, "know of no concepts, symbols, or images of God, Goddesses, gods, or divinity that I find intellectually credible, emotionally satisfying, or ethically challenging in the face of evil and the complexity of life." I do know, however, that, for now, I am able to find the meaning and the morality I seek in the work that I do, in the opportunity to learn from, and to help, others, in the people that I meet and in those I love, and in the pleasures that the simple things I take for granted provide me. I am willing to admit that, in many ways, I am a thorough-going, here-and-now, postmodern secularist, but one also with an indefatigable curiosity about the possibility of something else, something post-postmodern and post-secular. Why is it that I think I need something more than what I've already got?

These are my words. I choose, somewhat self-indulgently, I admit, to tell a bit of my own story here, because I think it captures important pieces of the narrative that I am calling secular humanism. I can be reasonably certain that in every course and workshop that I offer on any philosophical or religio-spiritual topic, there will always be secular humanists of varying ages and stages present. I am obviously partial to the secular humanist narrative because it is my own, but I can also be critical of it when I need to be. At this late stage in my career, I think I know where the narrative is appealing and where it is disappointing. I can see only too clearly its strengths and weaknesses in myself, and, as well, in all those humanists who find their way to my groups.

Most humanists in my seminars are asking my questions, making my assumptions, and are plagued, in their own ways, by my doubts about secular humanism, although many are reluctant to admit it. I actually relish this unwitting *affirmation* and *refutation* of the things I believe, whenever secular humanists in my dialogue groups talk about their convictions. This is one of the reasons I teach, I suppose—to hear in others' constructions the sense and the nonsense in what I hold to be true and good. For example, I admire secular humanists' passion in affirming the value of life in the here-and-now, and in exhorting the rest of us to accept the reality that we are masters of our own destiny, left alone in the universe to decide our fates together. However, I also wince at their passion in refuting as ignorant superstition all supernatural forms of religion and spirituality. I think this attitude is too facile, even anti-intellectual, in that it discards in a flash 3,000 years of collective religious wisdom and resourceful narrative-making.

When I use the term *secular humanism* in this section, I am not referring to Greek, Christian, Renaissance, academic, or therapeutic forms of humanism. While I value the utility and the legacies of all these expressions, I am using the term here mainly to represent a more general and cumulative worldview, a *this-worldly* (secular) approach to telling a particular story about reality. It is an approach based on the scientific worldview and on the efficacy of reason, and it tends to be highly suspicious of organized religion. It is also politically progressive. I prefer Corliss Lamont's (1965) definition of humanism in general for my purposes here:

> Humanism is a philosophy of joyous service for the greater good of all humanity in this natural world, advocating the methods of reason, science, and democracy. . . . Humanism is the viewpoint that men [sic] have but one life to lead and should make the most of it in terms of creative work and happiness; that human happiness is its own justification and requires no sanction or support from supernatural sources; that in any case the supernatural, usually conceived of in the form of heavenly gods or immortal heavens, does not exist; and that human beings, using their own intelligence and cooperating liberally with one another, can build an enduring citadel of peace and beauty upon this earth. (pp. 12, 14)

These points can be found in the various editions of "A Humanist Manifesto," a statement of 15 principles, first published in 1933 (reproduced in Lamont, 1965), and signed by such intellectual luminaries as John Dewey, Bertrand Russell, Edwin H. Wilson, and many others.

It is striking how many of the principles stated in the 1933 "Manifesto" hold up even today, when viewed from the vantage point of the twenty-first century. Although I have never met a single secular humanist student, administrator, or faculty member who has ever read the 1933 "Manifesto," I am confident that each would enthusiastically support the central theme in the secular humanist narrative: "This life is all and enough" (Lamont, 1965, p. 81). They would also endorse the Manifesto's persistent, this-worldly penchant. In addition, they would second the Manifesto's ultimate faith in the power of human beings to solve their own problems by using their reason and science, along with their courage and vision.

It is important to understand that, since the Renaissance and the Enlightenment, secular humanism has come to represent an *atheistic or agnostic viewpoint.* Ironically, these historical movements forced the Catholic and Protestant churches to put less emphasis on sin, redemption, and the afterlife and more on the intrinsic value, dignity, and intelligence of human beings (Rohmann, 1999). This loosening of traditional theology inadvertently set the stage for later, nonbelieving thinkers such as Sigmund Freud (1865–1939), who found the source of religion to be a group neurosis and the idea of God to be a father projection; and Charles Darwin (1809–1882), who located the origin of human beings in natural selection, rather than divine genesis.

Despite secular humanism's unrelenting critique of organized religion throughout history, however, it is intriguing to note that the signers of the 1933 "Manifesto" refused to expunge the word *religion* from their secular vocabulary. In fact they referred to their worldview as "religious humanism," in order to connote what they thought was a natural progression from a God-centered universe to a human-centered one. They simply redefined religion to mean a "quest for abiding values, an inseparable feature of human life" (cited in Lamont, 1965, p. 286). Thus, they succeeded in de-divinizing religion, and, in the process, according to some critics (e.g., Connolly, 1999), inadvertently elevated science, technology, reason, nature, culture, politics, and democracy to near-God-like status throughout the modern world.

The 1973 "Manifesto," and the 1981 "Secular Humanist Declaration," no longer referred to Humanism as a religion, however. In fact, the 1981 "Declaration" upped the ante, making religious skepticism a major tenet of secular humanism (both documents cited in Nord, 1995). The latest "Manifesto 2000" advocates a "planetary humanism" as the wave of the future. This manifesto is particularly critical of postmodernism in universities, which, according to manifesto writer, Paul Kurtz, undermines the "basic premises of modernity and humanism, attacking science and technology, and questioning humanist ideas and values" (quoted in Cimino, 1999, p. 3).

Finally, I am sure that secular humanists on the nation's campuses would celebrate the 1933 Manifesto's ultimate moral and political objective: the achievement of economic, cultural, and ethical happiness for all humankind—irrespective of nation, race, politics, or religion. Friedrich Dürrenmatt (quoted in Rohmann, 1999) captures the Manifesto's secular intent in concise language: "What the world needs is not redemption from sin but redemption from hunger and oppression; it has no need to pin its hopes upon Heaven, it has everything to hope for from this earth" (p. 185).

There is increasing evidence that, at the present time, a cadre of young secular humanists is beginning to organize on campuses throughout the country. While the overall number is comparatively tiny—consisting of no more than a few thousand members—it is growing. A national group called the Council for Secular Humanism, based in Amherst, New York, under the aegis of its founder, the aforementioned philosopher Paul Kurtz, has been active on more than 70 campuses in supporting a sense of community, identity, and security for student atheists and agnostics. The college chapters at these institutions are known as the Campus Freethought Alliance. Although, at this time, the chapters have little influence on other students, and attrition through graduation and dropouts is predictable, student interest continues to intensify at such places as Marshall, Harvard, SUNY at Buffalo, Maryland, and Webster. These chapters offer such bonding activities as Superstition Bash Day, Darwin Day, Banned Book Week, and Freethought Day (see Cimino, 1999).

Derek Araujo, president of the Freethought Alliance at Harvard, typifies the kind of secular humanist who would join such a group (Reisberg, 1998). He says: "Religious extremists have demonized atheism to the point where declaring one's non-belief is like admitting to eating babies. Christians feel free to display their faith by wearing crosses, but even I would not feel comfortable walking down the street wearing a T-shirt that says, 'Atheist'" (p. A44).

Typical too is Gabriel Carlson, a once-devout Italian Catholic, and current political liberal, who supports racial equality, women's rights, gay and lesbian liberation, sexual freedom, environmentalist causes, and the separation of church and state. He declares:

> I really tried to convince myself that there is an afterlife. My dad was a psychologist, so I used a writing assignment as a pretext to ask if, under hypnosis, people could be convinced to believe in the afterlife. I tell that to Christians a lot: If I could believe and have any intellectual integrity, I'd do it. Human mortality is a very positive thing, actually, since it really forces me to seize every day. (quoted in Nussbaum, 1999, p. 35)

And listen to D. J. Grothe, who came out as both a homosexual and an atheist at Ambassador University, an evangelical Christian college in Texas. After clandestinely reading Karen Armstrong's *A History of God* (1993) in his dormitory room late at night, and realizing that God appears to be nothing but a human construct, differing from culture to culture and time to time, he began to seriously question his Christian faith. He says:

> I found Nietzsche. When you begin having a dialogue with yourself, the whole thing crumbles. If God exists, you ain't gonna prove it on paper. You need personal experience. And I never had it. God never spoke to me. When I came out as an atheist [which he reports caused more turbulence at his college than coming out as a gay man], I wasn't exactly shunned, but it was a shock, and it sent ripples. I got e-mails saying "you of all people; this is a test of your faith; you'll be a minister, just wait and see." (quoted in Nussbaum, 1999, pp. 35–36)

D. J. Grothe is now a graduate student at Washington University in St. Louis, and a proud member of the Washington University League of Freethinkers. At Washington University, his organization and the local Campus Crusade for Christ often cosponsor friendly debates with each other, demonstrating, at least on this campus, that genuine religious pluralism is possible and need not necessarily result in Christian or atheist bashing.

In October 1999, the highly respected journal of academic life, *Lingua Franca*, ran a cover story on what it called "the campus crusade for secular humanism" (Nussbaum, 1999). The article tells the story of how many agnostic and atheistic students on college campuses throughout the United States are feeling great pressure to be "spiritual," as the more conservative religious revivals on college campuses begin to take on a huge momentum of their own. Campus Crusade for Christ, for example, numbering about 25,000 students nationally, has been known to villainize atheists, depicting them as immoral and anarchistic. Other evangelical campus ministries are also ratcheting up their efforts to proselytize and convert students, increasingly spreading the message that secularism, atheism, and agnosticism are the true enemies of a Christian way of life (Nussbaum, 1999; Reisberg, 1998).

In the face of what they perceive to be mostly subtle, but nevertheless insidious, pressure to become theists, many secular humanist students I know propose a counter-narrative they would like to enact in the academy. Like Derek Araujo, Gabriel Carlson, and D. J. Grothe, whom I quote above, they want it known that students ought to place their faith, not in revealed gospel truths or church dogmas, but in the awareness that *they* alone—not popes, prophets, or messiahs—are the social constructors of their religions and spiritual realities. What matters, therefore, is what works best for individuals and groups, not what is given by some transcendent force or ecclesiastical superauthority.

For these students, grand, all-enveloping religious and spiritual narratives are not only out of fashion; they can be dangerous. They too often weaken students' resolve to stand on their own two feet. They offer false hopes of an afterlife, thereby distracting students from the hard work they need to do to make *this* world a safer and fairer place. They provide a bogus sense of consolation at a time when young people need to face their problems head-on, if they are ever to solve them. Worst of all, though, they too often become aggressive in trying to make converts, and in the process, they risk turning universities into warring religious enclaves.

Some secular humanists in my courses and workshops have a tendency to be obstreperous in their disdain for all absolutisms, especially the religious kind. They relish going on the attack. They often remind me of Madalyn Murray O'Hair (1919–1995), at one time the most famous atheist in America, who never overcame the stereotype of anti-religious rabble-rouser in the public's eye. I think it is safe to say that O'Hair (1970), for all the good that she did, probably set back the cause of secular humanists in this country several decades because of her unrelenting and obsessive denigration of religion. She always seemed clearer about what she hated in organized religion (e.g., school prayer, tax-exempt churches) than what she stood for. Her invectives drowned out her convictions, and these were increasingly expressed in a number of court cases she initiated against local school districts, the Internal Revenue Service, the media, and the United States Government.

During her lifetime, O'Hair was an unyielding and notoriously uncivil propagandist for atheism and separation of church and state. I think of self-righteous secular humanists like her, with vindictive scores to settle and ideological battles to wage, as atheistic militants, the orthodox believers of disbelief. Although I may agree with many planks in their platforms, I for one do not appreciate it when they cross over the line that separates civility from outright hostility.

More attractive to someone of my temperament and philosophy, and also to those who join them in classes or in workshops, are the secular humanists who have no need to scream their truths at others. Let me call them the existential humanists with an ironic postmodern flair. Confident, but not smug, about their narrative, and genuinely open to dialogue with the opposition—like D. J. Grothe at Washington University—they go about their lives with a quiet assurance that they have discovered an important truth: *What makes life truly worth living, both privately and publicly, is that it is full of contingency, irony, and doubt. Because God has long since disappeared from the scene, no truth or revelation can ever be divine or final. However, this is no reason to despair, because now life can be full of incredible possibility, surprise, opportunity, and hope.* Existential humanists appreciate the autonomy they have to doubt, to question, and to suspend judgment in the face of all religious, political, and scientific claims to absolute truth. This, they believe, is a radical, individual freedom that empowers them and others to construct their own lives, according to their own best judgments.

I find something resonant and touching in this humanist affinity for existential ideas, even though few young people I know today bother reading such classical existential thinkers as Kierkegaard, Sartre, or Camus in the original texts. I once asked a dialogue group of students, staff, and faculty to answer the following question in ten different ways: *Even if you are postmodernists, what do you think are the "givens" in life that are inescapable for all of us, regardless of our unique interpretive frames, genetics, backgrounds, present situations in life, and future possibilities?* Only the secular humanists consistently mentioned those perennial existential themes related to human finitude (see Yalom, 1989, for a similar take on existentialism):

- the inevitability and finality of death awaiting all of us someday and how to cope with, and overcome, the anxiety usually associated with this reality;
- the dilemma of how best to use our hard-won freedom from the older, dominating myths in order to create ourselves and our world in the absence of gods and authority figures—to whom we have looked for answers in the past;
- the isolation and solitude that are the inescapable destiny of each and every human being, and the challenge to reach out to others in order to form relationships and community, in spite of this isolation and solitude;
- and the double paradox of needing to find a meaning in a life that has no intrinsic meaning and to realize that meaning-making is largely a by-product of living a life of activity and purpose rather than something consciously sought.

I am never exactly sure how to respond to the overtures of those secular humanists who will sometimes ask me to become more actively involved with them as a group outside of classes and workshops. Knowing that I lean philosophically in their direction, some of them sense a kindred spirit in their midst. A group of undergraduate and graduate students once sounded me out on the possibility of my being an unofficial adviser for a chapter of the Campus Freethought Alliance in the event that they were able to start one on my campus. I thought a long time about their offer, but eventually I turned them down. Admittedly, I was concerned about publicly affiliatiating with any religio-spiritual group because I did not want to be seen by other students as taking sides. I was also fearful of losing whatever pedagogical neutrality toward religion and spirituality I might be able to muster in the classroom and in my consultancies. For a very long time after I said no, however, I honestly did not know whether I had made the right decision.

Then one day, I happened to read the following poetic lines from Sara Maitland's book *A Big-Enough God: A Feminist's Search for a Joyful Theology* (1995):

> What I am suggesting here is that an honest, open-minded inspection of the creation, intimately including our own selves—with blood on its paws and death in the pot for the living's food—will not reveal directly the sort of God that we might like. For every pretty rainbow and golden sunset there is a child-abuser, a parasitic worm, a senseless randomness, or a lethal power. *There is also, more confusingly, a terrible tenderness.* It is as much our love as our malice and thoughtlessness that intrude into nature's careless but passionate commitment to change and growth, to evolution. We spare the mutants, treat the infertile, heal the sick, feed the hungry, breed pet dogs, cherish our teddy bears, stalwartly refuse to expose brain-damaged babies on mountain sides. Where does it come from, *this dangerous compassion,* for we did not learn it from nature, nor from the voracious black holes that spin and suck out there. (p. 37) (italics added)

I have no idea where "this dangerous compassion," "this terrible tenderness," come from, but I cannot stop thinking about Maitland's question. I also want to understand how it is that each of us can still commit to live a life of integrity, decency, and joy, knowing that, in the end, there are no definitive answers to the existential givens I mentioned above. Perhaps my need to understand these dilemmas is a residual narrative theme left over from my abandoned Catholicism. Perhaps not. I do know, however, that, amidst my own personal dither about the unanswerable questions of theodicy, I am still not ready to give up on the unlikely possibility of catching fleeting glimpses of transcendence in the universe.

To be sure, I am an existential humanist, secular to the core, with a postmodern flair, but I am also a closet explorer, always looking, forever on the prowl for something more. Pulitzer-Prize winning Annie Dillard (1999) once said that, despite writing all her best-selling books about spirituality and nature, she still "didn't know beans about God" (p. 169). In my opinion, the most eloquent and honest answer that anyone can give to the problem of evil, to the countless incidences of human woundedness that appear preventable but are not, to the nadir of the mystery of a God who drops out of sight when Her creatures are most in need of Her loving presence, is Dillard's. "I don't know beans about God." Her wonderful book, *For the Time Being* (1999), ought to be compulsory reading for adherents of each of the narratives I recount in these last two chapters, because Dillard is an important reality check on all our narrative excesses.

Further, I would say, no one else knows beans about God either—not the orthodox believers or the activists, and not the mainliners or the humanists. Every narrative, in its own way, is full of beans. This is what makes so many of them appealing and alienating at the same time. They are the best we can do, and so we need to be wary and humble, skeptical and grateful, whenever we are tempted to herald their virtues. Frankly, I do not meet many secular humanists who give one whit about Maitland's "dangerous compassion," or signals of transcendence. However, I give more than a whit, and I always will, even though I continue to be the first one to challenge all the too-easy religio-spiritual answers to the truly complex questions that my students ask about meaning. This is why, after much soul-searching and many second doubts, I think I did the right thing in turning down those secular humanists who wanted me to be their adviser.

Here are the types of questions that secular humanists often hear from others in my classes and workshops:

- If it is true that theists have demonized secular humanists, how can secular humanists avoid demonizing theists? Put another way, is the secular humanist narrative capacious enough to embrace the theist narrative, or is it more likely to be the other way around? Or are both narratives forever destined to be at war with one another, because of the radical incompatibility of their basic beliefs?
- How can secular humanism avoid the temptation to become simply another religion, with its own "sacred scriptures," "chapels," rituals, conversion tactics, cliquishness, and money-raising? Or is this creep toward institutionalization on campuses an inevitable by-product of trying to establish a corporate identity?
- Is the secular humanist narrative mainly reactive rather than proactive? At what point should it emphasize the values it stands for rather than the ideas it repudiates? Is the narrative likely to draw the support it needs on campuses in order to stay alive, if it is seen only as a critique of Christianity or other theistic religions? Or are critique and confrontation what make the secular humanist narrative genuinely unique and attractive, given the hegemony of Western religions on most college campuses?
- If some secular humanists feel threatened by the hegemony of theistic religions on their campuses, is it possible that some theists feel threatened by the habitual naysaying of the more militant, atheistic humanists? In some ways, do theists and atheists mirror each other's weaknesses and strengths? Do they fear the same things about each other?

- Are atheist fellowships, freethought alliances, and freethinker associations simply euphemisms for churches for the unchurched? Or is the need for community and affiliation so basic to human beings that both disbelievers and believers would be missing something vital without it?
- How can a secular humanist be moral without a belief in God or without belonging to any organized religion? If there is no Divine reward or punishment for behavior, why be good at all? Are all secular humanists moral relativists, who choose an ethic depending on whether it makes them feel good? Or does the secular humanist narrative actually tell the best story of ultimate personal responsibility, because, absent a Deity, individuals alone must be held accountable for their own behavior?
- Is secular humanism just an excuse to deify human beings? Is this naive, given the propensity of human beings to commit the most atrocious acts against one another? Or is there something truly God-like in all human beings, thereby rendering invalid the need to look to the heavens for a God?
- How is the secular humanist explanation for the presence of evil in the world an improvement over the explanations offered by all the world's religions? In the end, isn't the test of which narrative is best how comforting it might be to those who suffer? Or is the secular humanist explanation the most consoling of all because it says that some evil is simply a product of blind chance (a design flaw in natural selection) and, therefore, uneliminable, while some is correctible, given the will and the resources? Therefore, it is up to us to know the difference.

Before I close this chapter, I want to mention some assumptions I automatically make about religio-spiritual narratives and the people who tell them, whenever I teach a course, design a workshop, lead an all-campus dialogue group, or give an interactive lecture. I find that once I get clear about my own assumptions, then the subsequent teaching process seems to go a little more smoothly:

- People have religious stories they want to tell me (Bruner's "itch" to share construals of meaning), particularly if I can create a safe and mutually respectful space for this to happen.
- To this end, I must always ask these questions of each and every person:

What do you believe?

Why does this belief have such strong appeal to you?

Where, in your opinion, is your belief strongest and weakest in its *storytelling* appeal?

Where, in your opinion, is *my* belief strongest and weakest in its *storytelling* appeal?

What, in *your* narrative, do you think might, and might not, work for me, and *vice versa*?

- What is more, people want their religious stories to be heard, understood, and appreciated—*before they are evaluated*—by me.
- What is more still, it is possible that in the mutually empathic exchange of religious stories my own religious story might be deepened and enlarged, maybe even challenged, better, maybe even lived more genuinely.
- And if it is, wonderful; and if it is not, what have I truly lost? What am I afraid of? What have I got to prove? Why?
- After all, the religious story I hear from any storyteller is the story that makes sense to that storyteller. Thus, the most honest and respectful question I can ask of the storyteller is why? The most honest and self-respecting question I can ask of myself is why not?
- However, the two questions I must always remember to ask of both the storyteller and myself are these:

Why does any story have to be the only true story?

What does your particular need to have others adopt your religious story tell you about yourself (and the rest of us)?

Now I turn to one of the most difficult questions facing secular college campuses today: What role, if any, should religion and spirituality play at a college or university in the promotion of values, in the teaching of ethics, and in the formation of moral character?

Chapter 5

The Role of Religion in Fostering Values on a Secular Campus

The point which I should first wish to understand is whether the pious or holy is beloved by all the gods because it is holy, or holy because it is beloved by all the gods.

—Plato, *Euthyphro*

The attempts to found a morality apart from religion are like the attempts of children who, wishing to transplant a flower that pleases them, pluck it from the roots that seem to them unpleasing and superfluous, and stick it rootless into the ground. Without religion there can be no real, sincere morality, just as without roots there can be no real flower.

—Leo Tolstoy, *Selected Essays*, cited in Louis P. Pojman, 1995

I can only state my convictions that there is no cogent, positive argument for the existence of a God, that the problem of evil constitutes an insuperable difficulty for any orthodox theism, that the advance of scientific knowledge renders a theistic view superfluous as an explanatory hypothesis and utterly implausible, and that no specific revelation has reliable credentials. . . . [thus] moral distinctions do not depend on God any more than, say, arithmetical ones, hence ethics is autonomous and can be studied and discussed without reference to religious beliefs, [and] we can simply close the theological frontier of ethics.

—J. L. Mackie, *Ethics: Inventing Right and Wrong*, 1977

Universities . . . should model something for students besides the ideal of individual excellence. . . . If institutions that purport to educate young people don't embody society's cherished ideals—community, cooperation, harmony, love—then what young people will learn will be the standards the institutions do embody: competition, hierarchy, busyness, and isolation. A [university] community is a partnership of people committed to the care and nurturing of each other's mind, body, heart, and soul through participatory means.

—William H. Willimon & Thomas H. Naylor, *The Abandoned Generation: Rethinking Higher Education,* 1995

"I Am Comfortable Talking About Values . . . Not Religion"

I recently received an e-mail from a high-level, student-development administrator in another part of the country who read my first chapter while it was in rough draft. Her criticisms were both pointed and helpful, and they subsequently provoked much of what I intend to write about in this chapter on the connections between religion and values. Here is what she said:

> I want you to know that I liked your first chapter, and I intend to order your book for every one of my staff members when it is published. I am concerned, though, that you hardly mention the words *values* or *morals* in your first chapter. Shouldn't the primary purpose of higher education be to foster the right values in our students? This is what we try to do in our own office here on my campus as part of what we call the *extra-curriculum*. I'm not sure that putting so much emphasis on religion is going to achieve this objective. While I obviously love it that you ascribe a pivotal educational role to administrators like myself, and while I couldn't agree more with you that some students' religious and spiritual beliefs are key to what it is they value, I feel much more comfortable about leading cross-campus discussions about values than I do about religion. Values are the real stuff of meaning-making, wouldn't you say?

> I contend that it is important for us to decouple values and religion. Certainly, the former is crucial in the work that we do as student development educators, but the latter, though important and certainly central to my life, is far too controversial for us to expose to the light of day in a secular institution. Besides, administrators like myself don't know anything about the academic study of religion. How many of us were even religious-studies majors in college? I would argue that we must completely secularize the teaching of values. I don't even know how to talk abstractly about religion without embarrassing myself and anyone who is within earshot of what I am saying. I'm not trained to lead discussions on religion. Religion is just too much of a distraction when it comes to discussing values, I'm afraid.

> One more thing that I find disturbing about your chapter. Why do you let faculty off the hook? Why shouldn't they be the major players in promoting the kind of cross-campus, multifaith dialogue on religious pluralism that you are advocating? Don't tenure and academic freedom allow more latitude for this kind of discussion? Isn't the seminar room the best place for intellectually challenging conversations about religion, morality, and values? Why can't faculty get students to discuss these issues? Is it really because students are so busy vying for grades and letters of reference that they won't open up in classrooms? Or is it because too many faculty choose to be remote from students' lives more than they were even a few decades ago? I hope you promote your book among your academic colleagues as well as among administrators.

By the way, I must share with you that I'm beginning to see troublesome signs of religious bias on my campus. The other day a very outspoken, conservative Christian group recently broke up a public meeting of Neo-Pagans on my campus by shouting such slogans as "Jesus loves you, even though you are sinners," and "Satan is not the way, Jesus is the way." The Neo-Pagans, in turn, responded by counter-shouting "Jesus was really a witch," and "If Jesus were alive today, he would be a Neo-Pagan." So, maybe you're right after all. In this case, how can we ever get these students to talk about values without taking into consideration their strong religious beliefs? I know that I'm contradicting myself, but, what the hell, I'm confused. I admit it. This is why I am going to buy your book.

The e-mail writer raises four questions that I will try to address in these final two chapters. They are:

- What ought to be the role of religion and spirituality, if any, in fostering values on a college campus?
- What is it that educators—both faculty and administrators—need to know by way of academic content if they are to be effective values educators?
- What is it that faculty and administrators need to know by way of dialogue skills and understandings if they are to be effective values communicators?
- How might faculty and administrators, indeed educators throughout the entire campus, work together in order to teach values?

Learning About Earning Is Not What College Is All About

If my main thesis in this book is accurate, education for many young people in the academy today is as much about making meaning—and this includes religio-spiritual meaning—as it is about making money. I say this, despite what appears to be conflicting data in the *The Chronicle of Higher Education Almanac* (1999) that "being very well-off financially" (about 75%) is the chief objective for first-year students attending college. Upon closer look, however, the data show something else as well: About one-third, 35%, want to "influence social values." Approximately two-thirds, 65%, want to "help others who are in difficulty," whereas 40% want to "develop a meaningful philosophy of life." A combined 80% want to "clean up the environment," "participate in a community-action program," or "help to promote racial understanding." Another 32% want to "become community leaders." Also, 60% want to "gain a general education and appreciation of ideas," 35% want "to become more cultured persons," and 73% want to "learn more about things that interest [them]." These statistics have remained fairly constant over the last ten years in Almanac issues.

My own experience in teaching over two hundred courses in applied ethics, moral and character education, philosophy of education, and religion, spirituality, and education confirms the validity of these percentages. While it is undeniably true that most students who find their way to my seminars and dialogue groups pursue a college education in order to earn a decent living, most also want to know how to live a decent life. Earning money and making meaning do not have to be mutually incompatible goals. Neither does having fun in college and having a purpose in life. In fact, I find that most students understand all too well that riches and pleasure alone do not guarantee happiness or meaning. At some subliminal level, they know, in the words of Martin Luther King, Jr., that "the richer we have become materially the poorer we have become morally and spiritually" (quoted in Willimon & Naylor, 1995).

One request I frequently make of my students when the semester gets underway and we have had some practice talking about values is this: "Tell us all in just a few sentences what it is you value; I think this will go a long way in helping us, and you, to determine who it is that you are striving to become." This latter claim, although presumptuous, alerts students to just how important all of our subsequent conversations about values will be. I maintain that what students are publicly willing to admit they value invariably signals the kind of life-story they are in the process of constructing for themselves.

Here are the types of responses I often get, not listed in any rank order, and they echo the findings in the *Chronicle Almanac* issue: friendships, relationships, intimacy, family, satisfying work, helping others, personal integrity, honesty, care, compassion, freedom, social justice, health, security, fun, pleasure, happiness, nature, knowledge, education, God, spirituality, church, success, liberty, power, financial stability, independence, interdependence, community, adventure, peace of mind, making a difference, and self-esteem.

This list summarizes very well what I find to be most important to many students on campuses today. It demonstrates that students are far more than mere "hedonist machines," hell-bent on experiencing one pleasurable sensation after another while in school. In spite of the oft-repeated stereotypes that college students today "party hard" and "work soft," and that they go to school mainly for a one-way ticket to the high-paying professions and corporations, a list like this demonstrates a very compelling counter-truth. For many students, earning a decent living and living a morally fulfilling life can be complementary objectives. It is important for me to point out that I hear these and similar values expressed by students of all ages in cross-campus dialogue groups throughout the country. What is more, I take students at their word whenever they tell me that these are the values that are truly paramount for them.

Furthermore, many of these students continue to look without embarrassment to religion and spirituality for defining a moral meaning that is important to them. The comment of one mainline student in an all-university ethics colloquium I moderated recently says it well:

> My morality is actually the particular religious teaching I am trying to put into practice at any given moment. Without my religious convictions, and my church to support me, I've got no morality, period! Here I am ready to graduate, and today is the only time that I have ever been encouraged to discuss either my values or my religious beliefs in an academic setting. For all my professors and classmates know, I'm just a grade-making, tuition-paying robot, motivated mainly by the prospect of making big bucks in the real world later on.

What constantly amazes me, in the face of all the overwhelming evidence that I have cited throughout this book, is that each year the pollsters for *The Chronicle* never even bother to include a religio-spiritual "reason" or "objective" in their values categories for why students might decide to attend college. The pollsters appear to make the assumption that religion and spirituality have little or no role to play in motivating students to attend college, even though their own findings show that 81% of college students frequently attend religious services (*The Chronicle*, 1999, p. 22). Do the pollsters honestly think that *all* college students are prone to compartmentalize their lives—that they restrict religion and spirituality to just an hour or so one day a week, while going about their business on all the other days of pursuing an education and constructing a life-narrative totally devoid of religious values? Do the "experts" truly believe that all students live such schizophrenic, radically disjunctive existences?

In contrast, and based upon three-plus decades of experience in hearing students' stories, I can always make three warranted predictions about students, religion, and values at the beginning of each semester:

1. Students will jump at the opportunity in my courses to talk about what it is they genuinely value, even with minimal goads on my part to do so.

2. Students will find it very difficult to avoid discussing religion and spirituality in connection with their values, even if it is only to demonstrate that they have thoroughly rejected organized religion's influence.

3. At least a few students will ask this question at some time during the semester: "Just what do you mean by values, and whose values are we talking about anyway?"

If it is true, as I contend, that we all live in narratives because stories are indispensable for construing our lives in such a way as to be consistent, purposeful, and worthwhile, then, given the right circumstances, the fact that students will readily narrate their stories, values and all, is actually an easy prediction for me to make.

Another important example of how leaders in higher education ignore or underplay the significance of religio-spirituality in the formation of students' values is Willimon and Naylor's very popular book *The Abandoned Generation: Rethinking Higher Education* (1995). Among its insights is the laudable proposal that higher education ought to be centrally commited to helping students find a meaning in their lives, one that "integrates the spiritual, intellectual, emotional, and physiological dimensions of life" (p. 163). While I agree wholeheartedly with the authors' central objective, I disagree strenuously with their derogatory stereotypes of college students. The overall impression the reader is left with from their book is that the vast majority of students today are alcoholic, indolent, excessively careerist, consumerist, fragmented, apathetic, partying, anti-intellectual, lonely, isolated, plagued by an all-pervasive sense of gloom and despair, and self-centered (several of these adjectives appear throughout their book many times to describe current college students). Also, I am left completely mystified as to why the authors never once bother alluding to the specific role that religion or spirituality might play in the fostering of values and in the making of meaning among college students. It appears the authors are implying that religion and spirituality are completely beside the point for anyone who wishes to pursue meaning.

Is there a college mission statement anywhere in the United States that fails to mention the central importance of cultivating *values* as part of an institution's overall philosophy of education? Whether these values are environmental awareness, critical thinking, community-building, service-learning, volunteerism, human wellness, inclusiveness, multiculturalism, social justice, or civic responsibility, and so forth, the message from universities is still the same: There ought to be more to the pursuit of a college degree in institutional mission statements than merely promoting the goals of self-advancement, material success, and a life of hedonistic leisure (Ehrlich, 2000).

I would argue that the types of values found in college mission statements would take on added moral force for many students, if they could locate them in a context of religion and spirituality. All of the above values, however meritorious on their own terms, require a set of background beliefs, a framework of meaning, that will make sense to those students who do not find it easy to separate their religious leanings (or spiritual yearnings) from the rest of their lives. I contend that most of the values that tend to show up in college mission statements derive whatever philosophical or political rationale they might have from the teachings of the major religions. Such religious virtues as self-sacrificing love, binding people together in community, helping one's neighbor, and stewarding the earth's resources, add spiritual depth and resonance to the matter-of-fact value rhetoric of catalogue mission statements. I quote Warren A. Nord (1995) in this regard: "The idea that students can be educated about how to live, what kind of a person to be, and how to act, without taking religion seriously is at least illiberal and quite possibly absurd" (p. 351).

To their credit, Willimon & Naylor (1995), in the quotation that opens this chapter, say it well: The university ought to be about advancing such "core" values as care and nurture, cooperation and love because if it fails to do this, then students will learn only the worst standards that colleges embody. They will become competitive, driven, and eventually isolated. However, just as in Willimon & Naylor's influential text, one must search far and wide for even an oblique reference in most college mission statements to the role that religio-spirituality might play in helping students to develop such core values as the above.

It Is Neither Possible Nor Desirable
to Decouple Religion and Values

Whenever I use the word *value* in my teaching, I mean for it to be synonymous with the technical term *axiology*. According to the *Cambridge Dictionary of Philosophy* (1999), axiology (from the Greek, *axios*, meaning worthy or valuable) is the branch of philosophy that deals with the aesthetic value of beauty; the ethical values of right, good, and virtue; the moral principles by which people ought to live their lives; and the epistemological (Greek, *episteme*, meaning knowledge) values of how we can go about either justifying or criticizing particular claims to truth, including the religious, moral, and ethical. My approach to values in all my courses is wide-ranging, and although many philosophers use the term *values* in a more restricted sense—e.g., to examine whether some values are intrinsic or extrinsic, relative or absolute—I do not.

I initially use the term the way my students do, in a common-sense manner. Values refer to what it is they regard highly, what makes their lives worth living, what gives their lives meaning, what makes them happy, what is of ultimate concern to them. Then, when we dig more deeply into the concept, the term inevitably evokes the religious and spiritual ideals that guide their lives, the moral principles and codes they believe in, and the character qualities they would like to possess. It does not take long for all of us to be doing axiology.

My e-mail writing colleague at the beginning of this chapter urges me to "decouple" talk about values and religion on secular campuses. I can honestly say that I do not know how to do this, for the reasons just mentioned. Moreover, I do not think this cleavage is educationally desirable. As I pointed out in chapter 2, I refuse to bind cross-campus dialogue on values and religion by allowing secular *value-talk* full expression in the public sphere, but confining *religion-talk* to the closets of the private sphere. Religion-talk, like value-talk, is an important intellectual and emotional resource, and, I for one, want to use it to full advantage in helping students to become informed meaning-makers.

Let me try to be as clear as I can at this point about my own personal beliefs concerning the relationship of religion to values. Philosophically, I agree that religious ideas can be logically independent of values in the sense that people can reason and talk intelligently about values without necessarily referring to theological concepts. Value-talk and theology-talk are not mutually dependent on each other for coherence. However, this does not mean that I, therefore, ought to rule religion-talk out of order whenever students engage in value-talk. There are times when it is simply impossible to understand the force of some students' moral and ethical convictions without first grasping the influence of their religious or spiritual beliefs on these value convictions. For this reason alone, religion and values deserve equal air time, and this is precisely what they get in my courses and dialogue groups.

Let me also say that, in strictly practical terms, I believe that people can be moral without being religious or spiritual. So too it is possible for people to be religious or spiritual without being moral. Plato, in the quotation from *Euthyphro* at the beginning of this chapter, articulates well the dilemma of the relationship of religion to values: Is something good because the gods love it, or do the gods love it because it is good? Plato has Socrates come down on the side that believes something is valuable or good on its own terms, not on the gods' terms. In fact, the gods like the good precisely because it is the good. Therefore, one can do the good (be moral and hold values), a concept which precedes the gods, without necessarily believing in those gods. I agree with Socrates.

The converse, that something is valuable or good only because the gods like it, makes values wholly dependent on what the gods might prefer. If this statement is true, then what if the gods later change their minds, as many churches and religious leaders have done through the centuries? This makes values ephemeral entities, the playthings of fickle deities. If the assumption is true that something is valuable or good because the gods prefer it, then it renders nonsensical and redundant the notion that the gods are good to begin with. The concept of *good* must be logically prior to our understanding that the gods are indeed good; if not, then the concept of *good gods* has no coherent meaning to anyone, least of all to disbelievers and to people from other cultures and times who might construct narratives of *good (and bad) gods* in very different ways.

I strongly disagree with Tolstoy's contention in this chapter's opening quotation that "without religion there can be no real, sincere morality, just as without roots there can be no real flower." "Real," "sincere" morality, unlike a flower, needs many kinds of "roots" in order to survive, in addition to the religious. Not the least of these roots is the continuing support of the secular society in which morality might be located. Morality must have utility value for any society. When it does, according to Aristotle (1976), it requires constant habituation, modeling, and reinforcement, if it is to take hold and fortify what is in the society's best interests. When a morality narrative no longer serves the purposes for which society (or evolution) created it in the first place, then the narrative usually gets revised or rejected (Wilson, 1998). Thus, for me, morality is as much a social construct—measured for its efficacy by its adaptive value—as it is a timeless creation of the gods (a concept I reject but still find fascinating to contemplate).

Moreover, if I might challenge Tolstoy, it is entirely possible that religion needs the "roots" of morality for its survival rather than the other way around. The wholly secular morality that came out of the Enlightenment period, for example, with its emphasis on democracy, human rights, autonomy, reason, and liberty was certainly a vast improvement over what I would call the absolutist religious impulse. This is the impulse that, throughout history, has precipitated religious inquisitions and jihads, and supported slavery, suppression of women, and discrimination against homosexuals and Jews (see P. J. Gomes, 1996, for full documentation of these charges). One might say, that without secular morality to challenge its excesses and deficiencies, and to improve it, there can be no "real, sincere" religion. Of course, the reverse is also true. Without the "thick" values of religion—such as commitment, reparation, hope, faith, love, compassion, and forgiveness—secular values would remain "thin" and abstract.

As a secular humanist, I lean toward David Hume's thinking in the *Enquiry Concerning the Principles of Morals* (1902), first written in 1752. Setting aside the influence of religion, Hume believes that people are moral because they are naturally "benevolent." They are also motivated, in part, by "self-interest." Moreover, they wish to win the "good regard of others," just as they wish to achieve the "good regard of [themselves]." And they fear the "threat of civil punishment." I believe that, overall, Hume's thinking provides a reasonable explanation for why someone can be a moral person with good values without necessarily being a religious person.

Even though I am something of a Humean on the *origins* of the moral impulse, I must quickly say that I disagree strongly with J. L. Mackie's (1977) assertion that "ethics is [completely] autonomous and can be studied and discussed without reference to religious beliefs; [thus] we can simply close the theological frontier of ethics" (p. 230). Mackie is asserting something much more radical about morality and values than Tolstoy did, and I cannot go nearly as far as he. I do not believe that we can ever simply close the "theological frontier" of morality and values. Nor should we. While it is true that I personally believe I can live a morally valuable life without believing in a god or gods, this does not mean, therefore, that my belief is entirely satisfactory either to myself or to others.

Hume's reasons for acting morally are largely this-worldly and egoistic, grounded in self-interest. I cannot say definitively—in fact, I seriously doubt it—that self-interest is the most enduring and effective foundation for morality and values in any society, and neither can Hume. I think it fair to say that at least as much evil has probably been done in the promotion of self-interest throughout history as in the name of religion. Of course, it is true that self-interest and religion often criss-cross, and the evil that results from this mix can be especially deadly.

Hume's "reasons" for separating values and religion skirt the question of whether a secular morality *without* religious foundations is sufficient to address the overwhelming problem of terrible evil in the world. Here is J. C. A. Gaskin (1984) on this issue:

> only when set against the powers of an eternal or divine good or of a Satanic evil can the things we are now capable of be adequately experienced in moral terms. The genetic mutilation of all living things, the poisoning of the earth, the burning of most of the cities of the northern hemisphere: these are moral enormities of vast significance, but all our secular atheistic moralities allow us to talk about are social rights, utilitarian needs, proletarian demands, and sophisticated interpersonal relationships. These things are assuredly imortant, but they have deprived us of the language of absolutes, of moral eternities, just when we most need the depths of such languages to evaluate our own condition. (p. 164)

What Gaskin is implying is that if we take seriously Mackie's recommendation to "close the theological frontier of ethics," then we run the risk of impoverishing our moral consciousness. How would it ever be possible to find soul-satisfying answers to such difficult but persistent philosophical questions as "After all is said and done, why should I bother being moral anyway?" and "In the event that my self-interest and yours collide, why should I sacrifice my interests in order to do what might be right?" Also, as strict secularists, we lose the opportunity to look at such "moral enormities" as war, environmental devastation, genetic mutiliation, and genocide from the perspective of metaphysics, from the viewpoint of "moral eternities."

Edward O. Wilson (1998), the Pulitzer-Prize winning sociobiologist from Harvard and an atheist, holds that certain values and morals—e.g., cooperation, loyalty, promise-keeping, truth-telling—have evolved over many millennia because they conferred survival benefits, along with adaptable genes, upon human beings. These values have managed to endure right up to the present, because they have helped us to adjust to our environments to our mutual benefit. Eventually, Wilson claims, evolution will get it right and so will *homo sapiens*. However, until it does, it is up to us, *wise human beings*, to forge our future as a species, unencumbered by dysfunctional moral precepts and antiquated religious laws. Now we can be newly energized by the understanding that religion is just another "junk attempt at enlightenment" that can be explained as "brain circuitry and deep, genetic history" (pp. 260–261).

In spite of Wilson's brilliant recent attempts to construct a theory of "consilience," a unity of all knowledge, what I find missing in his evolution narrative is a sense of the numinous, grandeur, and humility present in all the sacred narratives of the world. For Wilson, everything is biological and material. Natural selection and perpetuating the gene pool are what life is all about. For me, there is far more sense of purpose, transcendence, and the tragic in the narratives of Hinduism, Buddhism, Sufism, Christianity, Judaism, or Taoism than there ever will be in the pallid narrative of Wilson's sociobiology. I have yet to meet a single student in over three decades who was able to summon up the kind of passion for the truths contained in evolutionary biology that I have experienced with my orthodox evangelical believers, activists, or explorers.

I have yet to meet a student or colleague who could even translate one of these evolutionary truths into a set of functional moral principles that a bright teenager might understand, and more importantly, be willing to use as a basis for constructing an ethical life. Passion and functionality do not settle the question of truth, of course. However, when it comes to what students might be willing to give their hearts to (the meaning of the Latin *credo* for creed or belief), a science that completely closes the frontier of religion will have few converts. Its hegemonic secular "creed" will hold little emotional appeal.

In my opinion, and even though my sense of morality is notably secular and humanistic, I would never opt to close any frontier of values, particularly the religious frontier. I prefer to locate the common points of agreement between religious and secular values, because I remain forever open to the possibility that there might be more overlap than separation between the two. I am also convinced that there are many worthwhile sources of values and moral obligation, including the scientific, and to close one frontier forever, the religious, is to cut us off completely from an historically and existentially vital source of meaning.

An Example of Coupling Values and Religion in a Colloquium

At this point, I want to give an actual example in my own teaching of how the coupling of value-talk and religion-talk can be both intellectually and morally beneficial. For a recent colloquium on religious pluralism, I asked participants to read Kay Haugaard's (1997) article "Suspending Moral Judgment: Students Who Refuse to Condemn the Unthinkable." Haugaard, an instructor of creative writing at Pasadena City College, assigned her adult writing class the short story, "The Lottery," by Shirley Jackson (no date mentioned in article), for discussion the following week. The story, according to Haugaard, portrays a warm, loving, earnest community of farming people who gather together each summer to participate in a lottery that is important to the crops. All of a sudden, without any warning, after Tess Hutchinson's husband draws a ticket from the black box, the village—including her husband and son—sets on Tess Hutchinson and stones her to death. The author's point is that when people simply "go along" habitually with a ritual like human sacrifice, when they continue to engage in unexamined acts of blind conformity, then terrible evil can be the result. Tess Hutchinson inexplicably loses her life simply because her name appears on a lottery ticket, the villagers think that the god who watches over their crops demands annual propitiation, and because the village has always held a lottery—whether or not the crops actually grow as a result.

What upset Haugaard about the story was her students' blase reactions to the horror of ritual murder and sacrifice. Not a single person in her class was willing to make a moral judgment about the villagers' behavior. In effect, she believed that her students were actually complicit with the evil-doing in the story because they refused to publicly condemn it. When she followed up with a reference to James Frazer's *The Golden Bough* (cited in Haugaard, 1997), which describes several cultures that approve of human sacrifice in order to make their crops grow, she got more of the same, morally noncommittal response. One older student ventured that, for certain cultures, ritualistic killings at strategic intervals were necessary in order to give people a sanctioned outlet to satisfy their need for spilling blood. Another student, a multicultural professional working in a hospital, refused to take a moral position on the grounds that "if some practice is a part of a person's culture, then we must teach people not to judge it, especially if it has worked for them" (p. B5). Haugaard, who was shaken at the reluctance of her adult students to draw any moral conclusions about "obvious cruelties and injustices," left the class that evening in stunned silence, "chilled to the bone."

I began our colloquium discussion by asking this question: "Why do you think that Haugaard's students refused to take a strong moral position against human sacrifice?" For the first half-hour, my colloquium students seemed to go out of their way to explain in the best possible light why Haugaard's class might have remained morally neutral. I heard several references to the need to respect the practices and moral codes of diverse communities and cultures. Some said that any critique of the "other," no matter how morally justifiable, is intolerant, unless the "other" is present to make a counter argument. Some students asserted that Western democracies too often attempt to impose their Judeo-Christian ethic on people in other cultures, and, to them, this is an act of religious and political arrogance.

A few students suggested that perhaps Haugaard's class did not want to come off sounding like "absolutists" or "moral fanatics." Others of a postmodern leaning offered the thesis that so-called "impartial" evaluations

of moral activity are impossible, given the influence of such social constructions as politics, class, and religion on our judgments. In reaction, at
least a few students pointed out the paradox that a stance of moral neutrality is itself actually a moral evaluation, based on a value system that
prizes nonjudgmentalism, tolerance, and respect for difference.

Finally, one student, quiet through most of the discussion, blurted out
something like the following:

> It seems to me that, in a weird way, we are doing just what Haugaard's class did,
> only we sound a little more intellectual. Well, I'll take a position, and I know that
> it will upset certain people here. I think her politically-correct class was cowardly.
> I also think that the whole idea of human sacrifice is immoral. Why do I say this?
> Because I can't imagine *my* God approving of such an activity. My God is a God
> of love, justice, mercy, and compassion. Human sacrifice is the work of Satan,
> not of God. I will condemn the practice of human sacrifice, for the same reason
> that I condemn the Holocaust, slavery, and oppression against women, homo-
> sexuals, and the poor. It is the handiwork of the Devil, carried out by sinful people
> who have turned away from God. One last thing, and if you don't hate me by now
> you will: Haugaard's class was afraid to make a moral statement, because her
> students probably had no solid religious ground on which to stand. If you are
> living your life without God, then you are building a moral edifice on quicksand.
> There's just nothing there that will hold you up when you need to take a stand.
> There, I'm glad I said it!

This student's comments injected an element of deliberate provocation
into a discussion that had become predictably nonjudgmental and open-
minded, and, truth to tell, a little boring as well. They also stimulated
others to display their own religious views, or lack of the same, on the
topic. The conversation took on a refreshing ebullience missing in the
previous half hour. I have often said that the whole of moral philosophy
and moral theology can be reduced to the choices in Plato's Euthyphro
dilemma which I quoted at the beginning of this chapter. If students are
able to grasp the full meaning of the simple question that Socrates posed—
is something good because God says so, or does God say so because
something is good?—then they have a sense of what is really at stake in
the value-religion dichotomy. Can we have values without religion, or are
values dependent upon religion? Can we take a moral position for or
against the practice of human sacrifice that is purely secular or purely
religious, or are the two inextricably linked? How is the secular position
on questions of human evil buttressed or weakened by the religious, and
how is the religious position strengthened or weakened by the secular?

The conversation that ensued after this student's outburst exposed
several religio-spiritual preconceptions that were lurking just below the

surface of our discussion. Each of the six narrative types that I discussed in the previous two chapters had their say. The orthodox believers sided with the speaker. They reasoned that because God is both good and just, good will always conquer evil, and evil is certain to be punished, if not in this world, then in the next. The wounded believers demurred, wondering just why the good, all-loving, all-powerful God of Christianity, Judaism, and Islam would allow human sacrifice in the first place. The mainliners suggested that perhaps the most we can realistically do about acts of cruelty in other cultures is to set a good example for the rest of the world by the way we treat each other in this culture, along with spending a lot of time praying together in our faith communities both for the victims and the offenders.

The activists talked about oppression and liberation. They argued that acts of unspeakable inhumanity are often the corollary of repressive, non-democratic governments and self-aggrandizing, Third-World leaders. The key is for liberationist churches and private religious groups to help citizens of other countries transform their own political systems from within, preferably by bloodless, democratic *coups d'etat*. The explorers taught us that some religions have always practiced human sacrifice, including the Marquesas Islanders in Polynesia, the Bambara of West Africa, and the Aztecs of pre-Columbian Mexico. Before we rush to Eurocentric, Judeo-Christian moral judgments, the explorers warned us to look beneath the surface. The Aztecs, for example, thought that sacrifice was necessary, because the human heart and blood were believed to be the ultimate source of power for the sun and deities.

The explorers also asked us to think about the fact that the survival of the Aztec state was threatened by overpopulation and limited food resources. Thus, human sacrifice was a form of population control (Levinson, 1996, pp. 201–205). Finally, the secular humanists took the position that it was important to condemn wrongdoing without adverting to religious mythologies for support. They argued that it is possible through critical moral reasoning, and vigorous dialogue and debate, to arrive at the proposition that violations of human rights around the world, and in our own country as well, warrant moral condemnation by all.

I would suggest that the kind of dialogue which took place in my colloquium demonstrates that it is possible for values and religion to be co-equal partners in cross-campus conversations. Our discussion on values and morals began with an emphasis on such desirable secular values as tolerance, nonjudgmentalism, respect for difference, open-mindedness, utility, and nonhegemony. Then, as often happens in my groups, a religious voice cried out to be heard. When one student made the decision to express a profoundly held religious view, the conversation grew more animated and intense. This student's example precipitated other spirited religio-spiritual responses to the question I asked.

The honest, yet empathic, give-and-take of contrasting narratives that followed not only enlivened the dialogue. More importantly, it demonstrated that taking values and religion seriously necessitates genuine encounter, sometimes leading to conflict. We had moved from a simple respect for religious difference to a willingness to mix it up in the rough-and-tumble arena of religious pluralism. This means taking risks, stirring things up a bit, knowing how to deal with controversy—all the while summoning up the courage to dig deeply and to speak honestly from the heart of the narrative where each of us lives.

We soon realized that there are lots of ways of talking about values, including both the secular and the religious. While the language and background beliefs of each may be very different—representing both poles, as well as every position in between, of Plato's Euthyphro Dilemma—there are bound to be some points of overlap. Where there is no overlap, the conversation takes a different turn, and people get a chance to consider the question from other perspectives. Initially, the secular narrativists carried the conversation in our colloquium. Their values set the tone and the agenda. In time, the religious narrativists asserted their views, and their values enlarged the scope of the conversation by taking it in another direction. The ultimate winner, of course, was the conversation itself, because, in my estimation, it took on new complexity, depth, and vibrance. Not a person left the room that day without remarking to me that something important had happened to all of us. I would agree. It is the reason why I teach, and why I continue to be excited by the educational potential of such controversial subject matter.

We Are All Values Educators

I have tried to make the case in this chapter that, to some extent, all of us who work as administrators and faculty on college campuses are values educators. How is it ever possible for even the most objective and dispassionate scholars and administrators to be consistently neutral on the things that they value with all their hearts and minds? These values have a way of seeping out. In fact, in the work I do, it is like taking candy from a baby to evoke values talk. Anyone can do it because I have never met one values-neutral, narrative-free person in my entire life. If, as an educator, I am able to implant the values itch deeply enough, the person will scratch.

A true values-neutral person, if there were ever to be such a creature, would be nothing more than a moral android, an inhuman construction of science-fiction writers.

On another campus, a well-known scholar, noted for his values-objectivity, had a very strong subjective response to my assertion that we should try to promote real dialogue on religion and spirituality across the university. He whispered to me at a private luncheon: "The best place for your kind of dialogue in a scholarly environment is the counseling center where this nonsense can be expunged once and for all! When did you get to be so sympathetic toward this kind of flummery [a Welsh word that means soft custard]?" This man was certainly no values-android, in spite of his national reputation for scholarly impartiality and open-mindedness!

Because I contend that values educators must take into account the unavoidable religio-spiritual convictions of their students in fostering desirable values, then we must have more than a nodding acquaintance with the content of religion and spirituality, if this project is to be successful. My e-mail colleague at the beginning of this chapter expressed considerable anxiety over her tongue-tied inarticulateness on religious matters, her inability to be coherent on such a complex topic without embarrassing herself. Hence, she opted for a radical "decoupling" of religion and values. I disagree strongly with her conclusion, and I told her so.

In these final sections, I am going to discuss the kind of academic preparation that I think is necessary for future leaders (administrators and faculty), and for students, to be able to open, and sustain, the cross-campus dialogue on religious pluralism that is sure to come in higher education. I will propose a radical, twenty-first-century revision of what, in nineteenth-century America, used to be called the senior "capstone seminar." I currently teach two of these types of seminars for graduate students, one in an Interdisciplinary Studies Program, the other in a nationally recognized Higher Education and Student Affairs Administration Program (HESA). I will talk here about what I do in the HESA capstone seminar in order to prepare future administrators and faculty to deal effectively with the reality of religious pluralism, and the central place of values, on campuses throughout the United States.

The content and purpose of my HESA seminar are constantly evolving; thus, the capstone course I offer today is different in many respects from what I have taught in the past. Originally conceived in the 1970s as a culminating, issues-oriented, group-bonding experience, in the late 1980s it evolved into a sharply focused applied-ethics seminar for future higher-education professionals. Now it has now become more of an all-purpose ethics-values-religio-spirituality course of study. I have lately begun to make the link between values, ethics, and religion far more directly and in depth than I have ever done. As a result, our capstone conversations are livelier, the professional applications are far more personal and honest, and the scholarly work considerably more interdisciplinary and creative. I have had dozens of students tell me over the years that, because of the capstone, they decided to take professional administrative positions only at those colleges and universities that invited them to be values educators. These students were unequivocal in asking for strong institutional support to encounter undergraduates where they really "lived": inside their religious and spiritual narratives.

I would also encourage educators to consider offering a similar type of capstone academic experience to undergraduates (revised to meet their particular readiness levels) at any point in their four-year experience. I believe that this experience would be a major advance in furthering an understanding of religious pluralism. After all, if training in multicultural sensitivity is an important component of an inclusive undergraduate education, so too is training in multireligious understanding. It is highly possible to develop a strong rationale for the placement of a capstone (the word means "crowning achievement") religion-and-values seminar either at the beginning, middle, or end of the college years. Crowning achievements can come anywhere during the course of a person's life, and are not necessarily tied to specific ages, life-stages, or grade levels.

The Nineteenth-Century Capstone Seminar

Capstone values seminars for undergraduates actually have something of a checkered history in the United States. The original impulse for these seminars was a laudable one: to form the moral character of young men about to enter the professions through a year-long, critical study of moral and intellectual philosophy. Unfortunately, these seminars were prone to turn into Christian indoctrination sessions. Frequently taught by college presidents with evangelical leanings, the capstone seminar focused more on matters of personal piety and character conditioning than it did on the intellectual life. The eminent historian of higher education, Frederick Rudolph (1990), describes the early capstone seminar in this way: "Although the course was everywhere accepted as philosophy, it was both in purpose and practice a mixture of religious orthodoxy and personal opinion. Mark Hopkins . . . was a college president . . . who earned a reputation . . . by teaching a course that was dedicated to the propagation of Christian dogma" (p. 141).

In general, throughout the eighteenth and nineteenth centuries, the mission of higher education was to mold moral character, prepare young white men for the ministry, medicine, and business, and to discourage serious intellectual activity. The colleges did all of this by promulgating Christian religious teachings at every turn. One president of an elite private college, in 1852, typified the mood when he said: "We have no faith in the capabilities of mere intellectual training." Another president, in 1868, wrote in his diary: "Without religion, a college is a curse to society" (cited in Rudolph, 1990, p. 139).

Religious pluralism on these campuses during the nineteenth century was virtually nonexistent, as religious dissent was intentionally stifled and driven underground. The small numbers of students with cerebral inclinations, who were also disbelievers and secular humanists, were likely to join the extracurricular debating clubs and literary societies. These were the only places available on campus for any kind of robust intellectual exchange. These disbelieving students, seeing themselves as heirs of the secular Enlightenment, put their faith in the power of reason and science to eventually overthrow religious orthodoxy. It goes without saying that these students were hardly a revered presence on their conservative campuses. For other students who might have craved social freedom more than intellectual stimulation, the fraternities and sports teams provided less-heretical havens of dissent during the nineteenth century.

Now, at the beginning of the twenty-first century, the rules of academia have changed drastically from those of the nineteenth-century college. At the present time, many academicians in the nation's secular colleges have effectively disestablished religion, particularly the conservative brands, because they think them to be repressive, reactionary, and anti-intellectual. They dismiss, or worse, scoff at claims of religious revelation as unscientific and superstitious. The only "spiritual" enlightenment they are willing to countenance in secular academia is the rational and the scientific, and occasionally the Eastern, as long as the latter concentrates on desacralized practices and avoids mystical excess. In the place of religion, some faculty have established, as a matter of de facto policy, a preference for intellectual skepticism and secular humanism. The nineteenth-century version of a capstone values seminar would be as alien, and unacceptable, to the twenty-first-century secular university as compulsory chapel attendance and Jim Crow discrimination laws. Well it should.

My e-mail colleague asks me why I tend to let my faculty colleagues off the hook in promoting cross-campus, multi-faith dialogue on religion. I do not and I will not. In fact, I am urging just the opposite: Faculty need to become full dialogue partners with the thousands of professionals I have called the "hidden educators" on campuses throughout the United States. We need each other in this venture. But before my faculty colleagues and I can become a positive force in enacting such a project, we must shed our instinctive suspicions of students and others who are not ashamed to go public with assertions of strong religious belief. We must learn how to engage in respectful give-and-take with those students who refuse to confine their religious enthusiasms to the usual private spaces on a college campus. The simple fact for hundreds of thousands of students across America is that they do not think of their religious faith as an intellectual irrelevancy. And neither should we. I contend that many of us need to learn how to get over our gut-level religio-phobia.

Is the American Professoriate Actually Religio-Phobic?

Before I describe my capstone seminar in the next section, it is important at this point to return briefly to a neologism that I first coined in chapter 1—*religio-phobia*. I am fully aware of how difficult it will be to involve some faculty in the dialogical venture on religion that I am describing in these pages. Huston Smith, in a hard-hitting, semi-autobiographical book, *Why Religion Matters: The Fate of the Human Spirit in an Age of Disbelief* (2001), traces what for him is a depressing trajectory from belief to nonbelief to disbelief throughout the twentieth century in the academy. It is irrefutable, according to Smith, that a large number of university faculty, particularly in the social and natural sciences, have moved historically beyond active sympathy (at one time, the term *college* denoted cloisters of monks), through a detached agnosticism, to what today might reasonably be called outright hostility toward religion, or, in my word, *religio-phobia*. The reasons for this marked disdain for religion, according to Smith, are many, but they can be summarized in one major assertion: The scientific worldview reigns supreme in the academy, and the religious worldview grovels in its wake.

Smith argues that as Western society has become increasingly secularized, *progress* in the name of technology and science has become the post-Medieval substitute for *salvation of the soul* in the name of God. As most undergraduate students in the twenty-first century know all too well, science, business, management, and engineering are the lucrative fields of study in higher education. Religion, philosophy, literature, and the other humanities are seen by many as merely marginal and ethereal intellectual pursuits, delivering no salvation that is financially worthwhile. Education for career (a word that denotes a "racetrack") preparation overwhelms an ideal of education as preparation for a lifelong calling, a *vocation* in the most basic, religious sense. Naturalism and pragmatism, Smith contends, have become the ruling scientific narratives for explaining the world. Idealism and metaphysics are pre-scientific atavisms whose time has long since come and gone.

Smith, a devout, albeit ecumenical, theist writes with passion, and much of his argument seems plausible on its face. However, I do not accept his basic assumption that there will always be such an irreconcilable disparity between the two opposing views of truth—faith versus reason—in the academy. Actually, Smith's words and mood appear angrier in *Why Religion Matters* than in other books of his that I have read. He clearly manifests symptoms of battle fatigue here, probably the result of having valiantly fought the humanities-science war in higher education for over 50 years. I, for one, cannot accept his opinion that the contrast between the two contesting narratives among the professoriate is as severe, indeed as lethal, as he tries to depict it. In Smith's construction, science will always *devour* religion whenever the two camps attempt to dialogue with one another.

From where I sit, the picture is at once far more complex and far more hopeful. Accounts of recent attempts to discover a science-religion rapprochement are becoming more common in the academy (see Begley, 1998, for an excellent overview). For example, the John Templeton Foundation spends fourteen-million dollars annually on interdisciplinary science-and-religion courses and scholarly conferences, as well as sponsoring a wide range of cooperative research efforts. Moreover, the Center for Theology & the Natural Sciences, founded in 1981, in Berkeley, California, is directed by a scholar, Robert John Russell, who is both a scientist and a Christian (see Wheeler, 1997). Scientists come together with theologians at the Center to explore the possibility of a "not-so-random universe." Conversations at these gatherings are often heated, frequently polarized and unsettled, but always respectful and civil.

Furthermore, evangelical scholarly publications such as *Books & Culture* and *Intervarsity Press* are increasingly sponsoring works that explore creative ways to deepen and enrich the religious worldview by incorporating unorthodox secular ideas from postmodern theory (see Allen, 2000). John Milbank, a professor at the University of Virginia and an evangelical Methodist, refers to this new theological movement as "radical orthodoxy," an attempt to integrate the logic of postmodern secularism and the logic of the sacred (see Sharlet, 2000). A good example of one evangelical author's efforts to chart the postmodern landscape is Stanley J. Grenz's (1996) *A Primer on Postmodernism*. In his own words: "Our critical reflections must lead us to determine the contours of the gospel that will speak to the hearts of postmodern people. We must engage postmodernism in order to discern how best to articulate the Christian faith to the next generation" (p. 174).

More importantly, however, I believe that despite their disciplinary and philosophical differences, most faculty, like their students, are inescapably engaged in a search for meaning. Most faculty, whatever their backgrounds, must inevitably come to terms with what Smith calls the "ultimate questions," questions that all human beings might very well be genetically programmed to ask (see Shermer, 2000, pp. 63–69). Moreover, most faculty members are acutely aware that these insistent questions are unanswerable because, in the end, they are simply beyond the province of the natural sciences, the social sciences, and the humanities. After all, how can these disciplines ever provide satisfactory answers to what philosophers call "zero-level" inquiries about the ultimate meaning of existence? Why would they even want to?

Finally, and more personally, I have found that even allowing for the presence of the inevitable dogmatists at the furthest ends of the science-religion continuum, many faculty whom I have encountered in the academy refuse to succumb to the easy temptations of religio-phobia. Even the more hard-bitten skeptics I have met, with a few notable exceptions, try very hard to maintain an open mind on questions of religion and values. The vast majority of scholars I know are simply unwilling to discredit a student's genuine quest for knowledge, even when it veers off in a religio-spiritual direction, and even if that direction is resolutely orthodox. Perhaps I am an incurable optimist, but, I believe that Smith himself, despite the occasional petulance in *Why Religion Matters* (2001), says it best in his epilogue: "We could [all] be siblings yet" (p. 271).

My Capstone Seminar on Religion and Values

My own version of the capstone seminar bears little resemblance to my nineteenth-century ancestors' version. I do not want my capstone religion-and-values seminar to be indoctrinative or repressive. I have no particular ideological or religious axe to grind, except for the strong conviction that energetic, cross-campus dialogues on issues related to values and religious pluralism have the unlimited potential to make the academy an intellectually richer, more vital place to live. However, even this assumption is open to rebuttal, and I do everything I can to expose it to critical scrutiny. I strive always to uphold the principles of open and reasoned dialogue: critical thinking, tolerance, and civility—principles, by the way, that I hold with tenuous tenacity. I know full well that, despite their strengths, these principles are also deeply flawed (more on how I think we ought to dialogue with tenuous tenacity together about values and religion in the last chapter). This means giving a fair and impartial hearing to both sides of Euthyphro's dilemma, while also encouraging hard questioning of each of the two positions and all the perspectives in between—including, of course, my own.

There are no absolute commandments in my seminar, as there were in the nineteenth-century capstone, and this includes the aforementioned "liberal" commandments of diversity, pluralism, and civil discourse. What Nicholas Wolterstorff calls our "control beliefs" (cited in Marsden, 1997, p. 50) are always open to dialogue. I welcome the religiously devout into the conversation, just as I welcome the irreligiously devout, and also the apatheists. I stress that no participants will ever have to deny their special "devotions," be they religious or secular, if and when they are ready to go public with them. I also stipulate, however, that, in the interest of educating each other, students ought to be willing to explain, and, when necessary, to defend their particular "devotions." Stephen L. Carter (1993), a strong advocate of the right to express one's religious faith in the public square, nicely captures my intent:

> What is needed, then, is a willingness to listen, not because the speaker has the right voice but because the speaker has the right to speak. Moreover, the willingness to listen must hold out the possibility that the speaker is saying something worth listening to; to do less is to trivialize the forces that shape the moral convictions of tens of millions of Americans. (p. 231)

At the beginning of my capstone seminar, I distribute a personal memorandum to my students. I prefer the memorandum format as an information-dispensing medium, because it is less formal and longer than a syllabus. It is also more personal in tone. It conveys the meaning that what I have to say in this personal note is something I want my students to remember (the Latin root is *memorare*, to remember), because the sentiments I express are very important to me, and I hope to them as well. After all, if we are going to be talking about subject matter as salient as values and religion for an entire semester, I need to establish my own justification-narrative for the capstone as clearly and as sincerely as possible. Candor also helps, of course. Thus, what follows is the memorandum that my students read on the first day of the capstone. I think it encapsulates in a fairly unique way the content to be covered in my seminar, and the communication process that I prefer.

A Personal Memorandum to My Students on the Capstone

Greetings to all of you. I want this personal memorandum to be my unique way of welcoming you to our capstone seminar on values and religion. We will be spending an intensive semester together examining material that only infrequently comes out into the open in the American university. I can think of nothing more important for us to do for 15 weeks, and I hope you feel the same. As I begin the term with you, I find myself making the following assumptions about our subject matter. I am interested in what you might think of them. Let's discuss them together when you finish reading. What, I wonder, might be some of the assumptions that you are making about the material as we begin the semester?

- *Too many colleges and universities are fearful about opening up academic dialogue on religion and values outside of religious studies departments. They think that open expressions of personal values, particularly as these might relate to religious faith, are too controversial, and too private, to deal with fruitfully in an academic setting. They prefer to confine these topics to such safe spaces as dormitory rooms, chapels, and religious-studies classrooms, or perhaps to an ethics seminar in philosophy. They also think of values-talk as perhaps too subjective, maybe even anti-intellectual, and, therefore, peripheral to the formal academic experience. I, for one, believe that these perceptions are unfortunate and need to be corrected.*
- *The secular worldview currently predominates in the humanities, social sciences, and sciences, and, in many (not all) colleges and universities, it tends to dominate all other alternatives. Therefore, whenever students bring up religious and spiritual issues in the classroom and at open forums, these views sometimes tend to get a quick dismissal. They make many intellectuals very nervous. The unintended message sent by nervous professoriate and administrators is that through omission, secular humanistic values are "superior" to religious values. In contrast, I think that all values—secular, humanistic, and religious—deserve a fair and open hearing in academic settings.*

- *Religion is such a fundamental part of human existence that students simply cannot understand the history or politics of most societies, including the United States, without a serious examination of religion's central role in producing both good and evil throughout the world during the last three millennia. I want all the disciplines to examine the impact that religion has had on the construction of human knowledge in each of these content areas. I believe that some type of religious study ought to be required of all students in higher education for the same reason that other subject matter is seen as necessary for a liberal education: Not only is there undeniable functional utility in becoming a religiously informed citizen in a pluralistic world; but religion is also a subject worthy of study for its own sake. I think of the content in this capstone as an excellent example of a functional liberal education both for preprofessionals and for in-place professionals.*
- *Moral education at any level of schooling is ultimately incomplete unless students have the opportunity to gain a serious understanding of religion's contributions (both positive and negative) to ethics, morality, and the formation of moral character. For example, I cannot separate the work we will be doing on moral development from faith development; or the identification and adjudication of ethical dilemmas in the profession from the impact that your religio-spiritual convictions (or lack of them) might have on your ethical understandings.*
- *At a time in our society when the study of multiculturalism is de rigueur in our colleges, I submit that the study of religion is crucial for the same, important reasons. Religious difference is as important to many students as is racial, ethnic, gender, sexual, and political difference. We in higher education must be very careful to consider the intellectual needs and rights of all students, both secular and religious, disbelieving and believing. Pluralistic educators committed to diversity, who want to understand the "whole person," need to know as much as possible about the actual religious content of what their students believe, and students need to know this content about each other as well.*
- *College administrators and educators need a sustained, in-depth opportunity to examine their own background beliefs regarding morality, religion, and spirituality. Whether we educators know it or not, these background beliefs keep getting in the way of*

our professional work. Religion can be a fascinating field of study, as much for disbelievers as for believers. In particular, religious literacy works, not just for our benefit, but for students' benefit as well, because most of them come out of some kind of religious context. Religious literacy and self-understanding will help all of us to understand the extent to which we are implicitly or explicitly taking a position for or against religion, thus making ourselves vulnerable to the charge from our students that we are unfairly advantaging, or disadvantaging, religion.

As I think at the outset about the content we will be covering in this capstone, here are some questions I am asking, and some personal concerns I have as well. What do you think of them, and which ones would you add to (or remove from) the list?

- *How can we talk about religion and values in both public and private settings in a way that does not offend a number of differing, sometimes contentious, constituencies? Conversely, is this offensiveness inevitable, given the nature of the subject matter? I am interested in what you might think of my "moral conversation" as one way of talking about very controversial topics.*
- *Will a narrative approach to talking about the religio-spiritual search for meaning "de-divinize" the subject matter enough so that students can genuinely appreciate the cultural, aesthetic, literary, philosophical, and political components of the religious experience?*
- *What particular religions and values do we open up for public conversation, and how do we do this? Does this include the full expression of agnosticism and atheism? Should we try to countermand, reinforce, or take a neutral stance regarding the religious upbringing some students might receive in their particular faith communities? Are these "at-home" religious teachings a priori untouchable, or are they, too, up for grabs? Or is it naive to assume that the majority of young people receive any substantive religious or values training at all in their own communities?*
- *Is values education, by definition, indoctrination, and, thus, an oxymoron for administrators and professors in secular colleges? How can educators remain impartial when discussing such con-*

troversial, heart- and soul-felt subject matter? Is it possible, or even desirable, to remain value-free when teaching such value-loaded subject matter as religion or ethics? What if we genuinely believe, for example, that religion or democratic values have been major sources of evil, or good, in the world? Why should we suppress our deepest convictions on such powerful forces?

* *How can we realistically separate the cognitive subject matter of religion as a field deserving of lively and candid discussion for its own sake from the emotional experience of students who might also happen to be believers or seekers? After all, what might be merely a "worldview," or a "story," or an object of curiosity for some is likely to be a "revealed, eternal Truth" to others, indeed a matter of life and death.*

* *What religious narratives make the most valid truth claims, or is it even right to ask this kind of question in secular, pluralist educational establishments that, in the past, have emphatically ruled this type of inquiry out of order? How should we handle the delicate, potentially volatile questions that students themselves sometimes raise about the "truth" of particular religious claims, some of which appear to be in direct conflict with each other?*

* *Does the religious worldview with its objective truths, supernatural realities, and authoritative doctrines and rituals clash irreconcilably with postmodernism's tendencies toward agnosticism, relativism, secularism, and skepticism? If so, do we risk speaking an unfathomable, indeed fanciful, language to those students who belong to Generation-X, and who often subscribe to a variety of "New-Age" values, predicated on a position of nonjudgmentalism, relativism, and subjectivism?*

My intellectual perspective on the subject matter in our capstone is interdisciplinary. Our readings will include works on religion, spirituality, values, moral development, and ethics. I also intend for our seminar to be a very personal one, and so I want each of you to undertake your own search for meaning in a very personal way. Think of helping me make this capstone seminar a model of how we might engage students, staff, and faculty who are on similar journeys. I will ask you to write your papers in a personal-narrative format. I will also ask you to come up with your own grade by turning in an extensive self-evaluation narrative at course's end. It should go without saying that I will expect each of you to do all the assigned reading and writing, to immerse yourselves in the various seminar activities, and to carry your fair share of the responsibility to present, discuss, and actively participate throughout the semester.

As a professor of educational philosophy, moral education, higher education, and applied ethics, I have directly examined religious, ethical, and educational issues in my work with thousands of educators and administrators in almost 35 years of university teaching. I am someone who is vitally interested in the intersection of religion, values, modern culture, educational policy, leadership, teaching, and the American university, and I have written extensively in all these areas (e.g., Nash, 1996b, 1997, 1999). Obviously I cannot make you religious studies scholars, values experts, or ethicists in one short semester, nor would I want to. What I hope can happen this term, though, is that, in time, all of you can become just a little more literate about (and appreciative of) moral and religious matters, especially as these impinge on our work as adminstrators and teachers.

Regarding the actual subject matter, I have organized the course into three parts. Part I, what I call "Setting the Values Stage," will provide an overview of the meaning of meaning, moral- and faith-development theory, the intersection of values, morals, ethics, and religio-spirituality, and how to talk productively about controversial value issues—with an emphasis on religious values. Part II I refer to as "Studying the Religio-Spiritual Narratives." During this unit, we will examine several representative religious narratives that we are likely to find on college and university campuses today. These will typify the journeys of believers and disbelievers of all ages. We will also examine a variety of ways to initiate and sustain constructive religious dialogue on secular campuses. We will spend some time talking about the perils and the promises of sponsoring, and leading, such campus-wide conversations. Part III will emphasize what I call "Thinking About Moral Character and Applied Ethics." Here we will explore theories of character development and approaches to ethical decision-making that go hand-in-hand with the two previous units.

I want to say something about the various narrative categories I will be using throughout the semester. The actual labels are my own; you may or may not like them. Obviously, I cannot cover every religious or moral narrative in a single, short semester; thus, some important religious perspectives will be left out, unless you take the initiative to introduce them as we progress this term. Equally as obvious, my categories are only as useful as categories tend to be, warts and all. I do not mean for them to be exhaustive, stereotypical, or disparaging. At their best, it is my hope that the categories can be intellectually suggestive, synthetic, and efficient as ways to organize huge masses of data and conceptual material. Speaking from experience, I can only say that it will help immensely if each of you resists the ever-seductive temptation this semester to find a suitable religious or value label for your own beliefs. Instead, think of these categories as fluid and heuristic educational devices, not as fixed, religio-moral identity boxes.

Now let me say a few words about religious and values narratives. In my opinion, the study of religion and values usually goes much better when I can get my students to think about the various orientations as stories. Stories help us to shift perspective more easily, to assume the vantage point of the other. The Greek word for stories or narratives is mythoi, the root of "myths." For example, in the study of religion, narratives, like myths, are neither true nor false; instead, they function more neutrally to remind us that people construct religious stories to explain the nature of life, and to provide a sense of cosmic purpose, personal identity, and morality. A good religious narrative, therefore, helps believers to make sense of their lives, because it gives them a satisfying account of where they came from, why they are here, and where they might be going.

Thus, in my view, even though we will be reading no fiction this semester, each of the texts we will be studying, like each of the religious perspectives we will be exploring, is actually telling a story of its own: Each has a set of distinctive characters, a plot, a climax, a lesson to teach, lots of description, and a unique setting. Sometimes a religious text tries to inspire, other times to persuade, or teach, or defend, or criticize, or laud, or regale. This semester I want us to read all of our texts, but particularly our religious texts, as stories. We ought to listen to each other's declarations of meaning as stories, because I believe it is often more fruitful (and far less argumentative and hurtful) to concentrate on whether our texts and our presentations are imaginative, provocative, powerful, and compelling at the level of narrative, than on whether they are true or false at the level of propositions or, in the case of religion, divine revelation. I prefer to ask: Does the story touch our lives in some ways? Does it hold together? Does it accomplish what its author might have set out to do?

Does the story transport, or entertain, or excite, or edify us? Does it help us to see the "real world" in a more imaginative way? Is the lesson in the story clearly rendered? defensible? realistic? useful? What do you think of the author's use of language?

Now let me talk briefly about a dialogical process I call moral conversation. This semester, I want us to be able to talk with each other about controversial, and heartfelt, religio-spiritual-value topics without attacking, or boring, each other to "death."

I hope we can learn how to engage in a respectful, to-and-fro movement in dialogical encounters with each other. The purpose of such encounters is to find common ground as well as to identify irreconcilable differences, to bring religious groups together rather than to pit one group against another. Each one of us should ask: How can we talk honestly about controversial topics not just to those who might agree with us, but to those who might disagree with us? How can we encourage open, candid, respectful, and critical dialogue among believers and disbelievers in the pluralistic campus setting, a dialogue that recognizes and respects the irreducible diversity of voices throughout the campus? How can we promote a conversation that will effectively forestall the imposition of a uniformity, or, worse, a values-correct blandness, on everyone, along with the mind-numbing, passion-killing repression that usually accompanies such an imposition?

How can we further a dialogue that seeks not so much to persuade one another to accept a particular truth, but to help one another to understand our differences so that we might actually live together for 15 weeks in some kind of accord? To do this, we will have to enlarge the conversational space about religion and values without asking adherents of the various narratives to bracket their own strong beliefs. We must be able to find ways to engage with intellectual integrity in a postmodern, pluralistic values-dialogue without asking people to voluntarily annihilate a significant piece of themselves in the search for common ground—absent all the sectarian particulars.

Finally, I would like to say something about what I consider to be the fragility of religious faith and moral conversation, and the durability of love and forgiveness. I do want to warn those of you whose faith is fragile (and whose isn't?) that, as your instructor, I am not here this semester to reinforce anyone's particular religio-spiritual beliefs. Neither am I here to destroy them. If you need someone in a position of authority to reassure you at this time in your life that your religiosity or spirituality do indeed possess the ultimate answer for everyone, then you will not find such reassurance in this capstone course. Remember I am a thorough-going, existential agnostic on any type of Ultimate Truth claim. Although I will work hard to remain genuinely open-minded and generous regarding the possibility of your particular answer, I tend to agree with Richard Rorty on the implausibility of arriving at certainty in religion, or in any other area of values for that matter. For Rorty (1982), what is really important is the following: "In the end . . .what matters is our loyalty to other human beings clinging together against the dark, not our hope of getting things finally right" (p. 157).

The overall goal of moral conversation is to get you to talk with one another, and with me, about the subject matter in this capstone seminar in a spirit of mutual vulnerability and regard, generosity and support. I want to put the emphasis this semester less on critique, conversion, or confrontation and more on connection; more on "clinging together against the dark" than on letting go of each other because some of us have found the saving light and others haven't. In my own fallible opinion, I ask each of you: When all is said and done, who can ever be absolutely sure that a particular set of values, a personal spirituality, or an assortment of religious doctrines, no matter how comforting or authoritative, represent the final truth? Doesn't it all depend on your narrative perspective, your particular standpoint, the way you were brought up? In my mind, the theologian Reinhold Niebuhr (1952) said it best regarding the importance of humility and love on the matter of ultimate truth:

> Nothing that is worth doing can be achieved in our lifetime; therefore, we must be saved by hope. Nothing which is true or beautiful or good makes complete sense in any immediate context of history; therefore, we must be saved by faith. Nothing we do, however virtuous, can be accomplished alone; therefore, we are saved by love. No virtuous act is quite as virtuous from the standpoint of our friend or foe as it is from our standpoint. Therefore, we must be saved by the final form of love which is forgiveness. (p. 63)

I want to close by mentioning some selective readings on the topics we will be covering in this capstone that have made a tangible difference in the way I currently think, and feel, about religion and values. These readings are not meant to be exhaustive, far from it. Instead, they represent my "short list" of works that I hope will whet your appetites for more than the required course texts (which will appear on the course syllabus I intend to distribute later). I offer this personally annotated bibliography to you, in Nel Noddings's (1993) words to describe what all teachers should be doing, as a "gift freely given" (p. 134). It goes without saying, of course, that you have every right to refuse this gift. At the very least, though, I hope that you will take the time to browse through the list, and that my brief, personal commentaries on each of the books will help you get to know me a little bit better. I also believe that all of these books will help you to think of yourselves in a new way as values educators. If you let them, each of these readings can help you in the construction of a defensible moral-religious "point" on which you can "stand." I list the works in alphabetical order:

- Armstrong, Karen. (1993). *A History of God: The 4000-Year Quest of Judaism, Christianity and Islam.* New York: Alfred A. Knopf.

Nobody today writes about religion with as much flair and intelligibility as Karen Armstrong, a highly respected authority on Judaism, Christianity, and Islam. A former Roman Catholic nun, Armstrong explores the many ways that the concept, and the experience, of God have changed through the centuries among the monotheistic religions. Her general thesis is that an idea of God will survive only if it works for those who believe it. Thus, the idea of God is as much a pragmatic social construction as it is a divine reality. Despite her own agnosticism, Armstrong is realistic, and optimistic, about the survival of religion, because she believes that the pursuit of a desirable symbol to represent the never-ending search for God is a natural aspect of humanity. I find Armstrong's views on religion very compatible with my own, and I concur with the following remarks:

> the statement "I believe in God" has no objective meaning, as such, but like any other statement only means something in context, when proclaimed by a particular community. . . . If we look at our three monotheistic religions, it becomes clear that there is no objective view of "God": each generation has to create the image of God that works for it. The same is true of atheism. . . . Despite its otherworldliness, religion is highly pragmatic . . . it is far more important for a particular idea of God to work than for it to be logically or scientifically sound. . . . Yet my study of religion has revealed that human beings are spiritual animals. . . . religion has been an attempt to find meaning and value in life, despite the suffering that flesh is heir to. (pp. xix, xx, xxi)

- Bellah, Robert N., Madsen, Richard, Sullivan, William M., Swidler, Ann, & Tipton, Steven, M. (1985). *Habits of the Heart: Individualism and Commitment in American Life.* Berkeley: University of California Press.

In my estimation, this book represents the single best examination of American culture and moral character since deTocqueville's classic, *Democracy and America* and David Riesman's *The Lonely Crowd*. Bellah et al.'s 1985 examination of the two dominant moral languages in America—individualistic and biblical-republican—set the stage for 15 subsequent years of sociological-philosophical analysis of American life. No study that I know of has improved on *Habits*, however, whose insights have held up surprisingly well since the time it was published in 1985. I was so impressed with this book when I first read it that I and a colleague did an essay-length review of it for the *Harvard Educational Review* in 1986. I have never received more response from readers to an essay review of mine than to this one. Each new year, Bellah et al. seem to speak to something powerfully resonant in the American character—the overwhelming tension that continues to exist between our private and public lives, as well as between our faith and our doubts:

> human life is lived in the balance between faith and doubt. Such a vision arises not only from the theories of intellectuals, but from the practices of life that Americans are already engaged in. Such a vision seeks to combine social concern with ultimate concern in a way that slights the claims of neither. Above all, such a vision seeks the confirmation or correction of discussion and experiment with our friends, our fellow citizens. (p. 296)

- Carter, Stephen L. (1993). *The Culture of Disbelief: How American Law and Politics Trivialize Religious Devotion.* New York: Basic Books.

It was Stephen Carter who first gave me the idea to invite religious believers to become active participants in scholarly conversations on college campuses. This pioneering text on the relationship between law, politics, and religion in the United States is still being debated in the courts and in government circles today. In brief, Carter, a Yale University Law professor, argues that religious values can strengthen democracy, because, at their source, they are consistent with what most Americans hold dear. In Carter's words:

> democracy is best served when the religions are able to act as independent moral voices interposed between the citizen and the state, and how our tendency to try to wall religion out of public debate makes that role a harder one to play . . . we should stop the steady drumbeat . . . for the proposition that the religiously devout are less rational than more "normal" folks and that we should avoid the pat assumption, all too common in our rhetoric, that religion is more dangerous than other forces in American society and must therefore be more carefully reined in. (p. 16)

- Cone, James H. (1997). *God of the Oppressed* (Rev. ed.). Maryknoll, NY: Orbis Press.

Cone was the first Black Liberation theologian I had ever read back in 1975 when his book was initially published. I found myself very excited about the content of his theology, but also put off by his angry, almost dismissive critique of white Christians and white theology. It was only after teaching Cone's book several times that I began to understand his animosity. He wants black Americans to draw less from conventional Euro-American conceptions of theology, including Latin American liberation theology and feminist theology, and more from their own unique experiences as an oppressed people. For Cone, the God of biblical faith is a Liberator of the oppressed from bondage. Therefore, throughout his book, Cone turns to black spirituals and gospel music, Fannie Lou Hamer, and Martin Luther King, Jr., for inspiration. His is an important voice for all of us to hear, as we encourage all types of religio-spirituality—including the African-American—to enter the campus-wide dialogue. Here is an example of Cone's passionate writing:

> Jesus Christ is the subject of Black Theology because he is the content of the hopes and dreams of black people. He was chosen by our grandparents, who saw in his liberating presence that he had chosen them and thus became the foundation of their struggle for freedom. He was their Truth, enabling them to know that white definitions of black humanity were lies. When their way became twisted and senseless, they told Jesus about it. He lifted their burdens and eased their pain, thereby bestowing upon them a vision of freedom that transcended historical limitations. (p. 30)

- Cupitt, Don. (1997). *After God: The Future of Religion*. New York: HarperCollins.

Don Cupitt is often called the "atheist priest" and the "heretic's heretic." Cupitt, an ordained Anglican priest and a renowned, emeritus scholar at Cambridge University, has written a series of very controversial works that, for the last quarter of a century, have challenged the religious establishment. Cupitt is an outspoken, postmodern, post-Christian philosopher of religion whose views I find very consistent with my own, with some important philosophical and stylistic differences. These will become clearer, I am sure, as the capstone progresses. For one, his writing style is decidedly more polemical and combative than mine. While many of my students, both believers and disbelievers, do not like him, they never forget him. I also find that, of all the authors I have assigned in my courses in recent years, Cupitt is the one most likely to disturb tenaciously held religious beliefs. His views always provoke passionate, sometimes heart-wrenching conversations. Here is a memorable example of his deliberately disturbing prose:

> Today, however, the whole cosmological or grand narrative side of religion has totally collapsed. We know, if we know anything, that there is no rationally ordered scheme of things out there, no grand-narrative meaning-of-life already laid on for our lives to be fitted into. We know, if we know anything, that there isn't literally any supernatural order, and there is not literally any life after death. This is all there is, and, as everyone knows, when you're dead you're dead. (p. 103)

* Dillard, Annie (1999). *For the Time Being*. New York: Alfred A. Knopf.

This is the best treatment of good and evil that I have ever read. I agree with those who have said that through the centuries more faith has probably been lost over the question of theodicy than over any other issue. Dillard's book is a "non-fiction first-person narrative," written by a believer, who wrestles in very personal terms with the paradox of a God who is all-powerful and all-loving, yet who permits the most unspeakable evil to exist in the world. Dillard asks innocently enough: "Does God cause natural calamity? What might be the relationship of the Absolute to a panicky lost schoolgirl in a plaid skirt? Given things as they are, how shall one individual live" (p. x)? And later, she observes: "Many people cannot tolerate living with the paradox [of good and evil]. Where the air is paradoxical, they avoid breathing and exit fast" (p. 197).

* Eck, Diana L. (1993). *Encountering God: A Spiritual Journey from Bozeman to Banaras*. Boston: Beacon Press.

Eck, the director of the Pluralism Project at Harvard University, is probably the foremost comparative-religion scholar in the United States today. She is also one of the leading advocates of religious pluralism, following in the footsteps of her mentor, Wilfred Cantwell Smith. My own views on religious pluralism owe a great deal to her work, particularly the distinctions she makes between exclusivist, inclusivist, and pluralistic conceptions of religious belief. Eck's book is a spiritual memoir that chronicles her lifelong attempt to reconcile the differences between Christianity and Hinduism in her own religious practice. Her basic argument is that continuous dialogue with people of other faiths is today more necessary than ever, if we are to come to terms with religious difference throughout the world. Here is Eck on genuine religious encounter:

> Both within and between religious communities, criticism must finally be safe and accepted if there is to be relationship and if knowledge of one another is to be

more than superficial. It is well known that absolutism cannot abide criticism, which is one reason that absolutists and exclusivists will not place themselves in the interchange of dialogue. But if even the pluralists and the inclusivists within each tradition do not welcome criticisms in dialogue, then the dialogue becomes merely another form of dogmatism. Dialogue is not a debate, but a search for a wider understanding of Truth. (p. 223)

- Frankena, William K. (1973). *Ethics* (2nd ed.). Englewood Cliffs, NJ: Prentice-Hall.

I have written and spoken widely on the subject of ethics for over 25 years, but Frankena's slim volume is still the gold-standard textbook in this area. I honestly cannot say that a single textbook on ethics, published since its first edition in 1963, has substantially improved on Frankena's fundamental insights. Frankena's work on egoistic and deontological theories, utilitarian, justice and love theories, moral value and responsibility, intrinsic value and the good life, and meaning and justification have set the ethics agenda for well over a quarter of a century of subsequent development by scholars. All of us have stood on Frankena's very broad shoulders in our work on applied ethics. I can say for certain that you will experience the full impact of his work in everything I will be saying about the study of morality, ethics, and values throughout our capstone this semester. Here is a wonderful statement of the author's attitude toward his own work as an ethicist, an attitude that I have tried to emulate for over three decades, but, I will wager, never as successfully as Frankena:

My arguments are meant as arguments for or against positions all right, as they should be in philosophy, but not as irresistible forces or immovable objects. Rather they are statements of my reasons for taking or rejecting a certain view and invitations to the reader to consider whether they convince him that he should do likewise. My point is not to push him around; it is to bring him to see what position seems most reasonable to him, when, with such help as I can give him, he thinks things over. He always can hold out against me; the question then is whether he thinks his position is the most sensible one to take—not whether he can take it but whether he is willing to take it. The method is that of Socrates. (p. xvi)

- Lamott, Anne. (1994). *Bird by Bird: Some Instructions on Writing and Life.* New York: Pantheon.

Lamott's very entertaining and inspiring book is about a great deal more than simply how to write. She is also teaching us how to live. There is a clear moral point of view exemplified on every page of this personal narrative. The chief lesson she teaches is that "the core, ethical concepts in which you most passionately believe are the language in which you are writing" (p. 103). Thus, her "instruction" to us on life is that we need to care about something passionately, if we are ever to write about it, or to live it, with conviction. Without the passion, our vital center is empty, and we will become spiritually and morally immobilized, both as writers and as professionals. I have met very few students who have read this book for one of my courses who fail to give it as a gift to a loved one. Some of my doctoral graduates openly acknowledge her assistance in completing their dissertations, for without her inspiring, no-nonsense advice like the following about writing, in all probability they would still be ABD's.

> So a moral position is not a message. A moral position is a passionate caring inside you. . . . So write about the things that are most important to you. Love and death and sex and survival are important to most of us. Some of us are also interested in God and ecology. . . . but remember, a moral position is not a slogan, or wishful thinking. It doesn't come from outside or above. It begins inside the heart of a character and grows from there. (pp. 108–109)

- Miller, Timothy (Ed.). (1995). *America's Alternative Religions.* Albany: State University of New York Press.

This is an excellent sourcebook for those of you who might need a quick study of the most prominent alternative religions in the United States. Estimates regarding the number of alternative religions in America range from 600 to 3,000. Miller's volume includes alternative Christian groups, contemporary Christian and Jewish movements, Asian religions, Middle East religions, African-American freedom movements, Ancient Wisdom and New Age movements, and secular religions. Each entry is written by an established scholar. Here is what Miller has to say about the staying power of mainline and alternative religions in the United States, despite reports of their imminent demise:

> Tomorrow someone will leave a mainline religious body and join an alternative religion, perhaps even marry someone with a very different religious background. Some friends and family members of the convert will be outraged by the move, but life will go on. The great vitality of religion in the United States will be alive and well. (p. 9)

- Noddings, Nel. (1993). *Educating for Intelligent Belief or Unbelief.* New York: Teachers College Press.

Noddings has been one of the major intellectual influences on my own scholarship in the fields of applied ethics and religious studies. This small book, written primarily for public school teachers, has immense relevance to the work that you and I need to do on college campuses in behalf of religious pluralism. Her approach to teaching about religion in secular settings is thematic, and she includes in her curriculum such issues as existentialism and metaphysics, the nature of the gods, belongingness, feminism and religion, immortality, salvation, pessimism, humanism and unbelief, and religious and secular ethics. Here is Noddings on her rationale for teaching about religion in the public schools, and she reaffirms my own approach to working with the same controversial subject matter in secular college settings:

> An education for intelligent belief or unbelief puts great emphasis on self-knowledge, and that knowledge must come to grips with the emotional and spiritual as well as the intellectual and the psychological . . . to believe without thinking through the questions that arise regularly in life—to merely accept or reject—is surely not intelligent. It is also unintelligent to ignore either the positive or negative side of religion. Education for intelligent belief or unbelief is as much education of the heart as it is education of the mind. (p. xiv)

- Nussbaum, Martha C. (1997). *Cultivating Humanity: A Classical Defense of Reform in Liberal Education.* Cambridge, MA: Harvard University Press.

Nussbaum, a philosopher and classicist at the University of Chicago, has written one of the best defenses of a liberal education I have ever read. Her three core values for liberal education—critical examination of one's values, world citizenship as a worthy purpose of higher education, and the cultivation of the narrative imagination—are entirely consistent with the methodology and the goals of this capstone seminar. In fact, Nussbaum could very well have written my syllabus. She believes that the classics are a prerequisite subject matter, along with a genuinely interdisciplinary, liberal studies curriculum, for anyone who today might want to be a values educator. I would submit that Nussbaum's proposal for a radically revised undergraduate education is an excellent preparation for the type of values work that I think needs to be done in the American university. Here is Nussbaum on the narrative imagination:

> This is the ability to think what it might be like to be in the shoes of a person different from oneself, to be an intelligent reader of that person's story, and to understand the emotions and wishes and desires that someone so placed might have. The narrative imagination is not uncritical, for we always bring ourselves and our own judgments to the encounter with another. . . . But the first step of understanding the world from the point of view of the other is essential to any responsible act of judgment. . . . (p. 11)

- Rorty, Richard. (1999). *Philosophy and Social Hope*. New York: Penguin.

For those of you who have never heard of Richard Rorty, here is a very readable compendium of his shorter essays written over the last decade. Rorty is unarguably one of the three or four most important philosophers in the world today, and the extent of his impact on my own thinking has been incalculable. This volume of essays, a kind of philosophical memoir, represents the most personal writing he has ever done. Rorty is a lifelong atheist and a secular humanist committed to the cause of social justice. While many of my students like Rorty, they have difficulty relating to his ironic writing style, and to what they think is his sometimes overly facile dismissal of all religiously based moral traditions. Here is a selection that is vintage Rorty:

> Critics of moral relativism think that unless there is something absolute, something which shares God's implacable refusal to yield to human weakness, we have no reason to go on resisting evil. . . . But to us pragmatists moral struggle is continuous with the struggle for existence . . . what matters . . . is devising ways of diminishing human suffering and increasing human equality, increasing the ability of all human children to start life with an equal chance of happiness. This goal is not written in the stars, and is . . . no expression . . . of the Will of God. It is a goal worth dying for, but it does not require backup from supernatural forces. (p. xxix)

- Sharma, Arvind (Ed.). (1993). *Our Religions*. New York: HarperCollins.

Sharma covers the same seven religious narratives as Huston Smith does below, with one major difference. He chooses as writers of each of the narratives those who are genuine adherents. Thus, the reader gets a believer's eye view of seven of the world's major religions. The writing is scholarly, clear, and loaded with valuable theological insights and historical details. Despite each writer's profound personal faith in the tradition being examined, each of the analyses is laudably balanced. I particularly like this assertion by Sharma that introduces his rich, packed volume because it raises the central issue regarding the study of religion that I touch on time and time again in my own writing and teaching:

> Two ends of the spectrum have often been played against each other in the study of religion: that one who knows one religion knows none and that one who knows too many does not know any. This book focuses not at the ends but at the colorful band that lies between these two ends. As the reader explores this band . . . he or she will have to decide whether the various religions of the world are hyphens that unite or dashes that divide, and in doing so will determine the grammar of religious discourse in times to come. (p. xi)

- Smith, Huston. (1991). *The World's Religions*. New York: HarperCollins.

Imagine a scholarly work on comparative religion that has sold upwards of two million copies! Imagine even more that the work is accessible, vibrant, and thoroughly engrossing. The author is a history- and philosophy-of-religions scholar who has been immersed in these disciplines for 50 years. His coverage of Hinduism, Buddhism, Confucianism, Taoism, Islam, Judaism, and Christianity is detailed, absorbing, and each of the chapters reads like a story. I began to think of religion and spirituality as a narrative response to life's persistent existential questions when I was in graduate school, and I first read Huston Smith. I quote Smith here on the challenge of religious pluralism, and I can only nod my head in vigorous agreement:

> How do we comport outselves in a pluralistic world that is riven by ideologies, some sacred, some profane? We listen. . . . Not uncritically, for new occasions teach new duties and everything finite is flawed in some respects. Still, we listen to it expectantly, knowing that it houses more truth than can be encompassed in a single lifetime. . . . So we must listen to understand, but we must also listen to put into play the compassion that the [world's religions] all enjoin. . . . God speaks to us in three places: in scripture, in our deepest selves, and in the voice of the stranger. (pp. 389–390)

Well, this is the end of my memorandum to you. Thank you for taking the time to read it. I would love to have a vigorous conversation about what you might have found agreeable and disagreeable in it. This will be a wonderful way to get us embarked on our semester-long journey together.

Robert J. Nash

The final chapter will explore in greater depth what I am calling moral conversation. Here I will attempt to tie up some loose ends, while commenting on such issues as faith development theory, postmodernism and religion, and working together with faculty and administrators in order to get the dialogue on religious pluralism started across the campus.

Chapter 6

One Group, Many Truths: Constructing a Moral Conversation

For those who say I can't impose my morality on others, I say just watch me.
—Joseph Scheidler, executive director, Pro-Life Action League, *Closed: 99 Ways to Stop Abortion*, 1994

It is not difficult to show, by abundant instances, that to extend the bounds of what may be called moral police, until it encroaches on the most unquestionably legitimate liberty of the individual, is one of the most universal of all human propensities.
—John Stuart Mill, *On Liberty*, 1852

Of course, there are those who do not want to listen, who have no interest in what the other side believes. They prefer shouting to civil conversation. But I am not talking about the extremists and the fanatics. I am addressing the conversation that might take place between people . . . of good will. . . . To them, I suggest that the conversation is more likely to continue if we can imagine the world from the other side of the barricade. Standing among "the enemy" for a moment, we might be able to see similarities between them and us, not some common 'human nature' or some ineffable "essence" shared by all, but the fact that we are all bundles of opinions and beliefs, of theories and prejudices about how we and our world are or ought to be.
—Edward Tivnan, *The Moral Imagination: Confronting the Ethical Issues of Our Day*, 1995

Crackpot cults prosper, manipulative sects thrive, discredited superstitions revive. Trapped between fundamentalists, who believe they have found truth, and relativists, who refuse to pin it down, the bewildered majority in between continues to hope there is a truth worth looking for, without knowing how to go about it or how to answer the voices from either extreme. . . . Everytime we take notice of each other, therefore, we get a little closer to truth. Those who refuse to acknowledge anyone's existence save their own must approach truth by imagining a variety of perspectives. To see things from no point of view is not even

theoretically possible. If we try to see from every point of view, we shall never attain our goal . . . [but] it is [also] literal nonsense to speak of seeing from none.
—Felipe Fernandez-Armesto, *Truth:*
A History and a Guide for the Perplexed, 1997

He drew a circle that shut me out—
Heretic, rebel, a thing to flout.
But Love and I had the wit to win:
We drew a circle that took him in.
—Edwin Markham, "The Man with the Hoe," 1899

"I'm Afraid to Open My Mouth in There for Fear of Getting Killed!"

My capstone was not going well. Three weeks into the semester, and the class was falling apart. I did not directly address the communication problems during class time, as I ordinarily would, because many of these students had taken courses with me before. I was confident that they would eventually come together on their own to resolve the difficulties, by using the familiar protocols of moral conversation that I had taught them. I also thought that they liked and respected each other enough to make the effort. I was wrong. They seemed ready to strangle each other and me, and my anxieties were growing with each hour I spent with them. I felt that I had lost control—and that I would never get it back. After a very difficult, often contentious, third meeting, several members of the capstone were waiting for me outside the seminar room. Their body languages spoke anger and disappointment. Their actual words were harsh.

Mary: "I'm afraid to open my mouth in there, for fear of getting killed."

June: "Where the hell is the respect for each other that we always talk about?"

Phil: "Is this what our discussions are going to be like every week? If they are, count me out. I'll just sit with my mouth shut, and let others hold court."

Reagan: "Did you see what they did to poor Nate? They jumped all over him when he started talking about his own lapsed Judaism, and how he never felt *he* needed the comforts of his religion *or* his ethnicity. He was perfectly happy just being an individualist. If I were him, I wouldn't open my mouth again."

Lawrence: "I didn't think you'd be able to pull this course off, given the controversial nature of the subject matter, Robert. There are just too many offensive know-it-alls in the group for us to go anywhere this term. If you turn this unruly mob around, you will really be a miracle worker."

David: "Why don't we talk about the readings more than we do? Why aren't people doing the writing? Why is everybody talking to *you*, Robert, instead of to each other? I don't mean to be negative, but there is no moral conversation in this group. Everybody is out to make everyone else look stupid. I'm beginning to think that moral conversation is a pipe dream when it comes to the real world."

Mary: "How can I ever talk honestly about my evangelical beliefs when the cynics are ready to rip off my head? Why do you let some people get away with rudeness and snideness? You wrote such great things in your Capstone Memorandum about respectful conversation, but I haven't seen any evidence of it yet in here. Was your Memo just a bunch of bullshit words?"

Chet: "My values and my spirituality are too brittle at this stage in my life to expose them to people who are always on the attack. Why do we all have to be so defensive? I'd almost prefer everybody to be politically correct, the way we were in our race-and-culture course when I was an undergraduate. Yeah, the conversation was dull a lot of the time. But, at least this way, I wouldn't have to duck the oncoming missiles whenever I open my mouth. Why should religion be a more explosive topic than race anyway?"

Armando: "I'd like to say something, and I'm not brown-nosing. Why are we getting on Robert's case? He's just one member of our group. It's true, he's the capstone leader, but he can only do his job if people are willing to make an effort to open up their minds a little bit and join him in real dialogue. Where's the cooperation? We've been scuffling with each other since the first hour of the first day of class. Everything we've learned about conversational civility in Robert's courses before this one we seem to have parked outside the seminar door here from day one. Why? Is this material so threatening that we need to turn to "Big-Brother" Robert all the time to protect us from each other? I don't know about you, but

> I'm ashamed of myself and the class. We're adults after all. Why did we feel the need to ambush Robert after three hours of what I'm sure must have been hell for him, too? He looks dog-tired to me.

Yes, I was "dog-tired." However, not tired enough to know that I wanted to kiss Armando at that moment, even though, in my opinion, he was among the worst of the capstone instigators. He was very bright, but he could also be very sarcastic, and he enjoyed pushing others around with the jaw-breaking jargon he had learned as an undergraduate religious-studies/philosophy major. For me, the bitter irony of this little "ambush" was that a few of the confronters were among the worst offenders of moral conversation, and they did not even realize it. Their view was that whatever problems we had in the capstone belonged to others, not to them. It was true: I had my work cut out for me with this crowd. Or better: They had a lot of work to do with themselves. Or better still: We all had considerable work to do to come together, without exceptions.

We did decide to begin the seminar the next week by talking about what had gone wrong in our group process and how we might correct it. I have believed for a very long time that how we talk to each other about the content in a seminar, or in a dialogue group, is at least as important as the content itself. Armando may have read everything in the religious-studies universe, but if he is intent merely on wielding his knowledge like a deadly rapier in order to pile up the bodies of his confreres, then he will be no help to us or to himself. He must learn to talk softly, and let his demeanor, not his rhetoric, exemplify his passion for the content. And, so, without hesitation, I started the conversation the following week with these comments:

> We will be spending many more weeks together talking about values and religion. I, for one, do not want to engage in mortal combat with anyone during this time, and I do not believe any of you do either. I also know that most of you genuinely want to be here, but you may not know how to address this material without inadvertently harming yourselves or others. Perhaps you fear the volatility of the content. I know I do in some ways. But I am convinced that we can salvage a great deal from the time we have already spent together, and that it will only get better if we renew our commitment to be here. What, in your opinion, might we do to make the last 12 weeks of the capstone something we can look forward to, indeed be proud of? I know that many of you do not like the way things have been going with us so far. What do you think, if anything, might already be working in our seminar, and what, in your mind, needs much more work?

The processing that we did on that afternoon was lively, at times a little frustrating, but, in the end, very helpful. After three hours, we arrived at

a consensus as to what we needed to do for the rest of the
These conclusions follow:

- Revisit, and reestablish, the principles of moral conversation during each and every class, if only briefly. These principles are at
once the most important guidelines for constructive capstone discussion, but they are also the easiest to set aside when dialogue
gets heated and the stakes get higher.
- Remember to ask these four questions about the readings at all
times:

  How do the author's own background beliefs influence the religious story
     being told?
  What exactly is the religious story that the author is telling?
  What do you think is the religious narrative's special appeal to its believers?
  What, in your opinion, are the narrative's strengths and weaknesses to you
     as a reader?

- Refer to specific passages and proof-texts from the readings as often as possible during class conversation, and always with an intention to "unpack" these in your own language.
- After the mid-class break, where appropriate, remind us to revisit
issues raised during the first half of class. Understand, however,
that because of time and content constraints, several issues each
week will necessarily be left up in the air for you to explore on your
own time.
- Remember always to talk to each other, instead of having a two-
way conversation with the instructor during class time. But do not
forget that the instructor is also a member of the group. Occasionally, a conversation with him is appropriate, particularly when reacting to something he says, and vice versa.
- Keep this in mind: We are all responsible for each other's success.
One of our duties during the conversation is to make each other
look smart, not stupid, and this includes you, the authors, and me.
Who among us is truly an expert in this material? Scholars write in
order to become more learned; at its best, the act of writing leads
to learning, which may or may not lead to expertise. Students read,
talk, and write in order to learn more about the things they do not
know but would like to. Instructors write, read, talk, and above all
listen, because they have as great a need as anyone to dig more
deeply into what they think they know, and to be able to voice this
a little more clearly and with a little more compassion and humility.

- E-mails outside of class time can be considered an essential part of our capstone conversation this semester. E-mails are one way of extending and enlarging the conversation beyond the three hours of class time each week, particularly when they do not degenerate into insidious gossip and chronic complaining. Learn how to use list-serve when you want to include all of us in the conversation. A good rule of thumb for e-mails: Would you want the comments of your messages to each other to be printed on the front page of the *Burlington Free Press* the next morning?
- Understand that each of us is a genuine seeker. Few of us have made up our minds once and for all on religio-spiritual issues and personal values. Thus, we need to treat each other with exquisite respect and sensitivity. Critique and feedback, when appropriate, ought always to come out of a framework of generosity and empathy, and always with an intention to make the other look good. Faith, whether sacred or secular, is, almost without exception, delicate.
- Realize that spirited and candid religious inquiry is more likely to occur when conversationalists feel safe and supported to speak their truths to others. In matters of religion and spirituality, the *receptive mode* of listening and responding in dialogue is far more effective than the *attack mode*.

Moral Conversation Versus Adversarial Discourse

Whether we are engaging in discussions about religion and values in the scholarly confines of the seminar room, or in large dialogue groups in public (hence more visible and intimidating) university spaces, or in more intimate and safe places like coffee houses, residence halls, chapels, and private offices, the challenge remains the same. How can we construct a framework for moral conversation that encourages the full and honest expression of many truths in one group? How, in Tivnan's word in the epigraph that begins this chapter, can we lower the "barricades" which so often polarize and paralyze us whenever we talk about controversial topics like religion? In the wonderful words of Edwin Markham, how do we "draw a circle that takes [others] in," not shut others out? How can we avoid stigmatizing people as "heretics, rebels, things to flout"? How is it possible for people like me to help the Marys and the Nates to open up in my groups without fearing they will "get killed" in the process? To my mind, the opposite of moral conversation is adversarial discourse, and the latter is always a threat to destroy my capstone seminar.

Several years ago, I began trying to construct a *modus vivendi* (a way of living together) for the classroom that would teach students how to dialogue with each other without reverting to monologue or diatribe. There is frequently too much posturing in seminar conversations in the academy, a lot of jockeying about to win favor or to destroy opponents. Deborah Tannen (1998) calls this "ritualized opposition," a time-honored academic ceremony that pits students against one another until the best debater or orator is left standing. To the losers, however, the experience can feel like an academic mugging or, worse, an intellectual execution. Sometimes, of course, these discussions can be animated and stimulating, and this is good. Often, though, they can be excruciatingly punishing. The victims are usually those students who sit silently week after week, either scared to death to get involved in the "contest," or completely uninterested in playing the game of impression-management and grade mongering.

Tired of discussions that went nowhere, that failed to produce honest, heart-felt dialogue, that too often deteriorated into an empty charade of scholarly name-dropping, textual nit-picking, and other forms of thinly disguised academic aggression, I decided to lay down some very specific ground rules at the outset. Much to my surprise, most students in my groups appreciated the structure. Today, at this stage in my teaching, I cannot imagine talking about religion and spirituality, or any topic that touches on the raw nerves of personal values, without adhering to my six principles of moral conversation. These conversational principles also seem to work very well in extra-classroom conversations. Imagine trying to discuss (and possibly reconcile) in public such potentially disabling religious dualisms as faith and doubt, reason and revelation, belief and disbelief, good and evil, religious community and religious individualism, transcendent and immanent meaning, church and cult, god and no-god, patriarchs and goddesses, morality and immorality, subjectivity and objectivity, mortality and immortality, and creation and evolution *without establishing some conversational ground rules beforehand*. In the past, I have tried to avoid such guidelines, and the results have been dreadful. Before I list and comment on the conversational principles I now employ, however, I first need to define two key words.

The Latin root of the word conversation, *conversari*, is to live with, to keep company with, to turn around, to oppose. A conversation is literally a manner of living whereby people keep company with each other, and talk together, in good faith, in order to exchange sometimes agreeable, sometimes disagreeable, ideas. A conversation is not an argument, although it can get heated. A conversation is at its best when the participants are not impatient to conclude their business, but wish instead to spend their time together in order to deepen and enrich their understanding of ideas. Tannen (2000) asks us to think of classroom conversation in the metaphor of a "barn raising instead of a boxing match" (p. B8). Students, in this image, become cooperative builders or story-makers not fighters, and they work at constructing a narrative that binds them together in a common edifice called a community of scholars rather than a "boxing ring" that leaves them bruised and battered.

A conversation that is moral, from the Latin root, *moralis*, is one whose *customs* emphasize the fundamental worth and dignity of each participant in the exchange, and this includes authors as well. The best way to get a person to talk is to treat that person with the utmost respect. Each person in the conversation lays claim to some share of truth. No single person alone inhabits the religious or moral high ground. No single person has the final word on on any issue. We are all *viators* (travelers with a purpose) on a journey to find meaning in the life we live. Furthermore, because our journey is our own and nobody else's, it possesses intrinsic worth, and deserves at least an initial consideration.

It gives me no satisfaction to repeat the commonplace that too often we academics set the supreme example for treating each other with disrespect on college campuses. Come to our scholarly conferences. Watch us in action in our faculty senates. Overhear our conversations in the faculty lounge. Be a fly on the wall at our departmental meetings. Read our essay reviews of each other's books. Listen to Alvin Snider (1999), a professor of English, rage that "institutionalizing civility" is nothing more than "bending the knee and embracing compulsory niceness." For Snider, civility is "bowing and scraping." He opts, instead, for colleagues to become "perpetual naysayers, fiery dissidents, and voluble curmudgeons" (p. A64). The sad upshot is that as students observe this, they tend to do this. We professors have long since forgotten Aristotle's insight that *mimesis* (imitation), rather than *phronesis* (practical wisdom), is often the best teacher.

In the academy, we see our colleagues less as fellow *viators* and more as predatory *violators* of one another's turfs and perks. We have learned well the art of intellectual intimidation and political terrorism. We are all too frequently alienated and aggressive in our dealings with each other. Although we talk the talk of civil discourse, and the importance of agreeing to disagree, our conversations are adversarial and competitive. In a recent, well-received article, the eminent Wellesley College classicist, Mary Lefkowitz (1998), implores us to stop "raging at each other," and learn to "observe the easy and supportive rules of etiquette that make productive

of information, critical thinking, even consensus and agreement—while certainly desirable achievements in many instances—are not the ultimate test as to whether moral conversation has been effective. Empathy, genuine dialogical encounter with difference, and mutual understanding are the key criteria for success.

Tivnan (1995) tells us that "conversation is more likely to continue if we can imagine the world from the other side of the barricade." Tivnan's point, where religion is concerned, is to avoid narrowing the conversation to one-way declarations of our unassailable beliefs to others. It is to realize that, no matter how different our views, "we are all bundles of opinions and beliefs, of theories and prejudices about how we and our world are or ought to be" (p. 250). This is simply to say that what we all have in common is the fact that our views are at one and the same time true and false, whole and partial, strong and weak, each in their own ways. We are each fallible containers of meanings, and admitting this, we need to turn down the volume in our moral conversations by turning up our empathy meters. We need to listen to others as we would be listened to. We need to question and challenge others as we would be questioned and challenged. And we must pontificate to others only under the condition that we want others to pontificate to us.

2. All views in moral conversation deserve at least an initial respect.

We are each unique makers of *meanings*, looking frequently to express them, hoping to find others to confirm them, and wanting to live our lives in a manner that is consistent with them. It is rare, however, that many of us will actively seek out others to change them. Mark R. Schwehn (1993) proposes that four virtues in particular—humility, faith, self-denial, and charity—are necessary for respecting, rather than changing, the views of others.

Humility presumes that we attribute at least a modicum of wisdom and insight to others. We should avoid too quickly dismissing the truth in another person's view until we have heard it and understood it from that person's perspective, as well as from our own. We should try to comprehend (from the Latin, *comprehendere*, to grab hold of, to seize) the other's truth from the inside-out as well as from the outside-in.

Faith means trusting that what we hear from others is worthwhile in some way. We need to have some confidence that what others have to offer us might indeed be able to enhance our own understandings. In the matter of religion, this does not mean accepting religious truths uncritically, but rather with an open mind, trusting in the fundamentally good intentions of the other. Schwehn (1993) puts it this way: "Believe what we are questioning and at the same time question what we are believing" (p. 49).

Self-denial suggests that at some point, we need to consider the possibility of abandoning at least a few of the beliefs we cherish. Self-denial is the core of intellectual integrity and honesty; without it, minds would never change, and mere opinions would ossify into sacred certainties. Schwehn says that we need to cultivate a "disposition to surrender ourselves for the sake of the better opinion" (p. 49). Self-denial is the inclination to give up the delusion that we are omniscient gods. Intellectual arrogance and selfishness are the vices that exist in opposition to the virtue of self-denial.

Finally, *charity* is all about "putting the best construction on everything," for example, attributing the best motive to those who are willing to express their most cherished religious truths to us. This does not mean ignoring or excusing errors in judgment, faulty reasoning, or one-sided zealotry. Rather, in Schwehn's terms, it means trying to be "more cautious in appraisal, more sympathetic with human failings, less prone to stereotype and caricature" (p. 51). Charity is all about generosity and graciousness, and it is a virtue tragically missing in higher education today.

3. *The golden rule of moral conversation is a willingness to find the truth in what we oppose and the error in what we espouse, before we presume to acknowledge the truth in what we espouse and the error in what we oppose.*

This concept is not to suggest that truth is always an illusion or that every view of truth is equally true or equally false. Truth-denial and truth-equivalence—what some call nihilism and relativism—have nothing to do with authentic moral conversation. Further, this principle is not meant to relieve truth-proclaimers (or truth-repudiators) of the responsibility to explain and defend their truths (or lack of them) or, even when necessary—under the weight of compelling, countervailing evidence—to modify them. There is nothing inherently erroneous or immoral about any initial presumption of truth in moral conversation. What is destructive of moral conversation, however, is the attitude that one individual (or group) possesses all the truth, and those who disagree do so because they are in error or there is something wrong with them. Barbara Herrnstein Smith (1997) puts it this way: "If orthodoxy is that which is manifestly true, self-evidently right, and intuitively and universally preunderstood, then how is it that its truth and rightness elude the skeptic? The orthodox answer to this question is familiar: profound defects and deficiencies of intellect and character . . ." (p. 83).

During moral conversation, students need to recognize that what might represent "definitive" or "inerrant" truth for some may represent just the opposite for others. Moreover, this does not mean that these others are necessarily defective in intellect, religious conviction, or moral character. In the matter of religion, a conflict of beliefs may be based less on a stubborn, ignorant, or "sinful" refusal to embrace revealed absolutes than on a sincere difference of opinion rooted in personal interpretation or perspective. It is necessary, therefore, for all of us to try to understand the special appeal of an opposing view to the actual truth-holder or truth-proclaimer. Asking these questions might help: What is there in the other's perspective, or interpretive framework, that makes the truth-claim ring truer than it does for me? Is there any validity to the other's truth-claim, no matter how slight it might seem to me, given the total narrative-context out of which the other is operating?

Notwithstanding truth's objective properties, though, a person's perception of truth is inevitably shaped by taste, temperament, perspective, and background. As Felipe Fernandez-Armesto (1997) says: "To see things from no point of view is not even theoretically possible" (p. 3). I would add: To see things outside of our socialization is an impossibility. Even when we might be in agreement that truth claims in religion need to meet one or another of the tests of objective revelation, coherence, logical consistency, tradition, self-interest, or practical utility, a person's perceptions of these criteria, like those of the truth-perceptions themselves, will always be mediated through particular sociocultural and psychological perspectives.

The conclusion is inescapable: In order to engage in empathic moral conversation, the reality of multiple perceptions of "invariant" or "objective" truths will require us to listen carefully for the impact of the socialization process on the other's proclamations of truth. Stated more simply, we must always work hard to detect even a little bit of truth in the biggest bunch of nonsense. What constitutes "truth" and "nonsense" depends, of course, on *our* perspective, just as it does on *theirs*.

4. *Either-or, all-or-nothing thinking is always a threat to destroy moral conversation.*

Either-or thinking oversimplifies complexity and dichotomizes diversity. Worse, when it dominates conversations about religio-spirituality, it frequently polarizes and anathematizes opposing narratives. Cognitive-behavioral therapists call this black-and-white thinking, and it is a common characteristic among psychological patients who suffer from anxiety disorders. These people tend to catastrophize by experiencing their lives in grave either-ors and false dilemmas. Deathly afraid of complexity, their initial inclination is to cut through it as if all issues can be resolved by a simple yes or no. This way their personal problems are manageable rather than overpowering.

In religious conversations, the disorder sometimes gets expressed this way: Either you agree with me or you disagree with me. Either you believe what I do or you are a . . . *select one*—heretic, infidel, apostate, recusant, renegade, backslider, deviationist, and so forth. Either you have seen the light or you are living in darkness. You are either with me or against me. Spare me the details—are you on God's side or the devil's side? Black-and-white religious thinking fails to capture the range of infinite variations of religio-spiritual belief. It is an angle on religious pluralism that wants to wrap it all up in one huge bundle called True Belief.

Joseph Scheidler (1994), executive director of the Pro-Life Action League, and a former Benedictine monk, quoted at the beginning of this chapter, is an either-or thinker. His position against abortion is absolute and beyond debate, so much so that he is *ever* on the ready to "impose my morality on others." Abortion, in his view, is always and everywhere the murder of an innocent child. There are no exceptions. Women who abort their children, and the doctors and nurses who assist them, are "baby killers." For Scheidler, the way to settle profound moral differences in the United States is to inflict his unimpeachable religious views on those who disagree with him and call them terrible names in the process.

Conversation, dialogue, and to-and-fro discussion are out because they are symptomatic of un-Christian, liberal dilly-dallying; religious prescription and proscription are in. There is no wish to compromise, no interest in pursuing a possible common ground. There is not a scintilla of recognition in Scheidler's anti-choice narrative that he might need contending visions of the truth to bump up against his so that his own Christian vision can be kept more honest, loving, and forgiving. His narrative, like all narratives, needs to be stretched and challenged. Who knows, it might even become less authoritarian and denunciatory in reacting to those whose viewpoints are different and as profoundly felt as his.

I am not overly optimistic, however. John Stuart Mill, quoted earlier, believes that the temptation to become a member of the "moral police" squad is "one of the most universal of all human propensities." Somebody like Scheidler believes he knows the truth, and he is convinced beyond any doubt that his truth will set all the rest of us free if only we will bend our knees to his moral and religious certainty. Such a stringent, all-or-nothing view, in my opinion, endangers the future of a pluralistic democracy. Sincere and thoughtful people on all sides—not the extremists or the fanatics—will always have serious, deeply held differences of opinion over such important topics as abortion, capital punishment, suicide, euthanasia, same-sex civil unions, and affirmative action. Scheidler's viewpoint stops moral conversation about these differences dead in its tracks, even before it begins. He seems temperamentally unable, or unwilling, to "imagine the world from the other side of the barricade" (Tivnan, 1995, p. 250).

Richard Rorty (1999) puts it this way:

> O.K., but since I don't think there is such a thing as the will of God, and since I doubt that we'll get anywhere arguing theism vs. atheism, let's see if we have some shared premises on the basis of which to continue our argument about abortion. [Why is such] a reply considered condescending and trivializing? . . . are we atheists supposed to try to keep the conversation going by saying, "Gee! I'm impressed. You must have a really deep, sincere faith"? Suppose we try that. What happens then? What can either party do for an encore? (p. 171)

F. Scott Fitzgerald once said that the test of a first-rate intelligence is the ability to hold two or more opposing ideas in the mind at the same time, and still retain the ability to function somewhat normally. I would go one step further. I think the test of a superior intelligence is to know that, on most political and religious issues, there are rarely clear and unequivocal opposites. There are only differences of degree and transitions. For example, on the issues of the previously mentioned abortion, affirmative action, and same-sex civil unions, either-or approaches will never be the best ways to resolve these disputes. Looking for what Rorty calls "shared premises" is a better way to proceed. I can only add to Rorty's suggestion that discovering "shared premises" is impossible without a commitment to moral conversation, as the following example will demonstrate.

On December 30, 1994, John Salvi entered two Planned Parenthood clinics in Brookline, Massachusetts, seriously wounding five staff members and killing two others. As a result of his 20-minute maiming-and-killing rampage, both pro-life and pro-choice leaders in Massachusetts were left appalled and grief-stricken, angry and terrified. Salvi's attack motivated six activist-advocates (all women) of both "pro-choice" and "pro-life" movements to meet together privately, away from the glare of the media spotlight, for more than 150 hours over a six-year period. This is an encounter that has continued up to the present time (Fowler et al., 2001). The stated purpose of these highly confidential meetings was to refrain from changing the other side's mind on an issue as complex, fixed, and inflammatory as abortion. Instead, it was to "communicate openly with our opponents, away from the polarizing spotlight of media coverage;

to build relationships of mutual respect and understanding; to help deescalate the rehetoric of the abortion controversy; and, of course, to reduce the risk of future shootings" (p. F2).

The official sponsor of this ground-breaking dialogue between two historically combative opponents was the Boston Public Conversations Project. The first meetings between the two groups were very difficult, often erupting in bitter clashes over such issues as the use of loaded language. Designations such as "pro-life" and "pro-choice," "fetus" and "unborn baby," "pro-abortion" and "anti-abortion," for example, ignited angry and defensive outbursts on both sides. As a result, the group members decided to establish a set of conversational guidelines which are very similar to the ground rules for moral conversation that I use in all my courses and dialogue groups around religio-spiritual topics. These included:

- Use only terms which are acceptable to all participants.
- No interruptions, grandstanding, or *ad hominem* attacks.
- Speak as individuals, not as members of organizations or interest groups.
- Keep everything confidential.
- Don't argue for a cause, but speak honestly and personally from the heart.
- Refrain from using deliberately polarizing rhetoric, such as "murderers," "baby killers," "genocide," "products of conception," and "termination of pregnancy."
- Stop thinking and speaking in stereotypes such as "religious fanatics," "anti-choice," "anti-women," "anti-child," "anti-men," and "anti-family."

Despite occasional recriminations, and feelings of disloyalty to such respective organizations as Planned Parenthood, the Religious Coalition for Reproductive Choice, Women Affirming Life, the Pro-Life Committee of the National Conference of Catholic Bishops, the National Abortion and Reproductive Rights Action League, and the National Committee for a Human Life Amendment, the members of the Conversations Project grew over time to respect and honor one other. While they may not have discovered any startling "shared premises" in their dialogues, they did realize that, in fact, they were able to agree on one major assumption: *Their two worldviews* ("narratives" in my language) *appeared to be "irreconcilable."* In spite of this, however, they still continued to meet for over six years because they wanted to stretch themselves intellectually, to truly understand the reasons for the intensity present in the opposition's position, and, most importantly, to experience something "radical" and "life-altering"—"the mystery of love" and, perhaps, a "common holy ground."

In the words of the authors (Fowler et al., 2001), the Conversations Project was a huge success:

> Since that first, fear-filled meeting, we have experienced a paradox. While learning to treat each other with dignity and respect, we all have become firmer in our views about abortion. But now when we face our opponent, we see her dignity and goodness. . . . We have glimpsed a new possibility: a way in which people can disagree frankly and passionately, become clearer in heart and mind about their activism and, at the same time, contribute to a more civil and compassionate society. (pp. F2, F3)

In a democracy, it is not by stricture or fiat that complicated social problems get addressed and resolved. It is through hard work, responsiveness, energy, constructing a case in behalf of a perspective, and reaching out to build bridges to others who do not share that perspective. It is also through generosity, humility, and, above all, realizing that, in a pluralistic world, visions of truth and reality are infinitely variable and interpretable and sometimes hopelessly incompatible. Thus, whenever we find ourselves, like Joseph Scheidler, clinging desperately and stubbornly to what we think is The Only Truth, we ought always to ask these questions: Why are we this insecure? What are we afraid of losing? Is a principled compromise truly impossible? Or, in the spirit of the Public Conversations Project, Why don't we try to avoid disparaging our opponents and, instead, learn to treat each other with dignity and respect, in spite of our radically opposed, apparently irreconcilable narratives? Moreover, how can we be so sure that somewhere, somehow, our diverging narrative threads do not, or will not, intersect, perhaps even on a mutually agreed upon "common holy ground"?

5. *In matters of religion, we do not live in reality itself. We live in stories about reality.*

It is self-evidently true, of course, that there is a material, "factual" world out there that all of us must consciously negotiate every day. There are traffic rules to obey, food to eat, grass to cut, pharmaceutical prescriptions to fill, weather to heed, gardens to tend, bills to pay, and so forth. However, this is a long way from saying that because the *material world* is "out there," so too is *truth* "out there." Religious truth is something far from being objectively verifiable—like rain and weeds and plumbing problems. It is not available to everyone in the same, unmediated way, if only we will open ourselves up to receiving one or another version of inerrant revelation, unwavering faith, or binding tradition. Religious truth is largely a product of the way we were raised to think and feel about religion, embedded as each of us is in our unique containers of contingent meanings.

Most important for moral conversation, however, is the understanding that our religious truths unavoidably take the shape of particular stories that enchant us. What we might find narratively enchanting, others might find revolting, or merely vapid. (It is almost impossible, for example, to get a room full of students to agree on the entertainment value of a particular film, novel, or popular song. Disagreements often get heated, because aesthetic tastes are so diverse and personal.) Thus, in my opinion, it is unlikely that there will ever again be a High Ground of Absolute Religious Truth for all to follow, if there ever was one, because there will never again be an All-Enchanting Narrative that will appeal to everyone, if there ever was one. No longer will it be acceptable to superimpose a religious exclusivity onto anybody's subjective story, unless, of course, this is done with the full, informed consent of each and every storyteller.

The upshot for moral conversations about religion and spirituality, then, is not for us to give in to the lure of skepticism or cynicism. Rather, it is to approach religio-spiritual dialogues with curiosity, modesty, humility, compassion, caution, and when fitting, with a sense of humor. It is to realize that nobody ever makes religious judgments outside of a particular narrative. When all is said and done, religious narratives will remain infinitely contestable, depending on one's aesthetic and theological perspectives. Thus, we need to learn how to engage in religious dialogues with an attitude about pluralism that says: "Let a thousand, even a million, alternative religious stories bloom. Who knows? Maybe some of them will correct the deficiencies in my own story, even while confirming its abundances."

In this regard, I am reminded of something that Voltaire (cited in Nord, 1995) once said about the necessity of religious pluralism: "If there had been in England only one religion, its despotism would have been fearful. If there had been two religions, they would have cut each other's throat. But as there are thirty they live peacefully and happily" (p. 191). Voltaire's insight for moral conversation is that by allowing for the full expression of multiple religious narratives in the American university, we are more likely to assure the protection of religious liberty on college campuses. By refusing to establish one particular religion (and this includes secular humanism) in higher education, we enable many to flourish. We also enhance the possibility that students will be able to talk about their stories without the threat of censure or rancor. If I have learned anything as a teacher, it is that there is only one thing better at making most students happy than narrating a story. It is narrating many stories. Voltaire was right after all.

Finally, Joseph Natoli (1997) recommends several good questions that we might ask ourselves in our moral conversations about religion and spirituality:

> Which world, or story of the world, is this that I am being confronted with? How do things come to meaning within this narrative frame? How do words signify within this narrative frame? How am I to place myself within this world in order to communicate effectively? What is it about this particular time and place that shapes my seeing and understanding here? What story of who I am is best able to deal with the reality here presented? What shared cultural stories forge a connection here? Why is this particular difference unsettling and offensive to me? What story of myself is here challenged and questioned? (p. 19)

6. *Moral conversation is not without internal contradictions, however, as its basic premises tend to lean leftward toward a liberal-postmodern view of the world.*

Thus, the way to improve moral conversation is to be as attentive to its political, philosophical, and theological biases as to its potential strengths. Stephen Carter (1993, 2000) has written frequently on the topic of religion and politics. Carter, a devout Christian, as well as a highly respected constitutional law professor at Yale, argues by inference that the kind of moral conversation I am recommending is not as religiously inclusive as I would like to think. Postmodern "liberals" like me, he suggests, hope

> to create a conversational space in which individuals of very different viewpoints can join in dialogic battle, in accord with a set of dialogic conventions that all can accept. The philosophical idea is that even though all of us have differing personal backgrounds and biases, we nevertheless share certain moral premises in common. If we then exclude what we do not have in common, what remains can be the basis for a conversation. (1993, p. 55)

What bothers Carter about this assumption, and it is one of the potential dangers in moral conversation, is that it (wittingly or unwittingly) excludes *religious* ideas from the mix, particularly those we do not share in common. It asks believers to act as if they are disbelievers, or, at the very least, religious nonpartisans. It requires that they bracket their deepest, self-defining convictions—that they remove from the public conversation the most distinguishing aspect of themselves—in order to inhabit a religiously neutral piece of the conversational space that a liberal democracy requires. Unfortunately, Carter believes, this forced denial of the spiritual self ends up reinforcing the anti-liberal stereotype that, on political matters, liberals want religious faith to remain intensely private and miles removed from the public political process.

While I am arguing for exactly the opposite outcome in cross-campus religio-spiritual dialogues, Carter's point is still well taken. I do not seek a denial of the spiritual self in higher education, but rather a spirited reclamation. Still, if I am being honest, I am talking about a conversation that celebrates religious diversity on *postmodern liberal terms*. I am asking that we allow a thousand narratives to flourish on equal standing in the dialogue, knowing that this may be theologically unacceptable to those who believe irreversibly in the religious exclusivity of their own narratives.

A pluralistic theory of conversation in the university, like the one I am proposing here, risks losing the very students it wants to include in the dialogue. It does this by sending them the message that they must disguise, or, worse, reconstruct their most essential religious premises, if they are to be accepted as full partners in cross-campus conversations. After all, for many of these students, issues like abortion, capital punishment, same-sex civil unions, and suicide are literally a matter of psychological and theological life and death, and are not to be taken lightly by professors like myself, whom they think of as secular relativists.

For most strong believers, religious truth does indeed have an irreproachable foundation. While it may be accurate to say that interpretation, context, and preference always bias one's view of truth, this, for them, does not mean that everything is, therefore, up for grabs. There are morally and theologically correct positions to take, positions that rest on objective moorings. These positions exist beyond the subjective reach of preference and perspective. A concept of moral conversation, predicated on the assumption that multiple narratives need to circulate freely, and that the most we can ever expect is to distill a small nugget of common truth from them, misses the point completely for convinced believers like the aforementioned Joseph Scheidler. For them, there needs to be a way to talk about morality, religion, and truth that finds perfect congruence among all three, and that eventually produces a conception of absolute truth upon which we can all agree and act. Proponents of moral conversation must understand that to say truth is infinitely contestable and interpretable is to take sides *ipso facto* against religious believers who think just the opposite.

I sympathize with all of these concerns. In respect to moral conversation, I can only say I agree that its basic premises seem to favor liberal understandings of civil dialogue. However, in a secular pluralist democracy, I cannot imagine how else we might be able to carry on peaceful and productive conversations with each other about such a controversial subject as religion. I agree by implication with Richard Rorty (1989) that if we make an honest effort to address the issue of religious pluralism on college campuses, then we might be able to achieve some kind of human solidarity. We might be able to discover some ways to stop inflicting pain and humiliation on each other whenever we display our different guiding narratives.

In principle, none of us can ever prove, once and for all, that our own favorite narratives will be the answer to everyone's problems. However, at a minimum, we can show the utmost respect for other narratives. We can go out of our way to understand them. We can practice empathy and restraint when we are tempted to ridicule them. Furthermore, when necessary, we can challenge them in a humble and nonviolent manner. On occasion, some of us might even embrace them. Moral conversation, when working well, can help fellow travelers inch a bit closer to some kind of mutually beneficial coexistence in the face of what can often be a fiercely contested terrain of religio-spiritual difference. It does this, not that people can finally get to the bottom of things, but that they might find out what they have in common, if anything.

This discovery of commonality is pressing because we are people who must somehow find a way to forge common agreements with one another. What is happening throughout the world today, evidenced by a number of bloody religio-nationalistic conflicts, makes this a crucial undertaking. Deadly disagreements about religion, politics, and geography that span many generations are rampant even as I write, in such places as Israel and Palestine, Northern Ireland, India, Sri Lanka, Indonesia, Sudan, Bosnia, Serbia, Tajikistan, Armenia, and Azerbaijan (Nord, 1995, p. 205). Believers persecute disbelievers, and disbelievers persecute believers. Tragically, all sides justify their cruelty in the belief that they alone have gotten to the bottom of things in God's holy name. In the presence of such zealotry, moral conversation withers and dies. A liberal, postmodern view of the world, despite its leftward philosophical slant, seems to me to be a far more humane alternative.

Finally, there is another way that moral conversation is politically biased, and this time the critique comes from the activist left. I remember a black student-activist once saying to me that she found it impossible to relate to my notion of moral conversation because it was too white and too middle-class. For her, the "civility movement" is "hung-up" on a politics of politeness; thus, it completely misses the need to attack at their source the basic social problems that plague America. Moral conversation, in her view, implies a kindness and empathy among opponents trying to deepen understanding of each other's perspective that is unrealistic in the face of tangible oppression and cruelty. Moral conversation is another example of the naivete implicit in white privilege, because often the only way that black Americans can get heard is when they raise their voices in anger.

There are times, she said, that the enemy does indeed need to be demonized, that evils like racism, sexism, and homophobia must be named for what they are, and times when truth needs to speak harshly to corporate greed and vested interests. Voices need to be strident (e.g., the Vietnam anti-war movement), and sometimes violent dissent is often the only way out of dismal social arrangements (e.g., urban riots against racism). Holstein & Ellingson (1999) argue that: "[c]ivility is not the language of urgency. It is not the language of people struggling to put food on the table or to stop the violence in their communities. It is instead the language of relative privilege, available to people who can afford to wait until some common areas emerge from ongoing conversations" (p. 14). To the activist left, moral conversation is nothing more than a tool of those entrenched in power, and this is the group that sets the terms of civil dialogue. The rules of civil discourse privilege the well-educated like myself, while penalizing those who do not care to speak empathically to their persecutors.

To this argument, I can only say, yes, of course. Dialogue definitely has its limits. Lowering the decibel level and making an all-out effort to truly hear the other will not, by itself, ever guarantee deep structural change, especially at the university. What, I ask, will? The anti-Vietnam war riots on college campuses in the late 1960s and early 1970s served mainly to alienate students (sometimes killing and maiming them as at Kent State University) and to polarize faculties and administrations (as at Columbia and Cornell Universities), often beyond the point of repair. I agree with my student's critical observation that moral conversation, if approached as a panacea, can easily lead to cooling out and cooptation. However, this is a serious abuse of the process I am describing. Moral conversation, at least as I am thinking about it here, is more concerned with procedure than policy. Its goals are small. Its main agenda is to provide a process whereby students with different religio-spiritual narratives can come together to talk, to listen, to learn, to question, and, sometimes, to find common ground.

On a college campus, perhaps one beset by the turbulence of an incipient and escalating religious pluralism, what is a better alternative than moral conversation? Name-calling? Strident us-versus-them rhetoric? Acts of violence in God's name? I take the position that in the academy we are more likely to address and solve our problems by displaying understanding and respect, particularly with those whom we call our adversaries. In my opinion, the models of moral conversation for the academy ought to be nonviolent activist-thinkers like Mahatma Gandhi, Martin Luther King, Jr., and Vaclav Havel (1990). What these men have in common is that they welcome many diverse voices into the public conversation.

Moreover, their civility is truly subversive, in the sense that they are always open to dialogue, hoping to find areas of overlap between and among contesting forces. Furthermore, whenever they have to resort to more active expressions of subversion in order to restore social justice, they do this in a religiously motivated way. They want first to love and only afterward to heal their enemies. They understand that nonviolent passion for a cause does not need to preclude compassion for the other, and that authentic civil dialogue is still the best tool for generating mutual understanding and, possibly, transformation—on all sides.

Are College Students Developmentally Ready for Moral Conversation?

I am often asked by university administrators if I think college students are mature enough to engage in moral conversation about religion, at least in the way that I envision it. After all, their reasoning goes, Gandhi, King, and Havel are hardly the developmental equivalents of the average college undergraduate or even of the older graduate student. My response is always the same: an enthusiastic but qualified yes. What troubles many administrators I have met is that my conception of moral conversation for college students does not always mesh with what they know of developmental theory.

Developmental or stage theory is the staple of most graduate programs in higher education administration. In fact, many of the best programs in the country feature a dominant developmental emphasis. There is nothing wrong with this disciplinary focus, of course, and what I have to say in the paragraphs that follow is not meant to be dismissive or overly critical. However, I think that educators need to be very cautious and selective when attempting to apply the insights of developmental theorists to moral conversation about religion on college campuses. Developmental theory is hardly the last word on which students may or may not be ready for moral conversation.

I will acknowledge that I have had my doubts about developmental theory, even though I have taught the stages of intellectual, ethical (Perry, 1970), and moral development (Kohlberg, 1984) many times. Generally, I find these stages of development a little too pat and formulaic, hierarchical, and too closely linked with age and gender. I for one have always resisted fitting the majority of my students' and colleagues' reasoning patterns into specific developmental boxes. Also, I find that stages can often become self-fulfilling labels, as some students search so eagerly (and desperately) for their appropriate niche that they breathe a huge sigh of relief (or frustration) whenever they think they have found it. Suddenly, the journey is over for them, and all is right (or wrong) with their worlds, depending on what they believe they have found out about themselves. Other students simply grow weary of trying to slot themselves, and they proceed to denounce the developmental approach in the strongest terms.

My biggest concern about stage development theory, though, is that like all theories it is nothing more, and nothing less, than a useful social construction. It is just another enchanting fiction—intriguing to be sure—this time created by social scientists, who think about morality and intelligence in certain normative ways. These constructions, I believe, are largely influenced by their creators' particular upbringings, value preferences, and academic training. In one sense, then, developmental theory is less science than story, almost entirely dependent on what an individual author deems intellectually and morally important in his own life. How could it be any other way?

Thus, for Lawrence Kohlberg, the Harvard University professor who also happens to be a middle-class, liberal male, the highest level of moral development is arriving at a rather abstract conception of justice, rather than achieving a more palpable sense of caring and compassion in relationships (Gilligan, 1982). Moreover, men (his early research involved no women) must pass through a series of invariant stages of reasoning in order to get there. There can be no shortcuts. So too, for William G. Perry (1970), the Harvard University professor who likewise happens to be a middle-class, white liberal male, all college men (his research involved only Harvard male undergraduates) must pass through a sequence of dualistic thinking to relativism to commitment. Perry's understanding of growth is less linear than Kohlberg's and more subject to fluctuations and spurts, but it is still hierarchical and formulaic.

While most college administrators know about Kohlberg's and Perry's work, I find that they know very little about James W. Fowler's (1981) research on stages of spiritual development. While I appreciate much of

Fowler's scholarship, I tend not to take it very seriously as a strictly *scientific* statement. What I do like is the existential capaciousness of his "dynamic triad" of faith. For Fowler, faith is social, relational, and philosophical. It is neither excessively orthodox nor excessively secular. Faith is grounded in a sense of community and in overarching loyalties to others. It is a way of knowing and seeking, more process than product, "a way of leaning into and finding or giving meaning to the conditions of our lives" (p. 92). This is a conception that is very compatible with my own formulation of faith as an ongoing search for narrative meaning, carried out in the spirit of honest doubt. I suspect that Fowler likes Paul Tillich's *Dynamics of Faith* (1957) as much as I do, because I find existential echoes of Tillich's work throughout *Stages of Faith*.

Like Kohlberg and Jean Piaget, Fowler is a stage theorist, and he is primarily interested in how adolescents and young adults conceptualize and develop their faith. His students begin at the "intuitive-projective" (faith as parental and authoritative) stage, progress to the "mythic-literal" (faith as personal and fantasy based), pass over into the "synthetic-conventional" (faith as interpersonal), transition into the "individuative-reflective" (faith as a search for meaning and responsibility), evolve into the "conjunctive" (faith as a deepening knowledge of self and others), and, if they are ready, end up in a final stage that is "universalizing" (faith as passionate commitment to love and justice).

The technical terms Fowler uses can be distressingly abstract, but Scotty McLennan (1999) breaks them down into commonsense language that, in my teaching, is suggestive. This is how he tracks the spiritual stages of his students at Tufts University. At first, they tend to experience God as an all-powerful, magical entity. Then God becomes more reality based, a person who can be influenced by good deeds. This is a cause-and-effect God. Then God becomes a parent, a God that renders students dependent on a personal relationship with the deity. Then God becomes a distant God, an impersonal force, not as significant as the inner soul or spirit that students feel. Then God becomes a paradoxical God, a deity of interdependence, whereby conventional religion once again is important for students, but so too is a more expansive spirituality. At this stage of understanding, truth is multidimensional and dialectical. Finally, students come to believe in an all-pervasive God, a God of unity, an Ultimate Reality that is cosmos, love, light, nature, and one.

It is interesting to note that McLennan is a Unitarian-Universalist minister, himself an activist and explorer, whose image of God is one of unity and love. His own troubled personal journey is the backdrop for his conceptualization of how students ought to develop their faiths. On one level, his entire book is a very readable, and enjoyable, personal narrative, calculated to get students from Stage One (magic) to Stage Six (unity). Thus, like Fowler's, his stages are more than simple, scientific descriptions of faith development; they are prescriptions for the way such things ought to be. More precisely, how things ought to be for Tufts University students in their spiritual development is the way things were and are for McLennan. Once again, how could it be otherwise?

Generally, I am drawn to McLennan's book, because he is very honest about his own spiritual preferences. He tells wonderful stories throughout, both personal and religious. In fact, his journey is similar to many of my students', particularly the explorers. Like Diana Eck (1993), whom I mentioned in an earlier chapter, McLennan (1999) believes that "religion is a process, not a product. It's a journey, not a destination" (p. 211). Also like Eck, McLennan suggests that "circling back to the religion of [one's] childhood" is developmentally appropriate, indeed even admirable in many instances. It is clear that McLennan, at mid-life, has "circled back" to the Christianity that he once cherished, albeit in a drastically revised version. McLennan's reconfigured faith has been cleverly depicted by his former Yale University classmate, Garry Trudeau, creator of the nationally syndicated, Doonesbury comic strip. McLennan is the inspiration for the somewhat-zany character of the Reverend Scot Sloan, pastor of the New-Age "Little Church of Walden."

What does all of this have to do with college students' readiness to engage productively in moral conversation about spirituality and religion? Certainly stage theory, for all the questions it raises, is instructive. Fowler and McLennan might say that students who are reflective and flexible in their thinking (4th stage and beyond) will be more adept at talking with one another in an open-ended, mutually respectful way about their faith commitments (or lack of them). I would agree, but with the important qualification that vigorous moral conversation requires students who represent all the stages of cognitive development. Monistic and dualistic thinkers, for example, have much to contribute to lively discussion because they can sometimes push people like me to reexamine some of the more heterodox religious assumptions I take for granted. Moreover, I believe that most students are able to learn and apply the rules of moral conversation, regardless of what stage of cognition or faith they might inhabit at any given time.

Also, I would strongly disagree with the inference in both Fowler and McLennan that those students who are "stuck" in the lower stages of faith development are more likely to be fundamentalist and authoritarian in their right-wing religious convictions. I have known social-justice advocates and members of the religious left, the developmental heroes in the Fowler-McLennan schema, who are as fundamentalist and authoritarian in their beliefs as many of their conservative counterparts. What, on principle, therefore, makes their commitments more noble? I also challenge the assumption that the only way to get to the later stages of faith development is to progress through the earlier stages. I have known hundreds of students who by-passed these stages altogether, or who constructed their own, far more creative stages. Finally, I would not link these stages so tightly to particular chronological periods, or present them as such rigidly linear constructions.

I have learned a few things about students during my three-plus decades of teaching, and one of them is this: Student development is fluid, diverse, and unpredictable, even more so where religio-spirituality is concerned. My experience in higher education with students of all ages (17–82) has been that some will think about religio-spirituality primarily in interpersonal terms. Others will be deeply introspective and private. Some will develop a passionate religious commitment to social-justice causes. Others will spurn social-outreach efforts entirely and express their faith commitment in alternative ways, perhaps through their jobs, intimate relationships, or love of nature. Some will grow in their faith. Others will find a new faith. Still others will lose or renounce their faith for good, and become apatheistic, agnostic, or atheistic. A few will even do all of these things at one time or another, either on or off schedule.

The lesson here for moral conversation is that we should strenuously resist making normative judgments about which stage is "higher" or "lower," and then go on to idealize and universalize these constructions. Fowler, echoing Kohlberg and Perry, thinks that the "universalizing" stage is the developmental zenith for human beings. He reserves this stage mainly for martyrs and heroes like Martin Luther King, Jr., Mother Teresa, and Dag Hammarskjold—saints who would give up their lives in order to advance the cause of social justice. It is also evident that, for McLennan, the "unity" stage is the spiritual apogee. He designates this stage for those people who are ego-free, beyond paradox and ambiguity, and panentheistic (God is in everything, everything is in God). This is the place where the Dalai Lama and Thich Nhat Hanh are said to reside.

While I myself respect the same people that Fowler and McLennan admire, some students do not know these figures well enough to have an opinion about them one way or the other. They have their own heroes, and few of them are likely to be political leaders or Buddhists. In general, I have found that students resent "higher" and "lower" value designations when they involve matters of faith and values, *particularly when the designators pretend to be context-free or narrative-neutral in their judgments*. Most students today are fairly sophisticated postmodernists, and they are wary of intellectuals who claim to be scientifically objective, and who then go on to establish their personal preferences as hierarchical and universal. Of course, they are equally suspicious of people like me— as well they should be—who make no claim to scientific objectivity, but who then go on to assert their postmodern preferences as if these too were objective and universal.

So here is my own preference, and I say it with tenuous tenacity. I do not believe that there is some highest developmental stage that is beneath or beyond socialization, that exists outside the impress of our personal histories, languages, cultures, tastes, and temperaments (all of these are the raw material for our narratives). These contingencies always affect our viewpoints about which stage might be higher or lower; as I have already said, we do not construct these normative perspectives out of thin air. In contrast, developmental theorists posit noncontingent Truths in the shape of invariant and universal stages that are cross-cultural, even transcendent. They strive to create a once-and-for-all developmental narrative that goes by the name of "grand theory." Its intention is to tie up morality, faith, and cognition in one neat bundle. In the process, they end up forcing individuals into a single meta-narrative wherein one size fits all. However, they never really succeed in replacing the messiness of pluralism with the tidiness of monism.

While there is admittedly a whiff of determinism in what I am saying about contingencies, I can only reiterate that I concur with Richard Rorty (1989) that "socialization goes all the way down" (p. xiii). Nothing defines us as moral or religious beings except for our contingent historical circumstances—except for what has been socialized into us by family, friends, teachers, and religious communities, as well as by a variety of cultural and social institutions. Even though I say this, however, I must also emphatically declare that I am not a fatalist. I believe enthusiastically in the ideal of self-creation and change, but only within the reasonable limits of what postmodern philosophers call our "historicity." According to Rorty (quoted in Malachowski, 1991), this is the view that it is "impossible for any of us to step completely outside our skins—the traditions, linguistic and other, within which we do our thinking and self-criticism—and compare ourselves with something absolute" (p. 27).

I agree with Martin Buber (1958), the Hebrew mystic, who believes that around each of us is a circle (what he calls our "destiny") beyond which we cannot pass, but within which we have far more freedom than we might think possible. For Buber, it is first necessary for each of us to become aware of our contingencies (what he calls the world of the "it"), those external conditions and contexts that shape our behavior, in order to enlarge the circles that currently enclose us. Buber believes that the key is not to limit ourselves to the world of the "it," but to "continually leave it for the world of relation."

He puts it this way:

> Destiny and freedom are solemnly promised to one another. Only the man [sic] who makes freedom real to himself meets destiny. He who [knows] what is caused and [then] makes decision out of the depths . . . is a free man, and destiny confronts him as the counterpart of his freedom. It is not his boundary, but his fulfillment; freedom and destiny are linked together in meaning. And in this meaning destiny, with eyes a moment ago so severe now filled with light, looks out like grace itself. (p. 53)

Moral conversation is my way—a la Buber—of helping students to enlarge the circle of religious meanings that contain them. I want them to confront their "destinies" (their "its" or contingencies) by engaging in vivifying and self-transforming dialogues with each other. I am offering students the possibility of a world of "relation" that introduces them to different languages, narratives, and perspectives on religion. What ultimately held my capstone group together after the "ambush" that fateful day was a hard-won commitment to encounter each other from the "depths" of their most heartfelt religious narratives. They agreed to do this with meticulous respect, generosity, compassion, and, yes, love. We spent much time and energy in successive meetings dealing with our individual "its" in order to unite as a community. After a while, these "boundaries" became our freedom, and we grew very close to one another. I cannot in truth say that our "destiny" ever looked exactly like "grace itself," but it was transformed into something very good and very satisfying. Moreover, I must add that, in my opinion, we came together *in spite of* where individual students might have been developmentally.

Establishing a Culture of Dialogue on College Campuses

I begin this section with an hypothesis: *What works to promote learning in a classroom can also work to induce learning campus-wide.* I am first of all a classroom teacher. It is in this space that I have discerned how to teach and, better, how to learn with others. I have drawn freely throughout this book from my own experiences as a veteran classroom teacher because I believe that good pedagogical principles are universally transferable. If engaged, open, and vigorous moral conversation about controversial issues can happen within the confines of a cozy seminar room or in a large, sterile classroom, or even in an impersonal, cavernous lecture hall via small-group discussions, then I believe it can occur anywhere else on a college campus. The same teaching-learning principles will apply regardless of the site.

On another note, I do not intend for an instant to underestimate the difficulties in promoting campus-wide dialogue on religio-spirituality. I have failed often enough in my own change efforts through the years to understand the folly of being overly optimistic whenever it comes to advocating for something innovative in the campus academic culture. However, I have also had my moments of success, owing to the tireless and enthusiastic assistance of others in helping me to bring something new and (I hope) vital to the university. I am convinced, after all my years in higher education, that the American university can become a true culture of dialogue, one characterized by what Eck (1993) calls

> a truth-seeking encounter. . . . [W]e do not enter into dialogue with the dreamy hope that we will all agree, for the truth is we probably will not. We do not enter into dialogue to produce an agreement, but to produce real relationship, even friendship, which is premised upon mutual understanding, not upon agreement . . . a culture of dialogue creates a context of ongoing relatedness and trust in which self-criticism and mutual criticism are acceptable and valuable parts of the interreligious exchange. (pp. 197, 225)

These are the questions I hope to touch upon in this section: What is the best way to implement a culture of dialogue around religio-spiritual issues? How can we get college adminstrators together with faculty and other interested participants to lead these dialogues? Where are the best locations for these unbounded dialogue spaces? What are some innovative dialogue configurations that might enhance moral conversations? What are some potential problems that might arise as students, administrators, and faculty enter into dialogues that involve not just "relatedness and trust" but also "self-criticism and mutual criticism"?

What follows are four tentative responses to these questions that I know will seem exasperatingly brief. We in the academy are at such a primitive stage of thinking about how to build an all-university culture of

religio-spiritual dialogue that I can only of
gestions for its initial formation and imp
ing and complete prescriptions. I formu
of tersely stated propositions, listed in

1. *Student affairs administrato*
each other as adversaries, at leas
We must agree to come together at stra
educational allies bent on a single mission: the esta
and informal cultures of dialogue throughout the campus, w
press purpose of initiating and sustaining moral conversations that truly
speak to students' cries for meaning. One powerful thematic focus for
creating genuine "living-learning communities" (particular types of educational spaces that currently represent a high priority for many student
affairs administrators) on college campuses is the religio-spiritual quest for
meaning. What better way to bind together a group of students, faculty,
and staff than the mutual give-and-take exploration of what, if anything,
gives proximate and ultimate meaning to particular lives? This exchange
would be an experiment in pluralistic living and learning that would be
virtually unprecedented in the academy.

However, this coming together will only happen when administrators
and faculty can set aside their differences and create collaborative dialogue teams whose primary purpose is to smooth the way to meaning-
making. It is essential that in the beginning adminstrators take the initiative to form these alliances because most faculty are encapsulated within
their own disciplines and because interdisciplinary partnerships among
faculty—both within and between academic departments—are difficult
enough to establish in their own right. Often what is needed is outside
instigation. However, this will not happen by issuing a series of administrative memoranda. Faculty are much too independent for that. The best
approach will be one of experimental suasion—appealing to some faculty
members' wishes to try something different in order to touch their students' lives in a very special way.

The key is for administrators and faculty to recognize the special tal-
ents and understandings that each brings to the venture. Contrary to
general administrative opinion, not all faculty members demean the intellectual contributions of student affairs leaders. Moreover, contrary to general faculty opinion, not all student affairs administrators diminish the
student-development contributions of the professoriate. Working together
on a college campus to create cultures of dialogue on topics of intellectual

oth parties is an excellent way of overcoming the hoary and
g stereotypes that many administrators and faculty tend to propa-
ut one another.

reotypes form because of different languages and mindsets. Stu-
t affairs administrators tend to speak the languages of corporatization
nd student-development psychology. Faculty members speak the languages of academic rigor and disciplinary loyalty. All of these languages
are valuable, of course, but they too often drive a wedge between the
administrative culture and the academic culture that ends in the estrange-
ment of both groups. When administrators and faculty members can come
together as educational partners in the venture I am recommending here,
willing to listen *to* each other and to learn *from* each other, then it is
possible for suspicion and misunderstanding to give way to trust and mutual
appreciation.

2. *We must be prepared for conflict in moral conversations about
religion.*

An administrator or a faculty member who is trained in conflict resolution and mediation would be a good addition to the educational alliance I
am advocating. I remember a professor of philosophy once remarking to
me when I was a graduate student at Boston University that to think
deeply about anything worthwhile will result eventually in growing angry.
Anger is inevitable whenever people get below the surface of thoughts
and feelings, and nothing penetrates the surface of everyday life like honest and probing religious conversation. I can recall very little in my experience that ignites conversations better than an uncensored disclosure
about one's own, or another's, religion or spirituality, particularly when
the disclosure might contain a direct or implied critique of somebody
else's beliefs.

Misunderstandings are bound to arise in moral conversations about
religion because narratives and languages are so diverse and frameworks
of interpretation (what Charles Taylor, 1991, calls "backgrounds of intelligibility" or "horizons") so multiple and unique. Feelings will get hurt,
people will be miffed, and some students will intentionally or unintentionally lob a sabotage bomb or two into the middle of conversation. Instead
of panicking or downplaying conflict, we must learn to trust the process
in moral conversation. Inevitably, things will go wrong before they go
right. However, because participants will have agreed on the conversational principles at the outset, much conflict will correct itself and turn
into opportunity for understanding and growth on everybody's part.

Perhaps the best way to deal with conflict in moral conversations about
religio-spirituality, though, is to become less preoccupied with teaching

and telling, and more concerned with listening and learning. Rachel Kessler (2000, p. 65) mentions the importance of "returning the question" to students whenever they inquire about the mysteries of ultimacy, transcendence, personal meaning, and the ubiquity of evil in the world. Sometimes, the best way to let students know that we value their religio-spiritual inquiries is to give their questions back to them so that they can discover the answers in their own natural wisdom. Also, checking in frequently with participants as to how they are feeling and what they are hearing is an effective way to defuse the kind of conflicts that simmer and fester and eventually lead dialogue groups astray, often destroying them in the process.

The point here, though, is to resist succumbing to what I would call the "temptation to avoid giving offense." Victor H. Kazanjian, Jr., (2000) says it well in respect to his own institution, Wellesley College:

> Wellesley had fallen prey to the belief that in order to bring people of different traditions together, one had to find a common, neutral context in which everyone felt comfortable and in which no one was offended. The result was the stripping of all particularistic experience from community rituals and programs leaving a kind of universalistic mush in which no one's unique perspective was reflected. (pp. 216–217)

I strongly recommend Kazanjian, Jr.'s essay, "Beyond Tolerance: From Mono-religious to Multi-religious life at Wellesley College," in *Education as Transformation* (2000) for a number of very helpful suggestions to resist the temptation to avoid giving offense when discussing controversial, personal topics such as religion and spirituality. Genuine dialogue, built on a foundation of trust and mutual exploration, invites candor and critique, because it conveys the message that a "neutral" approach really does not take the other's point of view very seriously.

3. *We must be prepared for conflict between and among the vested professional interests on campus.*

Some campus ministers will complain that "me-first spirituality is a sorry substitute for organized religion on campuses." They will argue that to remove religion from the chapels, prayer rooms, and churches on campus is to downplay the importance of institutionalized religion in favor of an ephemeral spirituality that has no specific sense of practice, place, or community. Needless to say, the importance of campus ministers might be downplayed as well. As one campus chaplain said: "What we need is not more [cross-campus] calls for spirituality, but more money for chapels and chaplains" (Schaper, 2000, A56).

Some religious studies faculty (and other academicians as well) will criticize the "dumbing down" of religion whenever it leaves the seminar room and becomes the object of conversation outside the scholar's provenance. Many religious studies instructors are more comfortable teaching *about* religion (particularly its weaknesses) than facilitating conversations with people who *have* religion. In fact, two sociologists of religion, Rodney Stark and Roger Finke (2000), make the claim that religious studies departments throughout the United States are filled with "village atheists." They contend: "Clearly, today, the personal religious beliefs of students are treated with far more respect in social science courses than often is the case in religion or theology departments" (p. 20).

Some student affairs administrators, who see themselves more as managers than educators, will raise questions about cost effectiveness, crossing boundaries, accountability, potential student lawsuits, and the unworkability of teaching alongside professors. They will comport themselves chiefly as caregivers in the dialogue groups and defer to professors to do all the intellectual work in moral conversations about religion. For these professionals, the type of educational alliance between administrators and professors that I am calling for is bound to be experienced as a burden.

I can only say that on the campuses where I have worked and visited, there are many wonderful exceptions to these stereotypes. The trick is to find professionals who are as student-centered as they are content- and administration-based. It is also important to identify those professionals who are enthusiastic about new teaching-learning projects, and willing to take interdisciplinary and pedagogical risks. Sad to say, with some notable exceptions, academia does not generally reward risk-taking via collaboration with those who are not members of the same professorial or professional guilds. In spite of the obstacles, however, I know from firsthand experience that potential allies are everywhere.

In my own case, I actively sought out campus ministers who would help me get my venture off the ground. At least two at my campus were more than willing to cooperate and, even better, to take some specific operational initiatives. One even became a student (actually more of a coteacher) in my graduate course for an entire semester. I also found a number of academicians on my campus and elsewhere who were supportive, albeit mostly from afar. Those who wanted to play a more active role tended to come from the professional schools rather than from arts and sciences. Even so, still, a few colleagues from both religious studies and philosophy departments stepped forward with good ideas once I involved them in the preliminary planning.

My general rule of prediction around joint interdisciplinary activities is that many faculty and staff will always be threatened by the blurring of borders. Some faculty members, for example, are disciplinary purists, or intellectual loners; others fear facing the inevitable hazards of any kind of innovation. Some do not know how to reach out to (or be reached by) colleagues; while others zero in only on what they need to do in order to win scholarly acclaim, pay raises, tenure, and promotion. A few are just plain lazy. Interdisciplinarians are border-dwellers and border-crossers, by definition. They live at the margins of organized bodies of knowledge, and they straddle intellectual frontiers. I fully understand that not everyone is temperamentally or intellectually comfortable with the type of teamwork and moral conversation that I am advocating.

Having said all of this, however, I also need to add that I have met many enthusiastic border-dwellers in the academy, and I have worked closely with them. I have collaborated with student affairs professionals who were at least as knowledgeable as I regarding matters of religion and spirituality. I have talked at length with academic colleagues who cared at least as much as I about their students' search for meaning and the importance of moral conversations about what truly touches students' lives.

We must understand that where issues of personal meaning and purpose are concerned, all of us in academia are rank amateurs, learning as we go along. Everyone's journey is different and is to be honored. When it comes to the most complex existential questions—what the French refer to as *les profondeurs*—there are no certified experts. Consequently, the best traits for engaging in the type of experiment I am describing here are a profound sense of humility and a natural taste for adventure. It also helps to be intensely interested in people's religio-spiritual stories, particularly those I would call students' quest narratives. Mastery of academic content, while admirable, is helpful particularly when it goes hand-in-hand with the aforementioned traits.

4. *The diffusion of religio-spiritual content throughout the academy is vital, if we are to meet students where they live. Thus, new configurations of teaching and learning are necessary.*

As a professor, I have a natural fondness for the classroom. This is where I have practiced my craft for better than three decades, and I have witnessed some phenomenal intellectual growth there, including, not least, my own. But I am also acutely aware that wonderful learnings occur in other sites as well. Therefore, it will be necessary for all of us to emphasize the concept of diffusion in our educational efforts to promote a culture of cross-campus dialogue on questions of meaning and purpose. Diffusion entails dispersing teaching and learning about religion throughout the academy. In Diane Winston's (1998) words, diffusion "signals the scattering of religious ideas, beliefs, and behaviors in arenas ranging from medicine (for example, medical-school courses on spirituality and health) to computing (the magazine *Christian Computing*) to cyberspace (chat rooms and Web sites devoted to religious topics)" (p. A60). Winston goes on to recommend that professors encourage their students to discuss issues of meaning whenever they might be relevant to the topic at hand, not just in religious-studies seminars, but in courses representing all the disciplines. I certainly concur.

Nevertheless, I am going one major step further than Winston. I want the conversation about meaning to take place *outside as well as inside* the officially recognized academic structures, e.g., classrooms, credit hours, research papers, semester-long courses, lectures, exams, and so forth. I want to encourage us to think imaginatively about constructing new teaching-learning configurations throughout the campus, e.g., in coffee houses, cafeterias, residence halls, chapels, cultural pluralism centers, and student activities rooms. During a recent meeting I had with students, we brainstormed some innovative ways to encourage the search for meaning in *all* the campus spaces using some creative delivery systems. I list them below in no particular order of priority.

- all-campus town meetings with specific religio-spiritual themes
- mini-retreats for students, faculty, and staff emphasizing the quest for meaning
- special religious topics colloquia
- comparative religion institutes
- out-of-classroom dialogue groups
- leadership training institutes
- mediation and conflict resolution training sessions
- chapel services and religiously sponsored special events days
- a "first-lecture" series on "what I would like to learn about meaning"
- a "last-lecture" series on "what I think I have learned about meaning"
- brown-bag lunches
- off-campus ally groups for religious pluralism
- multi-faith centers
- deep-connection groups
- spiritual-renewal communities
- stillness centers
- safe spaces for border dwellers

- all-campus big-question sessions
- religio-spiritual journaling groups
- campus elders' sessions
- distinguished religio-spiritual speakers' series
- poets' corners
- philosophers' corners
- atheists' corners

I myself have had much success in working with small dialogue groups both in and outside the classroom. I usually organize these groups around the kinds of questions I have been asking throughout the book, but particularly the ones that follow each of my religio-spiritual narratives in chapters 3 and 4. I have also enjoyed setting up a series of Friday afternoon colloquia whose attendance is voluntary. Students, faculty, or administrators agree to present a formal paper or a series of short, personal reflections on a special topic. Then they open up the session to respectful and candid discussion. The primary ground rule is that the presenter must first respond to each question from the audience with a restatement of what the presenter has heard before formulating an answer. By like token, the initial questioner must frame the inquiry in terms that reflect that questioner's own search for meaning.

I remember that the first time I facilitated a Friday afternoon colloquium in my own college, over 40 students showed up on a sunny and warm April afternoon. I reminded the participants that, etymologically, a *colloquium* puts as much emphasis on listening as it does on talking. A colloquium is a coming together in conversation so that listeners might confer with one another on topics of mutual interest. The initial speaker was a graduate student who was doing an independent study with me on the implications of his newly constructed "postmodern Catholicism" for his future work as a college administrator.

After he presented the gist of his paper to the group, I asked him to provoke us with a series of personal questions that he was still asking himself as a result of doing his project. I stipulated that the questions be honest, meaning-centered, and provocative, with resonance for all the rest of us. I was only slightly surprised that a scheduled two-hour colloquium grew into a spirited and moving three-hour conversation. Those of us in the audience were as intensely interested in the speaker's personal questions as we were in the formal content of his presentation. This is always how such sessions proceed, especially when people feel safe enough to talk about what really matters to them.

The Widespread Yearning for Consoling Narratives of Meaning

I want to close this final chapter with an extended quotation from a writer I admire greatly. Peter Marin (1996) is a contributing editor to *Harper's Magazine*, and I have used his essay, "An American Yearning: Seeking Cures for Freedom's Terrors," on two different occasions in my all-college dialogue groups. The essay is a savage critique of a conference that Marin attended in Washington, DC, called the "National Summit on Ethics and Meaning." Marin is a religious skeptic, and he delights in exposing hypocrisy and posturing among the "spiritual elites" who sponsor expensive New-Age type conferences, ostensibly to help others grow, but who also pocket extravagant honoraria for their efforts. He is good at unmasking what he thinks are examples of monumental religious fraud throughout America.

What always catches my students' attention in the piece, however, is not the biting critical commentary. It is something very personal that Marin reveals about his daughter, something that sounds very much like a wistful parental aside, yet is of volcanic concern to many of my students.

> Let me be honest. I have a daughter in her mid-twenties, close to brilliant. She had a childhood she thought was perfect and a wild but satisfying adolescence, and then she sailed through the university studying the great books and philosophy and learning in the process how to excel in the academy and, at the same time, an immense disdain for it. She is astonishingly honest and self-possessed and capable of love and solitude, and she has a good job in Chicago and a sweet semi-slacker boyfriend. . . . she is also, at times, overcome with a despair so deep, and with so profound a melancholy, that she doubts life is worth living. Her grief at such times is all-encompassing, impenetrable, and as a father I grow helpless, bewildered, and afraid, unable to offer anything of use. I do not know what will help her or what she should do: change boyfriends or careers, exercise or sleep more, stop drinking, take vitamins or classes, start therapy, meditate, cut down on coffee or carbohydrates, or any one of the dozens of other antidotes and gambits that flood my mind. (p. 42)

Marin goes on to talk about how, at times, he would welcome with open arms the comforts of religion in his beloved daughter's life, no matter how foolish or absurd these comforts might seem to him. He would gladly swallow his pride, bite his skeptical tongue, and lovingly hold his daughter close to him. Most importantly, he would resist telling her that she must learn to live her life without myth or illusion. The majority of my students always see traces of themselves in Marin's daughter. She becomes an archetype for their own metaphysical journeys, their gnawing spiritual angst, their own desperate need for consoling narratives of meaning.

The plight of this young woman reminds them that their lives are fragile, that good and evil are often interchangeable aspects of their daily existence, and that the freedom they demand to construct their own narratives carries with it the terror of failure, isolation, and hopelessness. This, I suspect, is one of the main reasons why my course on religion and spirituality continues to fill up each semester. This is why I believe that America is currently undergoing a major religious revival in the midst of a soaring economy. Finally, this is why I have taken the time to write a book about the cry for meaning and religious pluralism on college campuses everywhere. I know too many young people who remind me of Peter Marin's daughter, and I am convinced that I am called at this time in my life to respond as best I can to their soulful entreaties. I can only hope that I am up to the challenge. Better still, I can only hope that *all* of us in the academy are up to the challenge.

Bibliography

Allen, C. (2000, December/January). Is deconstruction the last best hope of evangelical Christians? *Lingua Franca*, 47–59.

Allison, D. (1994). *Skin: Talking about sex, class, and literature*. Ithaca, NY: Firebrand Books.

Aristotle. (1976). *The ethics of Aristotle: The Nichomachean ethics* (J. A. K. Thomson, Trans.). New York: Penguin.

Armstrong, K. (1993). *A history of God: The 4000-year quest of Judaism, Christianity, and Islam*. New York: Knopf.

Bawer, B. (1997). *Stealing Jesus: How fundamentalism betrays Christianity*. New York: Crown.

Beaudoin, T. (1998). *Virtual faith. The irreverent spiritual quest of generation x*. San Francisco: Jossey-Bass.

Begley, S. (1998, July 20). Science finds God. *Newsweek*, 46–51.

Bell, J. L. (1993). *Bridge over troubled water: Ministry to the baby boomers, a generation adrift*. New York: Victor.

Bellah, R. N., Madsen, R., Sullivan, W. M., Swidler, A., & Tipton, S. M. (1985). *Habits of the heart: Individualism and commitment in American life*. Berkeley: University of California Press.

Bellah, R. N., Madsen, R., Sullivan W. M., Swidler, A., & Tipton, S. M. (1991). *The good society*. New York: Knopf.

Bloom, H. (1993). *The American religion: The emergence of the post-Christian nation*. New York: Touchstone.

Boorstin, D. J. (1998). *The seekers. The story of man's continuing quest to understand his world.* New York: Vintage.

Bromwich, D. (1992). *Politics by other means: Higher education and groups thinking.* New Haven, CT: Yale University Press.

Bruner, J. (1996). *The culture of education.* Cambridge, MA: Harvard University Press.

Brussell, E. E. (Ed.). (1988). *Webster's new world dictionary of quotable definitions* (2nd ed.). New York: Simon & Schuster.

Buber, M. (1958). *I and thou* (2nd Ed.). New York: Charles Scribner's Sons.

Buehrens, J. A., & Church, F. (1998). *A chosen faith: An introduction to Unitarian Universalism* (Rev. ed.). Boston: Beacon Press.

Callahan, D. (2000, January–February). Universalism & particularism: Fighting to a draw. *Hastings Center Report*, 37–44.

Carpenter, J. A. (1998). *Revive us again: The reawakening of American fundamentalism.* New York: Oxford University Press.

Carter, S. L. (1993). *The culture of disbelief: How American law and politics trivialize religious devotion.* New York: Basic Books.

Carter, S. L. (1998). *Civility: Manners, morals, and the etiquette of democracy.* New York: Basic.

Carter, S. L. (2000). *God's name in vain: The wrongs and rights of religion in politics.* New York: Basic Books.

Chronicle of Higher Education Almanac. (August 28, 1999), 22.

Cimino, R. P. (Ed.). (1999, October). Secular humanism optimistic and defensive. *Religion Watch: A Newsletter Monitoring Trends in Contemporary Religion*, 1–2.

Cimino, R. P., & Lattin, D. (1998). *Shopping for faith: American religion in the new millennium.* San Francisco: Jossey-Bass.

Cone, J. H. (1997). *God of the oppressed* (rev. ed.). Maryknoll, NY: Orbis.

Connolly, W. E. (1999). *Why I am not a secularist.* Minneapolis: University of Minnesota Press.

Constable, P. (July 15, 2000). A new assault on Christians: Violence by Hindus in India escalates in recent months. *The Burlington Free Press*, 2C.

Cox, H. (1995). *Fire from heaven: The rise of pentecostal spirituality and the reshaping of religion in the twenty-first century.* Reading, MA: Addison-Wesley.

Creedon, J. (July–August, 1998). God with a million faces. *Utne Reader*, 42–48

Crossette, B. (1998, July 5). The Shangri-La that never was. *The New York Times Week in Review,* 3.

Dewey, J. (1934). *A common faith.* New Haven, CT: Yale University Press.

Dillard, A. (1999). *For the time being.* New York: Alfred A. Knopf.

Easterbrook, G. (1998). *Beside still waters: Searching for meaning in an age of doubt.* New York: William Morrow and Company, Inc.

Eck, D. L. (1993). *Encountering God: A spiritual jouney from Bozeman to Banaras.* Boston: Beacon.

Ehrlich, T. (Ed.). (2000). *Civic responsibility and higher education.* Phoenix, AZ: Oryx Press.

Ellis, J. M. (1997). *Literature lost: Social agendas and the corruption of the humanities.* New Haven, CT: Yale University Press.

Fernandez-Armesto, F. (1997). *Truth: A history and a guide for the perplexed.* New York: St. Martin's Press.

Flanagan, M. (1999). *We are Unitarian Universalists.* Boston: UUA Pamphlet Commission Publication.

Fowler, A., Gamble, N. N., Hogan, F. X., Kogut, M., McComish, M., & Thorp, B. (January 28, 2001). Talking with the enemy. *Boston Sunday Globe*, F1–F3.

Fowler, J. W. (1981). *Stages of faith: The psychology of human development and the quest for meaning.* San Francisco: Harper & Row.

Foxman, P. (1997). *Dancing with fear: Overcoming anxiety in a world of stress and uncertainty.* Northvale, NJ: Aronson.

Freedman, S. G. (1998, May 24). Yeshivish at Yale. *The New York Times Magazine*, 32–35.

Freedman, S. G. (2000). *Jew vs. Jew: The struggle for the soul of American Jewry*. New York: Simon & Schuster.

Fuller, S. (1988). *Social epistemology*. Bloomington: Indiana University Press.

Fuller, S. (2000). *Thomas Kuhn: A philosophical history for our times*. Chicago: University of Chicago Press.

Gallagher, W. (1999). *Working on God*. New York: Random House.

Gaskin, J. C. A. (1984). *The quest for eternity: An outline of the philosophy of religion*. New York: Penguin.

Geertz, C. (1973). *The interpretation of cultures*. New York: Basic Books.

Gilligan, C. (1982). *In a different voice: Psychological theory and women's development*. Cambridge, MA: Harvard University Press.

Glover, J. (1999). *Humanity: A moral history of the twentieth century*. New Haven, CT: Yale University Press.

Gomes, P. J. (1996). *The good book: Reading the Bible with mind and heart*. New York: Morrow.

Graham, R. B. (1997, July 19). Boomers putting their stamp on spirituality. *The Burlington Free Press*, 6C.

Greeley, A. (1990). *The Catholic myth: The behavior and beliefs of American Catholics*. New York: Charles Scribner's Sons.

Grenz, S. J. (1996). *A primer on postmodernism*. Grand Rapids, MI: William B. Eerdmans.

Hanh, T. N. (1995). *Living Buddha, living Christ*. New York: Riverhead.

Hanson, V. D., & Heath, J. (1998). *Who killed Homer? The demise of classical education and the recovery of Greek wisdom*. New York: Free Press.

Harvey, A. (Ed.). (1996). *The essential mystics: Selections from the world's great wisdom traditions*. San Francisco: HarperCollins.

Hauerwas, S. (1977). *Truthfulness and tragedy: Further investigations into Christian ethics*. Notre Dame, IN: University of Notre Dame Press.

Haugaard, K. (1997, June 27). Suspending moral judgment: Students who refuse to condemn the unthinkable. *The Chronicle of Higher Education*, B4–5.

Haught, J. A. (1990). *Holy horrors*. Buffalo, NY: Prometheus.

Haught, J. A. (1996). *2000 years of disbelief: Famous people with the courage to doubt*. Buffalo, NY: Prometheus.

Havel, V. (1990). *Disturbing the peace*. New York: Knopf.

Hedin, R. (1995). *Married to the church*. Bloomington: Indiana University Press.

Holstein, M., & Ellingson, W. (1999, May/June). Voices from left field: Civil discourse from the edges. *The Park Ridge Center Bulletin*, 13–14.

hooks, b. (1994). *Teaching to transgress: Education as the practice of freedom*. New York: Routledge.

Howe, N., & Strauss, W. (2000). *Millennials rising: The next great generation*. New York: Vintage.

Hume, D. (1902). *Enquiry concerning the principles of morals* (L. A. Selby-Bigge, Ed.). New York: Oxford.

Hunter, J. D. (1991). Culture wars: The struggle to define America. New York: Basic Books.

Hunter, J. D. (1994). *Before the shooting begins: Searching for democracy in America's culture war*. New York: The Free Press.

James, W. (1961). *The varieties of religious experience: A study in human nature*. New York: Collier. (Original work published 1902)

Johnson, F. (1998, September). Beyond belief: A skeptic searches for an American faith. *Harper's*, 39–54.

Juergensmeyer, M. (2000). *Terror in the mind of God: The global rise of religious violence*. Berkeley: University of California Press.

Kazanjian, V. H., & Laurence, P. L. (Eds.). (2000). *Education as transformation: Religious pluralism, spirituality, and a new vision for higher education in America*. New York: Peter Lang.

Kessler, R. (2000). *The soul of education: Helping students find connection, compassion, and character at school*. Alexandria, VA: Association for Supervision and Curriculum Development.

Kintz, L. (1997). *Between Jesus and the market: The emotions that matter in right-wing America.* Durham, NC: Duke University Press.

Kohlberg, L. (1984). *The psychology of moral stages.* San Francisco: Harper & Row.

Kurtz, P. (1986). *The transcendental temptation: A critique of religion and the paranormal.* Buffalo, NY: Prometheus.

Lama, D. (1999). *Ethics for the new millennium.* New York: Riverhead.

Lamont, C. (1965). *The philosophy of humanism* (5th ed.). New York: Frederick Ungar.

Lamott, A. (1994). *Bird by bird: Some instructions on writing and life.* New York: Pantheon.

Larson, E. J. (1997). *Summer for the gods: The Scopes trial and America's continuing debate over science and religion.* New York: Basic.

Laurence, P. (1999, November–December). Can religion and spirituality find a place in higher education? *About Campus,* 11–16.

Lawrence, B. B. (1989). *Defenders of God: The fundamentalist revolt against the modern age.* New York: Harper & Row.

Lefkowitz, M. (1998, February 20). In wars of words, a role for rules of etiquette. *The Chronicle of Higher Education,* A64.

Levinson, D. (1996). *Religion: A cross-cultural dictionary.* New York: Oxford University Press.

Lewis, C. S. (1962). *The problem of pain: How human suffering raises almost intolerable intellectual problems.* New York: Macmillan.

Lewy, G. (1996). *Why America needs religion: Secular modernity and its discontents.* Grand Rapids, MI: Eerdmans.

Lush, T. (1999, August 4). Groups face off over right to marry. *The Burlington Free Press,* 1B.

Mackie, J. L. (1977). *Ethics: Inventing right and wrong.* New York: Penguin.

Maitland, S. (1995). *A big-enough God: A feminist's search for a joyful theology.* New York: Henry Holt.

Malachowski, A. (Ed.). (1991). *Reading Rorty*. Cambridge, MA: Basil Blackwell.

Marin, P. (December, 1996). An American yearning: Seeking cures for freedom's terrors, *Harper's Magazine*, 35–43.

Marsden, G. M. (1996). *The soul of the American university: From protestant establishment to established nonbelief*. New York: Oxford University Press.

Marsden, G. M. (1997). *The outrageous idea of Christian scholarship*. New York: Oxford University Press.

Marshall, G. N. (1999). *Challenge of a liberal faith* (3rd ed.). Boston: Skinner House Books.

McCourt, F. (1999). *'Tis: A memoir*. New York: Touchstone.

McLennan, S. (1999). *Finding your religion: When the faith you grew up with has lost its meaning*. San Francisco: Harper.

McMurtrie, B. (1999, December 3). Pluralism and prayer under one roof. *The Chronicle of Higher Education*, A48–A50.

McMurtrie, B. (2000, May 12). A Christian fellowship's ban on gay leaders splits 2 campuses. *The Chronicle of Higher Education*, A51.

Mendelsohn, J. (1995). *Being liberal in an illiberal age*. Boston: Skinner House Books.

Miles, J. (1997, December 7). Religion makes a comeback. *The New York Times Magazine*, 56–59.

Miller, D. W. (2000, June 30). Striving to understand the Christian right. *The Chronicle of Higher Education*, A17–A18.

Miller, K. R. (1999). *Finding Darwin's God: A scientist's search for common ground between God and evolution*. New York: HarperCollins.

Miller, T. (Ed.). (1995). *America's alternative religions*. Albany, NY: State University of New York Press.

Muzzey, D. S. (1943). *Ethical religion: Its historical sources, its elements, its sufficiency, its future*. New York: American Ethical Union.

Nash, R. J. (1996a, Vol. 7, no. 1). Fostering moral conversations in the college classroom. *Journal on Excellence in College Teaching*, 83–106.

Nash, R. J. (1996b). *"Real world" ethics: Frameworks for educators and human service professionals.* New York: Teachers College Press.

Nash, R. J. (1997). *Answering the "virtuecrats": A moral conversation on character education.* New York: Teachers College Press.

Nash, R. J. (1999). *Faith, hype, and clarity: Teaching about religion in American schools and colleges.* New York: Teachers College Press.

Nash, R. J., & Griffin, R. S. (1986, May). Balancing the private and public. *Harvard Educational Review,* 171–182.

Natoli, J. (1997). *A primer to postmodernity.* Malden, MA: Blackwell.

Niebuhr, R. (1952). *The irony of American history.* New York: Scribner's.

Noddings, N. (1993). *Educating for intelligent belief or unbelief.* New York: Teachers College Press.

Noonan, J. T., Jr. (1998). *The lustre of our country: The American experience of religious freedom.* Berkeley: University of California Press.

Nord, W. A. (1995). *Religion and American education: Rethinking a national dilemma.* Chapel Hill: University of North Carolina Press.

Nord, W. A., & Haynes, C. C. (1998). *Taking religion seriously across the curriculum.* Alexandria,VA: Association for Supervision and Curriculum Development.

Nussbaum, E. (October, 1999). Faith no more: The campus crusade for secular humanism. *Lingua Franca,* 30–37.

Nussbaum, M. C. (1997). *Cultivating humanity: A classical defense of reform in liberal education.* Cambridge, MA: Harvard University Press.

Oakeshott, M. (1950). The idea of a university. *The Listener,* 43, 420–450.

O'Hair, M. (1970). *An atheist epic: Bill Murray, the bible and the Baltimore board of education.* Austin, TX: American Atheist Press.

Otto, R. (1923). *The idea of the holy: An inquiry into the non-rational factor in the idea of the divine and its relation to the rational* (J. W. Harvey, Trans.). New York: Oxford.

Palmer, P. (1983). *To know as we are known: A spirituality of education.* New York: HarperCollins.

Palmer, P. (1998). *The courage to teach.* San Francisco, CA: Jossey-Bass.

Parks, S. D. (1986). *The critical years: Young adults and the search for meaning.* New York: HarperColllins.

Parks, S. D. (2000). *Big questions, worthy dreams.* San Francisco, CA: Jossey-Bass.

Perry, W. G. (1970). *Forms of intellectual and ethical development in the college years: A scheme.* New York: Holt, Rinehart, & Winston.

Peshkin, A. (1988). *God's choice: The total world of a fundamentalist Christian school.* Chicago: University of Chicago Press.

Postman, N. (1996). *The end of education: Redefining the value of school.* New York: Vintage.

Rauch, J. (1993). *Kindly inquisitors: The new attacks on free thought.* Chicago: University of Chicago Press.

Reese, W. L. (1996). *Dictionary of philosophy and religion: Eastern and Western thought.* Atlantic Highlands, NJ: Humanities Press International, Inc.

Reeves, T. C. (1996, No. 66). Not so Christian America. *First Things,* 16–21.

Reisberg, L. (1998, April 17). New groups unite in belief that one needn't believe in God. *The Chronicle of Higher Education,* A43–A44.

Reisberg, L. (2000, October 20). Campus witches may wear black, but don't look for hats or broomsticks. *The Chronicle of Higher Education,* A49–50.

Rockefeller, S. (1996). *Meditation, social change, and undergraduate education.* Williamsburg, MA: Seva Foundation.

Rohmann, C. (1999). *A world of ideas: A dictionary of important theories, concepts, beliefs, and thinkers.* New York: Ballantine.

Roof, W. C. (1993). *A generation of seekers: The spiritual journeys of the baby boom generation.* San Francisco: HarperCollins.

Roof, W. C. (1999). *Spiritual marketplace: Baby boomers and the remaking of American religion.* Princeton, NJ: Princeton University Press.

Rorty, R. (1982). *Consequences of pragmatism.* Minneapolis: University of Minnesota Press.

Rorty, R. (1989). *Contingency, irony, and solidarity.* New York: Cambridge University Press.

Rorty, R. (1998). *Achieving our country: Leftist thought in twentieth-century America.* Cambridge, MA: Harvard University Press.

Rorty, R. (1999). *Philosophy and social hope.* New York: Penguin.

Rudolph, F. (1990). *The American college & university: A history.* Athens, GA: University of Georgia Press.

Schaper, D. (2000, August 18). Me-first spirituality is a sorry substitute for organized religion on campuses. *The Chronicle of Higher Education,* A56.

Scheidler, J. (1994). *Closed: 99 ways to stop abortion.* Rockford, IL: Tan Books.

Schreiber, L. (1999, July 25, 1999). Spiritual matters: Colleges bending to address religious issues. *The Boston Sunday Globe,* C1, C14.

Schwartz, R. (1997). *The curse of Cain: The violent legacy of monotheism.* Chicago: University of Chicago Press.

Schwehn, M. R. (1993). *Exiles from Eden: Religion and the academic vocation in America.* New York: Oxford University Press.

Seok, K. (1998, December 3). Fight to control Buddhist order turns violent. *The Burlington Free Press,* 2.

Shapiro, R. M. (1998, July–August). God with a million faces. *Utne Reader,* 47–48.

Sharlet, J. (2000, June 23). Theologians seek to reclaim the world with God and postmodernism. *The Chronicle of Higher Education,* A20–A22.

Sharmer, A. (Ed.). (1993). *Our Religions.* New York: HarperCollins.

Shermer, M. (2000). *How we believe: The search for God in an age of science.* New York: W. H. Freeman and Company.

Shorto, R. (1997, December 7). Belief by the numbers. *The New York Times Magazine,* 61–62.

Showalter, E. (1999, January 15). Taming the rampant incivility in academe. *The Chronicle of Higher Education,* B4–B5.

Smart, N. (2000). *Worldviews: Crosscultural explorations of human beliefs* (3rd ed.). Upper Saddle River, NJ: Prentice Hall.

Smith, B. H. (1997). *Belief & resistance: Dynamics of contemporary intellectual controversy.* Cambridge: MA: Harvard University Press.

Smith, H. (1991). *The world's religions.* New York: HarperCollins.

Smith, H. (2001). *Why religion matters: The fate of the human spirit in an age of disbelief.* San Francisco: HarperCollins.

Smith, J. Z. (Ed.). (1995). *The HarperCollins dictionary of religion.* San Francisco: HarperCollins.

Smith, R. J. (2000, September 6). Vatican statement draws criticism. *The Burlington Free Press,* 12.

Snider, A. (1999, May 7). Stifling the naysayer in an age of compulsory niceness. *The Chronicle of Higher Education,* A64.

Stark, R. & Finke, R. (2000). *Acts of faith: Explaining the human side of religion.* Berkeley: University of California Press.

Steinfels, M. O. (2000, October 6). The homosexual agenda. *Commonweal,* 5.

Sullivan, J. L., Pierson, J., & Marcus, G. F. (1982). *Political tolerance and American democracy.* Chicago: University of Chicago Press.

Tannen, D. (1998). *The argument culture: Moving from debate to dialogue.* New York: Random House.

Tannen, D. (2000, March 31). Agonism in the academy: Surviving higher learning's argument culture. *The Chronicle of Higher Education,* B7–B8.

Taylor, C. (1991). *The ethics of authenticity,* Cambridge, MA: Harvard University Press.

TeSelle, S. (1975, July). The experience of coming to belief. *Theology Today*, 159–160.

Thurman, R. (1998). *Inner revolution: Life, liberty, and the pursuit of real happiness.* New York: Riverhead.

Tickle, P. A. (1997). *God-talk in America.* New York: Crossroad.

Tillich, P. (1948). *The shaking of the foundations.* New York: Charles Scribner's Sons.

Tillich, P. (1957). *Dynamics of faith.* New York: Harper & Row.

Tivnan, E. (1995). *The moral imagination: Confronting the ethical issues of our day.* New York: Simon & Schuster.

Ulstein, S. (1995). *Growing up fundamentalist: Journeys in legalism & grace.* Downers Grove, IL: InterVarsity Press.

Wheeler, D. L. (1997, April 11). A foundation seeks to create a discipline in the intersection of science and theology. *The Chronicle of Higher Education,* A15–A16.

Willimon, W. H. (1985). *Sighing for Eden: Sin, evil, & the Christian faith.* Nashville, TN: Abingdon Press.

Willimon, W. H. & Naylor, T. H. (1995). *The abandoned generation: Rethinking higher education.* Grand Rapids, MI: William B. Eerdmans.

Wilson, E. O. (1998). *Consilience: The unity of knowledge.* New York: Random House.

Wilson, J. (1999, September/October). Thou shalt not take cheap shots. *Books & Culture*, 3.

Winston, D. (1998, January 16). Campuses are a bellwether for society's religious revival. *The Chronicle of Higher Education*, A60.

Wolfe, A. (1997, September 19). A welcome revival of religion in the academy. *The Chronicle of Higher Education*, B4–B5.

Wolfe, A. (1998). *One nation, after all: What middle-class Americans really think about God, country, family, racism, welfare, immigration, homosexuality, work, the right, the left, and each other.* New York: Viking Penguin.

Wolfe, A. (1999, February 26). Catholic universities can be the salvation of pluralism on American campuses. *The Chronicle of Higher Education*, B6–B7.

Wuthnow, R. (1998). *After heaven: Spirituality in America since the 1950s*. Berkeley: University of California Press.

Yalom, I. D. (1980). *Existential psychotherapy*. New York: Basic Books.

Yalom, I. D. (1989). *Love's executioner: And other tales of psychotherapy*. New York: HarperCollins.

Index